The Business of Sports

The Business of Sports

Volume 1
Perspectives on the Sports Industry

EDITED BY BRAD R. HUMPHREYS
AND DENNIS R. HOWARD

Praeger Perspectives

Westport, Connecticut
London

Library of Congress Cataloging-in-Publication Data

The business of sports / edited by Brad R. Humphreys and Dennis R. Howard.

   p. cm.

  Includes bibliographical references and index.

  ISBN 978-0-275-99340-5 ((set) : alk. paper) — ISBN 978-0-275-99341-2 ((vol. 1) : alk. paper) — ISBN 978-0-275-99342-9 ((vol. 2) : alk. paper) — ISBN 978-0-275-99343-6 ((vol. 3) : alk. paper)

  1. Professional sports—Economic aspects. 2. Sports—Economic aspects. 3. Sports administration. I. Humphreys, Brad R. II. Howard, Dennis Ramsay, 1945–

  GV716.B89 2008

  796.06′91—dc22   2008008547

British Library Cataloguing in Publication Data is available.

Library of Congress Catalog Card Number: 2008008547
ISBN: 978-0-275-99340-5 (set)
      978-0-275-99341-2 (vol. 1)
      978-0-275-99342-9 (vol. 2)
      978-0-275-99343-6 (vol. 3)

First published in 2008

Praeger Publishers, 88 Post Road West, Westport, CT 06881
An imprint of Greenwood Publishing Group, Inc.
www.praeger.com

Printed in the United States of America

The paper used in this book complies with the Permanent Paper Standard issued by the National Information Standards Organization (Z39.48–1984).

10 9 8 7 6 5 4 3 2 1

Contents

Preface

From one perspective, the sports industry is just another industry in a modern economy. The sports industry, like the beverage industry, is a collection of firms producing an array of products and services that meet the demands of modern consumers. Bottled water and diet soda are commodities, as are tennis rackets and tickets to baseball games. The process of obtaining the financing needed to build a new bottling plant has many similarities to the process of obtaining the financing needed to build a new hockey arena. Zoning laws apply equally to package stores and health clubs. But from another perspective, the sports industry differs in profound ways from other industries. What other industry has an entire section devoted to it in most local newspapers across the country? Or a separate segment on local news broadcasts? Has anyone ever asked to have her ashes spread on the local used car lot after passing on to life's ultimate destination?

The sports industry contains some interesting features. Sport has the ability to elicit powerful emotions and inspire transcendent performances; yet every sporting contest by definition produces clear winners and losers, and the larger the stakes involved, the greater the potential gains and losses, the higher the highs and the lower the lows. The presence of a sports team is frequently linked to the status and prestige of cities, and the performance of national sports teams is closely tied to national pride and identity; but most sports are produced by profit-oriented, bottom-line-focused businesses.

The Business of Sports is a comprehensive examination of the sports industry. From its inception, our goal was to bring together a group of international scholars and industry practitioners who were passionately involved in the sports business from a variety of perspectives and turn them loose on the biggest issues facing the sports industry in the twenty-first century. Because sport is a universal phenomenon, we solicited contributions from authors all over the globe. From the outset, it was clear that the modern sports industry was too complex and diverse to be contained in a single volume.

Volume 1 of *The Business of Sports* explores the dimensions of the sports industry. The chapters in this volume explore the big issues in the sports industry, tackle the biggest problems, and highlight the global nature of the industry. One of the biggest unexamined questions about the sports industry is a clear definition of its size and scope. While a few newspapers have hazarded guesses about the size of the sports industry, there have been very few attempts to quantify the economic scale of sports in any economy. Brad Humphreys and Jane Ruseski assess the economic size of the sports industry in the first chapter of this volume.

Are professional sports teams profitable businesses? The answer to this question has important implications in many areas in the twenty-first-century economy. Sports team owners frequently claim that their businesses regularly lose money, but the fantastic prices paid for sports franchises suggest that these businesses may be very profitable. Professional soccer teams in Europe operate in a very different environment than their counterparts in North America—promotion and relegation leagues—and frequently encounter financial problems. Rob Simmons and Babatunde Buraimo address this interesting and important issue and compare the profitability of teams in European and North American sports leagues.

For Western readers, China represents both a great unknown and a tremendous opportunity in many commercial endeavors, and sport would rank near the top of any list of Chinese industries about which we know little. Adam Antoniewicz is a sports executive living and working in China. He has considerable experience working in the sports industry in China, and his chapter provides an interesting first-hand account of the development of the sport industry in China and contains deep insights into the nature of this largely unexamined industry with immense potential.

Mega-sporting events are the world's highest-profile contests. Cities, regions, and countries compete intensely for the rights to host these events, and the popular press contains many accounts of large economic benefits that these events generate. As part of the competition to host these events, governments spend large sums of money to upgrade their sports venues, tourist amenities, and infrastructure. Victor Matheson takes a critical look at the claims made by the proponents of sports mega-events and assesses the conclusions of academic evidence about the economic impact of these events.

The Olympic Games are, arguably, the highest-profile sports events on the planet. From the high-stakes bidding process that pits world-class city against world-class city, to the notorious excesses lavished on the committee that decides where the next games will be played, to the massive broadcast rights fees paid to beam the Games to the world, the Olympic Games are the world's most outsized athletic competition. Brad Humphreys and Andrew Zimbalist take an in-depth look at the financing and economic impact of the Olympic Games.

Radical changes have taken place in North American professional sports leagues over the past fifty years. In years past, professional athletes held second jobs in the off season to make ends meet, people who owned sports teams also ran run-of-the-mill businesses like car dealerships, and broadcast media paid little attention to sports. Today, athletes are multimillionaires, team owners are billionaires, and dozens of television channels show nothing but sports 24/7. The single factor that has brought about these changes in professional sports is the huge increases in revenues earned by sports teams. In addition, since 1990, almost $30 billion has been spent on the construction of new "fully loaded" sports venues in the United States and Canada. Currently, three stadiums under construction in the United States will cost more than $1 billion a piece, each the equivalent of the total spent on new sport facility construction for the entire decade of the 1980s. How is this unprecedented capital spending being sustained? Daniel Mason and Dennis Howard dissect the revenues earned by modern professional sports teams, document the ways in which the revenue streams of professional sports teams have changed in the twenty-first century, and speculate on the ways that revenue streams will continue to evolve in the future. Mason and Howard provide an in-depth examination of the latest revenue acquisition methods employed by professional sports organizations. While their analysis focuses on North American sports leagues, many of the innovative operational and capital financing techniques they discuss have relevance for teams and leagues around the globe.

The sports industry in Europe is as large and significant as the sports industry in the North America. The sports industry in Europe shares many common features with its North American counterpart: it consumes European sports fans just like in North America; the top players in European sports leagues are huge stars; the media exposure of sports in Europe is as large, if not larger than in North America. But the sports industry in Europe also has profound differences from the North American sports industry, in terms of league structure, player compensation, facility financing, and other important dimensions. Wolfgang Maennig and Arne Feddersen provide a thorough and engaging description of the sports industry in Europe, and highlight the similarities and differences.

The sports industry has undergone rapid and extreme changes in the past few decades. Despite these changes, sports fans are extremely resistant to change, and only grudgingly accept alterations to the beloved institutions they hold dear. If past performance is any indication of the future of the sports industry, sports fans are in for a wild ride in coming years. Rodney Fort, the dean of North American sports economists, polishes off his crystal ball and speculates on the future of professional and college sports in North America.

In many ways, college sports are the most interesting element of the sports industry. Unlike other sectors of the sports industry, college sports are produced by nonprofit educational institutions, and long after the Olympics abandoned the pretense of amateurism, college sports still clings to the amateur ideal. Yet college sports ranks among the biggest sports businesses and a large segment of sports fans in the United States fixate exclusively on college sports. Daniel Mahony and Timothy DeSchriver take a careful look at the state of college sports in the United States.

Sporting events first appeared on television in the 1930s. By the 1980s revenues from television and radio broadcasts revolutionized the business of professional sport, turning players into millionaires and team owners into multimillionaires. Like television generations ago, digital media are revolutionizing the sports business; unlike the television era, it clearly will not take forty years for new digital media to have a significant effect. Paul Swangard surveys the digital frontier in sport. This up-to-the-second chapter contains a comprehensive view of the many recent developments in this rapidly changing area of the sports business.

ACKNOWLEDGMENTS

A project on the scale of *The Business of Sport* is a huge undertaking. From inception to publication, it has taken a long time and a lot of work—more than either of us realized when we first took on this project. We could not have completed it without the help of many people, all of whom deserve our deepest thanks and appreciation. First and foremost, we thank each and every one of our contributing authors. We have been blessed to work with such a talented group, and we gratefully acknowledge the contributions of all of these hard-working individuals.

We also got a tremendous amount of editorial support from the staff at Praeger Publishers/Greenwood Press. Praeger is an excellent, professional, well-run publishing house, and the efforts of the editors there have made significant contributions to the project. We thank all of the Praeger/Greenwood editorial staff members who assisted us in the completion of *The Business of Sport* for their help. We also thank Jane Ruseski, Brian Soebbing, Dan "Professor Puck" Mason, Tiffany Richardson, Angela Ronk, Jill Gurke, Amie Cowie, Craig Depken, Andy Zimbalist, Rick Zuber, and Paul Swangard for their help, support, and valuable input. We couldn't have done this without you.

One

The Scope of the Sports Industry in the United States

Brad R. Humphreys and Jane E. Ruseski

Sport plays an important role in society. From the Olympic Games in ancient Greece, to the spectacles in the Coliseum in Rome, to tournaments in medieval Europe, to today's high-profile professional sports leagues, society has long celebrated and fixated on sporting events. Today, sport plays an important part in the fabric of society, including a prominent role in social discourse from the media to backyard conversations between neighbors. In this chapter, we document the economic scope of sport in the United States.

The first step is to define sport in economic terms. Economic activity is organized around markets, and economists commonly group markets with similar characteristics into an industry; so the first step in this exercise is to define the sports industry.

Sport is a multifaceted activity. It encompasses modern spectacles like the Summer and Winter Olympic Games and informal pickup games on urban basketball courts; a recreational jogger and a runner in the Boston Marathon—an event with thousands of participants—and the people watching the Boston Marathon on television are all taking part in sport in some way. Any activity this complex and varied is difficult to define precisely. For the purposes of this exercise, we define the sports industry as having three principal components:

1. Activities involving individual participation in sport.
2. Activities involving attendance at spectator sporting events.
3. Activities involving following spectator sporting events on some media.

While a number of activities related to sport are not included in these three components, all three are indisputably part of sport. These activities are easily defined and observed, which will prove useful when estimating the economic scope of these activities in the United States. We assume that any individual household or firm engaged in an activity that falls into one of these three areas is part of the sports market. We define the sports industry as all producers of the goods and services that fall under these three areas.

Given these definitions, this chapter examines the scope of the sports industry by documenting the extent of individual participation in these activities and estimating of the value of the economic activities in the United States related to these activities. Note that by focusing on the United States in this chapter, we do not intend to diminish in any way the importance of sport in other countries. We recognize that sport plays an important role in many societies, and that sports industries in other countries are large and well developed. However, we are familiar with the economy of the United States and the large number of data sources available to document the economic activities that take place in the United States. The focus of this chapter on the sports industry in the United States is simply a matter of convenience.

PARTICIPATION IN THE SPORTS MARKET

Individuals can participate in the sports market in three ways: by participating in a sport, by attending a sporting event, or by watching or listening to a sporting event on some media like television, radio, or the Internet. Each generates direct and indirect economic activity. All three take time, and economic theory tells us that time use has an opportunity cost. In this case, the opportunity cost of individual participation in sport is the value of the next best opportunity for an individual. For consumers of sport, this opportunity cost can be valued in terms of forgone wages or earnings. Furthermore, participating in sport requires equipment, fees, and potentially travel, all of which generate economic activity. Attending a sporting event involves purchasing tickets, travel, and perhaps other purchases like food and souvenirs. Watching or listening to sporting events requires equipment, in the form of televisions, radios, or computers, as well as subscriptions to broadcast services. Since all of these economic activities increase with the number of participants, documenting the number of participants is an important indicator of the scope of the sports market.

More important, individuals' participation in the sports market generates significant economic benefits beyond direct and indirect economic activity. Individuals derive satisfaction, or utility, from participation in the sports market, which has economic value. In the jargon of economics, individuals' participation in the sports market produces consumption benefits. These consumption benefits are not bought and sold like tickets, but they are important when assessing the overall scope of the sports market. Although placing a dollar value on sport-related consumption benefits is beyond the scope of this chapter, it is safe to say that the value of these consumption benefits rises with the number of participants in the sports market.

Participation in Sport

There are a number of sources of data on the number of individuals who participate in sport in the United States. The National Sporting Goods Association (NSGA) periodically produces estimates of the number of participants in sport in the United States.[1] The NSGA participation estimates are based on a national mail survey sent out to about 300,000 households. Table 1.1 shows NSGA's estimates of the reported number of participants

TABLE 1.1
Estimated Participants in Sport, 2005

Sport or Activity	Number of Participants
Walking	87,500,000
Swimming	56,500,000
Bowling	44,800,000
Health club memberships	37,000,000
Bicycling	35,600,000
Weightlifting	32,900,000
Running/Jogging	29,200,000
Basketball	26,700,000
Golf	24,400,000
Baseball	14,600,000
Soccer	14,000,000
Softball	12,400,000
Volleyball	11,100,000
Inline skating	10,500,000
Tennis	10,400,000
Mountain biking	9,200,000
Downhill skiing	6,400,000
Martial arts (2004)	5,400,000
Snowboarding	5,200,000
Ice/Figure skating (2003)	5,100,000
Cross-country skiing	2,600,000
Ice hockey	2,600,000

Source: Compiled from various National Sporting Goods Association (NSGA) reports, http://www.nsga.org.

for a selected group of sports in the United States for the most recent year available, 2005. Based on the information in Table 1.1, walking is by far the most popular sport in terms of total participation. This is to be expected, because walking is not a costly activity. Participating in walking requires relatively little equipment, few fees, and does not have to involve much travel, since many people can walk simply by stepping outside their home or workplace. Because of this, walking also generates relatively little economic activity. The other sports in Table 1.1 generate more economic activity than walking because they require more equipment, membership fees, and travel costs to participate in.

A simple total of the number of participants reported in Table 1.1 points out an important limitation of these estimates as an indicator of economic activity. Adding up participation in the individual sports suggests that over 484 million individuals participated in sport in 2005. Since the U.S. population was about 297 million, the methodology that generated these estimates involves counting some individuals multiple times. The NSGA survey question asks the respondents to list each sport participated in more than once in the past year and to list those sports every member of their household over the age of seven participated in more than once over the past year.

Clearly, any given individual can easily participate in both bowling and golf, so in one sense this accounting method is appropriate for assessing the scope of the sports industry. However, the economic activity associated with participation in any sport depends on the intensity of participation. For example, the participation count for golf in Table 1.1 treats equally a person who borrows a set of clubs and plays a single round, and a person with a country club membership who plays three rounds a week and takes a vacation to play golf every year. The total economic scope in terms of the direct economic activity, opportunity cost, and consumption benefits generated by these two golfers differs significantly. To the extent that a significant amount of heterogeneity in the intensity of participation in sport exists, the participation figures in Table 1.1 do not provide a great deal of information about the economic scope of sport participation in the United States.

A measure of participation in sport that accounts for intensity of use will be useful for addressing this problem. We turn to the Behavioral Risk Factor Surveillance System (BRFSS) for evidence on sport participation that accounts for intensity of use. The main component of the BRFSS is the Behavioral Risk Factor Surveillance (BRFS) survey, a nationally representative survey of the adult population of the United States conducted by the Centers for Disease Control and Prevention (CDC). The BRFS collects uniform state-specific data on health prevention activities, including physical activity. The BRFS employs a telephone-based survey methodology, meaning that individuals must live in a household with a telephone to be eligible for the survey.

The 2000 BRFS contained detailed questions about participation in sport. This included questions that asked respondents to list the sport that they spent the most time participating in, given that they reported participating in any sport. The specific BRFS question was: "What type of physical activity or exercise did you spend the most time doing during the past month?" Individuals who answered this question are not just casual, once or twice a year, participants in sport. So the sport participants identified by this survey question probably generate significant economic activity while participating.

Since the BRFS is a nationally representative sample, the results of this survey can be used to generate estimates of the total number of participants in various sports in the country. Table 1.2 shows the estimated number of participants for a selected group of sports from the 2000 BRFS. Many other types of physical activities, including gardening and housework, were reported as physical activities in the 2000 BRFS, but we consider the list in Table 1.2 to be the relevant group of sports for this analysis.

Again, we interpret the participation totals in Table 1.2 as reflecting frequent participants in these sports and the totals in Table 1.1 as reflecting both frequent and infrequent participants. The participation totals in Tables 1.1 and 1.2 show some consistencies. Walking has the most participants in both tables. About 70 million people, just under 25 percent of the population, reported walking frequently for exercise in 2000. About 87.5 million people, just under 30 percent of the population, reported walking for exercise either frequently or infrequently in 2005. The biggest difference between these two tables is the smaller number of frequent participants in all the sports except walking. For example, while only 2.3 million people reported swimming frequently for exercise, 56.5 million people reported swimming in the NSGA survey, which includes infrequent participants. This pattern can be seen in the participation counts for all the other sports.

In summary, the analysis of these participation data suggest that in any year over 50 percent of the U.S. population participates in some sport regularly, and a far larger number of people participate in some sport occasionally. By either measure, individual participation in sport in the United States is significant, and this participation generates a considerable amount of economic activity.

Attendance at Sporting Events

The NSGA also compiles total spectator attendance for a number of professional and amateur sports. Table 1.3 contains total attendance estimates

TABLE 1.2
Estimated Sport Participants, 2000

Sport	Estimated Number of Participants		
	Lower Bound	Mean	Upper Bound
Walking	68,600,000	69,301,784	70,000,000
Running/Jogging	12,500,000	12,901,119	13,300,000
Weightlifting	7,118,775	7,396,304	7,673,832
Golf	4,787,312	4,982,688	5,178,063
Bicycling	4,588,754	4,791,467	4,994,179
Aerobics	4,189,563	4,355,448	4,521,333
Basketball	3,276,901	3,461,372	3,645,844
Health club workout	2,375,871	2,510,246	2,644,621
Swimming	2,216,229	2,356,134	2,496,039
Calisthenics	2,054,979	2,208,816	2,362,652
Bike or rowing machine exercise	1,493,113	1,622,729	1,752,346
Tennis	1,072,147	1,171,802	1,271,457
Soccer	878,774	1,010,848	1,142,922
Martial arts	570,918	649,406	727,895
Skating (ice and roller)	544,010	633,485	722,960
Bowling	543,637	611,725	679,813
Volleyball	456,615	531,830	607,045
Snow skiing	315,119	373,660	432,201
Racquetball	298,842	359,900	420,958
Boxing	167,959	208,423	248,887
Touch football	133,717	179,878	226,039
Waterskiing	120,486	158,624	196,761
Squash	57,243	101,219	145,194
Surfing	57,243	101,219	145,194
Badminton	29,427	50,090	70,752
Table tennis	20,818	38,056	55,295
Handball	8,264	18,249	28,234
Softball	4,339	8,203	12,067
Total	118,481,056	122,094,722	125,702,581

Source: Author's calculations based on data from the Behavioral Risk Factor and Surveillance Survey, Center for Disease Control; http://www.cdc.gov/brfss.

for selected sports leagues in 2005. Professional baseball clearly draws the most spectators of any sport in the United States. Over 74 million people attended a Major League Baseball game in 2005, and an additional 15.6 million attended a minor-league baseball game. In part, this is because there are many professional baseball teams at the major- and minor-league level, and these teams play relatively long seasons. This provides consumers with many opportunities to attend baseball games. The next two largest sports in Table 1.3, in terms of total attendance, are college football and college basketball. These

TABLE 1.3
Estimated Total Attendance at Sports Events, 2005

Sport	Total Attendance
Major League Baseball	74,385,100
NCAA football	43,486,574
NCAA men's basketball	30,568,645
National Basketball Association	21,369,078
National Hockey League (2004)	19,854,841
National Football League	17,011,986
Minor-league baseball	15,636,000
NASCAR Winston Cup series	6,300,000
Minor-league hockey	6,179,000
Horseracing	5,979,000
Professional rodeo	5,429,000
NASCAR Busch Series	3,911,000
Professional Golfers Association	3,200,000
Arena Football League	2,939,000
Major League Soccer	2,900,715
Minor-league basketball	2,625,000
Professional tennis	1,970,000
Professional boxing	1,931,000
IndyCar racing	1,914,000
National Hot Rod Association	1,835,000
NASCAR Truck Series	1,708,000
Champ Car racing	1,490,000
Professional Bowling Association	1,310,000
Women's National Basketball Association	1,087,000
Professional lacrosse (MLL, NLL)	1,019,000
Major Indoor Soccer League	992,000

Source: Compiled from various National Sporting Goods Association (NSGA) reports; http://www.nsga.org.

totals reflect college attendance at all levels. Again, hundreds of colleges and universities have football and men's basketball teams, so this large total attendance is to be expected, given the ample opportunities to attend these sporting events. Some readers might be surprised to see that the National Football League (NFL) total attendance is smaller than the other major professional sports leagues—including hockey—and smaller than NCAA football and basketball. However, the NFL plays a relatively short sixteen-game regular season schedule and, as we will soon see, focuses on television viewing as its primary means of public exposure. NASCAR attendance is broken out into Winston Cup, Busch Series, and Truck Series in Table 1.3. Total NASCAR attendance was just under 12 million in 2005, and when the other car racing sports are added to this, total attendance at all professional racing events in 2005 was over 17 million, exceeding total attendance in the NFL. But total professional and NCAA football attendance, including arena football, at over 63 million in 2005, dwarfs total professional racing attendance.

Total attendance at the sports events listed in Table 1.3 was just over 277 million in 2005. This total includes many individuals who bought tickets to multiple games, including season-ticket holders who go to many games in one sport in a single year and people who attend many different sporting events in a single year. Still, 277 million tickets sold in 2005 is a large number compared to the total U.S. population of 296.6 million in 2005. This total represents quite a bit of economic activity. The opportunity cost of the time represented by this attendance is also considerable. Assuming the average sporting event takes three hours to complete, and an average of one hour of travel to and from the event, this total attendance represents the equivalent of approximately 138.5 million eight-hour workdays spent attending sporting events in 2005. The 2005 Economic Report of the President reports that average hourly earnings in 2005 were $18 per hour for the entire workforce. Based on this average, the total opportunity cost of time spent attending the sports events represented in Table 1.3 was $19.9 billion in 2005. Still, this estimated opportunity cost of time represents less than 0.25 percent of the $8.2 trillion of personal spending in 2005.

In addition to the opportunity cost of time, the 277 million people who attended professional and college sporting events in 2005 generated a substantial amount of direct and indirect economic activity. Tickets were purchased for each of these events, along with parking, concessions, and souvenirs. For those spectators who traveled long distances to attend a sporting event, attending the event also generated travel spending, including hotels and meals.

Viewing and Listening to Mediated Sport

Spectator sports play an important role in print and broadcast media. Almost every daily newspaper in the country has a sports section, and sports broadcasts can be found on many television and radio stations across the country. According to the *Vital Statistics of the United States* (2005), the total multimedia audience in the United States was 215,800,000.[2] This implies that, of the 295,194,000 people counted as the resident population of the United States in 2005, 73 percent had access to some form of media, including newspapers, television, radio, and Internet. The NSGA also estimates television-viewing audiences for a number of professional sports leagues. Unfortunately, estimated television-viewing audiences for NCAA football and men's basketball are not readily available. Table 1.4 shows the estimated television audiences for the professional sports leagues tracked by the NSGA in 2005.

The National Football League has the largest television viewing audience of any U.S. professional sports league. The 105-million-person NFL television audience represents over one-third of the total 2005 U.S. population. More than one of every three Americans watched NFL football in 2005. Following the NFL are Major League Baseball and the National Basketball Association, two other traditionally popular professional sports leagues.

One interesting feature in Table 1.4 is the relatively large TV audiences for professional golf (about 38 million viewers) and tennis (about 26 million viewers), and the 21.5-million-person TV audience for horseracing, a sport widely perceived to be in decline. The estimated television audience for these

TABLE 1.4
Estimated Total Television Viewing Audiences, 2005

Sport	TV Audience
National Football League	105,874,000
Major League Baseball	76,744,000
National Basketball Association	60,877,000
NASCAR Winston Cup Series	45,588,000
Professional Golfers Association	37,899,000
NASCAR Busch Series	27,981,000
Professional tennis	26,187,000
Horseracing	21,560,000
IndyCar racing	19,366,000
Professional rodeo	18,862,000
Professional boxing	18,094,000
Arena Football League	17,094,000
National Hockey League	13,870,000
Professional Bowling Association	13,470,000
Women's National Basketball Association	12,220,000
NASCAR Truck Series	12,073,000
Major League Soccer	10,010,000
Minor-league baseball	9,668,000
National Hot Rod Association	7,900,000
Minor-league basketball	7,126,000
Champ Car racing	6,678,000
Minor-league hockey	3,315,000
Professional Lacrosse (MLL, NLL)	3,103,000
Major Indoor Soccer League	2,338,000

Source: Compiled from various National Sporting Goods Association (NSGA) reports. http://www.nsga.org/.

sports may reflect the popularity of a few events, like the four "major" championships in golf, the U.S. Open and Wimbledon in tennis, and the Triple Crown races in horseracing. The popularity of these sports on television may not have the same durability of the NFL, MLB, and the NBA, which probably have a larger day-to-day following. Also, note that NASCAR has a very large estimated television audience; the total audience for the three NASCAR series is over 85 million, which placed it at a similar level to the Big Three professional sports. A caveat is that adding the three estimated television audiences may lead to a lot of double counting, as many of the people in the Winston Cup Series television audience are probably in the Busch Series and Truck Series audience as well.

These statistics illustrate the problems associated with adding up the estimated television audiences in Table 1.4 to estimate the total sport television audience. The NSGA estimates of total television size do not indicate how long an individual spends watching each sport in the average week or month, so we have no idea of the intensity of viewing. Also, unlike live-game attendance, the actual amount of time spent "watching" a sporting event on television is difficult to measure. A fan watching a sporting event on television could be doing a number of things at the same time. For example, while writing this section of the chapter, we had the live television coverage of the Tour de France on in the background. Was that time spent watching sports on television or working?

In any event, watching sports on television generates the smallest direct and indirect economic activity of any of the activities discussed so far. Watching sports on television requires the purchase of equipment (a television) and may also require a subscription to cable or satellite programming packages. Beyond this, the primary economic benefit generated by watching sports on television comes from the consumption benefits.

Aggregate data on the number of people who listen to sporting events on the radio are difficult to find. According to the *Statistical Abstract of the United States*, the estimated radio listening audience in 2005 was about 181 million people, a total that is not much smaller than the television audience.[3] Anecdotal evidence suggests that quite a bit of sports programming is available on radio, perhaps as much as is available on television for the NFL, MLB, and the NBA. So the opportunity cost of time for this activity may be a relatively large fraction of television viewing.

Determining the amount of sports viewing done over the Internet is also difficult to determine. The *Statistical Abstract of the United States* reports that about 138 million people had access to the Internet in 2005. Also, the fraction of surveyed internet users who reported "checking sports scores or information" was larger than those reporting downloading music, although smaller than those using the Internet for email.[4]

ESTIMATING THE VALUE OF ECONOMIC ACTIVITY IN THE SPORTS MARKET

The previous section documented the number of participants in sport, the number of spectators attending sporting events, and the number of individuals who watch and listen to sport through various media. This type of participation is one indicator of the scope of the sports industry. A second indicator is the dollar value of the direct and indirect economic activity that takes place in the sports market.

Economic theory tells us that markets are composed of two distinct parts: suppliers who make and sell goods and services, and demanders who purchase and consume goods and services. This distinction suggests two alternative methods for estimating the value of economic activity in the sports market. Either add up the value of output or revenues of all of the producers in the sports market, or add up the total spending of all consumers in the sports market.

How much direct economic activity, in terms of dollar value of goods and services produced and consumed, takes place in the sports market? The answer to this question is surprisingly difficult to determine. We can easily find out the total sales of the hotel industry for any recent time period ($170,767,400,000 in 2005),[5] and have some idea of the amount of economic activity that takes place in the market for hotel rooms in terms of the dollar value of sales made by all businesses selling short-term accommodations. This supply-side estimate is readily accessible because the accommodations industry has been defined and quantified by the U.S. Census Bureau; but we cannot find out the total sales of the sports industry so easily. The sports industry is not defined by any government agency that collects statistical data on economic performance in the United States. Because of the lack of a commonly accepted definition of the sports industry, any measure of the value of the economic activity in the sports market must be cobbled together from various sources.

In this section, we develop estimates of the dollar value of the sports industry in the United States from both the supply side and the demand side of the sports market.

Supply-Side Estimates of the Sports Market

The U.S. Census Bureau groups individual firms into industries based on the North American Industrial Classification System (NAICS). The NAICS includes the Arts, Entertainment, and Recreation industry (NAICS 71), which contains a number of subindustries that are clearly part of the sports market, based on the definition of the sports industry offered above. These include Spectator Sports Teams and Clubs (NAICS 711211), Racetracks (711212), Other Spectator Sports (711219), Golf Courses and Country Clubs (71391), Skiing Facilities (71392), Fitness and Recreation Centers (71394), and Bowling Centers (71399). The NAICS also identifies Promoters of Performing Arts, Sports and Similar Events (7113) and Agents and Managers for Artists, Athletes, Entertainers and Other Public Figures (7114), but these subindustries appear to include many activities outside sports. This group of subindustries in NAICS Industry 71 accounts for a large fraction of the businesses on the supply side of the sports industry. One important exception is manufacturers of sports equipment. These firms are primarily grouped in Sporting and Athletic Goods Manufacturing (33992).

There are several other sport related subindustries in the NAICS. These include Sporting Goods Stores (45111) and Sporting and Recreational Goods and Supplies Merchant Wholesalers (42391). These two subindustries are related to the distribution of sporting goods.

The primary source of economic data disaggregated to the four- to six-digit NAICS code level is the 2002 U.S. Economic Census,[6] which takes place every five years, most recently in 2002. The Economic Census is based on a complete census of firms and reports summary statistics such as total revenues, total payroll, and total employment for all of the industry groups in the NAICS. In addition, supplementary Economic Census publications contain detailed data on sources of revenues of firms in various industry groups. Both these data sources contain a rich variety of data on the supply side of various markets in the United States economy.

Table 1.5 shows some summary statistics for the NAICS subindustries identified above as part of the sports market. In terms of number of establishments and employees, the Fitness and Recreation Center subindustry is the largest of these, with over 25,000 firms employing over 445,000 people. In terms of total payroll, the Spectator Sports Team subindustry is the largest, with $9.1 billion in total payroll in 2002. Despite the small number of employees in this subindustry, the total payroll is large because professional athletes in the top leagues receive high salaries. In terms of revenues, the Golf Courses and Country Clubs subindustry is largest, generating about $17.5 billion in revenues in 2002. In total, these subindustries included 49,159 establishments employing 1,080,306 people in 2002. The total payroll for these establishments was just under $26 billion and the total revenues earned by establishments were about $71.5 billion. To put these totals in perspective, in terms of revenues the Computer and Peripheral Equipment manufacturing (NAICS 33411) subindustry is of similar size; in terms of employment, the Machinery manufacturing industry (NAICS 333) employs about the same number of people.

TABLE 1.5
Summary Statistics for Firms in the Sports Industry, 2002

Subindustry	NAICS Code	Establishments	Employees	Revenues	Payroll
Spectator sports teams and clubs	711211	674	40,746	$13,025,050,000	$9,106,388,000
Racetracks	711212	646	47,121	$6,702,456,000	$995,042,000
Other spectator sports	711219	2,752	19,860	$2,585,910,000	$664,504,000
Golf courses and country clubs	71391	12,261	312,812	$17,533,703,000	$6,656,680,000
Skiing facilities	71392	387	70,083	$1,801,235,000	$631,951,000
Fitness and recreation centers	71394	25,290	445,508	$14,987,674,000	$4,953,584,000
Bowling centers	71399	4,924	82,010	$3,074,777,000	$904,547,000
Sporting and athletic goods mfg.	33992	2,235	62,166	$11,855,949,000	$2,075,475,000

Source: Compiled from U.S. Census Bureau, 2002 Economic Census, Arts, Entertainment and Recreation—Industry Series. http://www.census.gov/econ/census02.

Table 1.6 shows some summary statistics on sources of revenue for the same NAICS subindustries shown in Table 1.5 (excluding Sporting and Athletic Goods Manufacturing). The primary sources of revenue differ slightly depending on the nature of the subindustry, but the main categories are admissions, revenue from radio and television, membership dues, and sale of food and beverages. In the Spectator Sports Team subindustry, 35.5 percent of the revenues come from admissions (about $4.6 billion in 2002) and 37 percent come from radio and television broadcast fees (about $4.8 billion in 2002). In the Golf subindustry 57 percent of revenues come from membership dues or admissions, and 24. percent from the sale of food and beverages. In the Fitness and Recreation Center subindustry, 57 percent of the revenues came from membership dues ($8.6 billion in 2002). No other single category of revenues contributed more than 10 percent to total revenues in this subindustry. Thus the operation of establishments in these subindustries differs considerably in terms of how they generate revenues.

We have not included the wholesale and retail subindustries in these tabulations of the size of the sports industry for two reasons. First, these establishments also sell general recreation goods like camping, hunting, and fishing supplies, which are outside the scope of the sports industry as defined in this chapter. Second, other wholesale and retail establishments handle sporting goods, so these subindustries would not reflect all of the sporting goods equipment sales in the United States. We turn to other sources of data to estimate the size of the sporting goods and supplies industry of the sports market.

One source of aggregate information regarding the size of the sporting goods and supplies subindustry of the sports market is contained in a recent industry profile published by Datamonitor (November 2006).[7] The market definition of sports equipment in this industry profile includes equipment for golf, fishing, tennis, physical fitness, gymnastics, archery bowling, billiards, winter and summer sports, fun sports, beach sports, racquet and indoor sports, outdoor sports and team sports. This market definition does not coincide exactly with the definition of the sports industry used in this chapter but it is an improvement over the NAICS subindustries because it does not include leisure-related vehicles such as boats, bicycles, motorcycles, and snowmobiles.[8] The market value of the U.S. sports equipment subindustry reached $23.3 billion in 2005, a 2.80 percent increase from 2004. Market values represent retail selling prices and include all applicable taxes.[9]

The industry profile further segments the sports equipment market into five areas: fitness and athletics equipment, golf, fishing, racquets, and other. Revenues from fitness and athletics equipment comprise 21.9 percent of total revenues or $5.1 billion. Sales of equipment for golf account for 16.5

TABLE 1.6
Sources of Revenue for Firms in the Sports Industry, 2002

Subindustry	NAICS Code	Admissions	Membership Dues	Sale of Food and Beverages	Radio and Television
Spectator sports teams and clubs	711211	$4,623,100,000	n/a	$171,502,000	$4,852,911,000
Racetracks	711212	$1,169,600,000	n/a	$260,384,000	$306,399,000
Other spectator sports	711219	$31,592,000	n/a	$8,184,000	$21,332,000
Golf courses and country clubs	71391	n/a	$5,904,724,000	$3,931,228,000	n/a
Skiing facilities	71392	$13,372,000	$138,071,000	$213,389,000	n/a
Fitness and recreation centers	71394	$636,766,000	$8,620,854,000	$641,056,000	n/a
Bowling centers	71395	$12,440,000	$381,000	$847,232,000	n/a

Source: Compiled from U.S. Census Bureau, 2002 Economic Census, Arts, Entertainment and Recreation—Industry Series, http://www.census.gov/econ/census02.

percent of the market values, or $384 billion. The combined market share of fitness and athletics equipment and golf equipment of 38.4 percent is close to the 51 percent share of the catch-all "other" category.[10]

The NSGA provides additional data on the size of the market for sporting goods and supplies in terms of annual revenues for vendors of equipment for sports, athletic footwear, and athletic apparel. The revenue data can be used to construct measures of market concentration in these three product areas and allow us to evaluate both the extent of competition in this area of the sports industry and trends in competition. Some understanding of the nature and extent of competition in the sports industry is useful because competition (or lack of competition) among firms in any industry has implications for consumer and social welfare. A highly concentrated market is a market in which there is not a great deal of price or quantity competition because either a small number of firms are producing and selling goods and services in that market or a couple of dominant firms and a large number of "fringe" firms are. In the latter case, the dominant firms have the lion's share of the market and may be able to exercise some market power in pricing and producing because of their large size relative to the other firms. The smaller, "fringe" firms will simply follow the large firms in this type of market. From an economics perspective, a highly concentrated, and therefore less competitive, market is likely to be harmful to consumers because prices are higher and production is lower than in a competitive market. In addition, it is possible the less-competitive markets produce goods and services of lower quality because they do not have to provide high quality in order to attract business.

The measure of market competition constructed is the commonly used Herfindahl-Hirschman Index (HHI). It is calculated as the sum of the squared market share of each firm in the study industry multiplied by 10,000. The HHI reflects the distribution of the market shares of the firms in the industry and gives proportionately greater weight to the market shares of the larger firms, which reflect their relative importance in competitive interactions. The HHI ranges from 10,000 for a monopoly to nearly 0 for highly competitive industries with many firms. The larger the HHI, the more concentrated the market. The merger guidelines employed by the U.S. Federal Trade Commission (FTC) and Department of Justice (DOJ) divides the spectrum of market concentration as measured by the HHI into three regions that can be broadly characterized as unconcentrated (HHI below 1000), moderately concentrated (HHI between 1000 and 1800), and highly concentrated (HHI above 1800).[11] We constructed HHIs for the athletic equipment, footwear, and apparel vendors separately.

Table 1.7 shows total revenues, market shares, and the HHI from FY2003 to FY2006 for manufacturers of sporting goods equipment. Total

TABLE 1.7
Revenues, Market Share, and Industry HHI for Equipment Vendors, FY2003–FY2006

Vendor	FY2006 Revenue (in million US$)	FY2006 Market Share (%)	FY2005 Revenue (in million US$)	FY2005 Market Share (%)	FY2004 Revenue (in million US$)	FY2004 Market Share (%)	FY2003 Revenue (in million US$)	FY2003 Market Share (%)
K2	1,384.70	17.42	1,313.60	17.46	1,200.70	16.97	718.50	12.13
Callaway	1,107.90	13.94	998.10	13.26	934.60	13.21	814.00	13.74
Icon	852.20	10.72	898.10	11.93	1,095.70	15.49	1,011.50	17.08
Oakley	761.90	9.59	648.10	8.61	585.50	8.28	521.50	8.80
Nautilus	681.50	8.57	633.10	8.41	523.80	7.40	498.80	8.42
Easton-Bell Sports	639.00	8.04	379.90	5.05	166.00	2.35	n/a	n/a
Brunswick Corp.	593.10	7.46	551.30	7.33	558.30	7.89	486.60	8.22
Head NV (Holland)	461.00	5.80	448.00	5.95	479.10	6.77	431.20	7.28
Remington	n/a	n/a	410.40	5.45	393.00	5.55	390.70	6.60
Johnson Outdoor	395.80	4.98	380.70	5.06	355.30	5.02	315.90	5.33
Collegiate Pacific	224.20	2.82	106.30	1.41	39.60	0.56	21.10	0.36
Escalade Inc.	191.50	2.41	185.60	2.47	220.70	3.12	221.70	3.74
Sturm Ruger	167.60	2.11	154.70	2.06	145.60	2.06	147.90	2.50
Smith & Wesson	160.00	2.01	125.80	1.67	119.50	1.69	100.00	1.69
Cybex	126.90	1.60	114.60	1.52	103.00	1.46	90.20	1.52
Adams Golf	76.00	0.96	56.40	0.75	56.80	0.80	50.90	0.86
Aldila	72.40	0.91	77.00	1.02	52.80	0.75	37.90	0.64
Everlast	51.90	0.65	43.30	0.58	45.00	0.64	64.70	1.09
Total	7,947.60		7,525.00		7,075.00		5,923.10	
HHI	984		957		1016		996	

Source: Compiled from various National Sporting Goods Association (NSGA) reports. http://www.nsga.org.

revenues increased from $5.92 billion in FY2003 to $7.95 billion in FY2006. This 34.1 percent increase in revenues occurred in part because data for Easton-Bell Sports were not available in FY2003. Easton-Bell's market share grew from 2.35 percent in FY2004 to 8.04 percent in FY2006 so the missing data in FY2003 probably results in overstating the overall growth in the size of the market. Three vendors, K2, Callaway, and Icon, have at least a 10 percent market share in each of the four years and have a combined market share of about 42–45 percent in any one year. Although the athletic equipment market appears to be dominated by three firms, a sufficient number of smaller firms in the market likely serve to discipline the market from a competitive standpoint. The HHIs in this market are under 1000 in every year except FY2004, which suggests that the market is not concentrated.

The revenues for equipment vendors provided by NSGA are somewhat similar to the industry profile of sports equipment provided by Datamonitor if the major component of equipment in the NSGA data is fitness and athletics equipment. Recall Datamonitor estimated the market value of the sports equipment market to be $23.3 billion in 2005, with the fitness and athletic equipment segment comprising $5.1 billion of the total $23.3 billion. The NSGA data put the size of the equipment segment at $7.5 billion in 2005. It is not clear what is contributing to the $2.4-billion difference between the two revenue figures but one reason may be that the sports equipment market is defined differently in the Datamonitor report. If the NSGA revenue data include other categories of equipment, such as bowling and golf, then the difference between the Datamonitor and NSGA revenue estimates is more difficult to explain.

The size and structure of the athletic footwear market is quite different from the athletic equipment market. Table 1.8 shows the revenue, market share, and HHIs for footwear vendors from FY2003 to FY2006. Note how much larger in terms of revenue the footwear market is compared to the equipment market. Total revenues from sales of athletic footwear were $25.7 billion in FY2003 and rose to $34.1 billion by FY2006, a 32.8 percent increase. This rate of increase is likely overstated because data for Reebok, a rather large player in the market, were not available for FY2006. Reebok enjoyed a market share of 12.07 percent in FY2005 so the omission of their revenues in FY2006 likely makes an important difference in the market revenue figures for that year. In terms of market share, Nike and Adidas are clearly the dominant firms with respective market shares in the neighborhood of 43 percent and 26 percent. The HHIs for the footwear market increased in every year from FY2003 to FY2006 with a noticeable increase of 561 (from 2795 to 3356) between FY2005 and FY2006. Unlike the

TABLE 1.8
Revenues, Market Share, and Industry HHI for Footwear Vendors, FY2003–FY2006

Vendor	FY2006 Revenue (in million US$)	FY2006 Market Share (%)	FY2005 Revenue (in million US$)	FY2005 Market Share (%)	FY2004 Revenue (in million US$)	FY2004 Market Share (%)	FY2003 Revenue (in million US$)	FY2003 Market Share (%)
Nike	14,955.00	43.85	13,700.00	43.62	12,300.00	43.32	10,697.00	41.65
Adidas (Germany)[a]	12,665.84	37.14	8,258.45	26.29	7,289.74	25.67	7,092.99	27.62
Reebok[b]	n/a	n/a	3,790.67	12.07	3,785.30	13.33	3,485.00	13.57
Timberland	1,570.00	4.60	1,565.70	4.99	1,501.00	5.29	1,342.00	5.23
Wolverine	1,141.90	3.35	1,061.00	3.38	991.90	3.49	888.90	3.46
Skechers	1,205.00	3.53	1,013.10	3.23	920.30	3.24	835.00	3.25
Stride Rite	706.80	2.07	588.20	1.87	558.30	1.97	550.10	2.14
K-Swiss	501.10	1.47	508.60	1.62	484.10	1.70	429.20	1.67
Rocky Brands	263.50	0.77	296.00	0.94	132.20	0.47	106.20	0.41
Crocs Inc.	354.70	1.04	108.60	0.35	13.50	0.05	1.20	0.00
Deckers	304.40	0.89	264.80	0.84	214.80	0.76	121.10	0.47
Heelys, Inc.	188.20	0.55	44.00	0.14	21.30	0.08	n/a	n/a
Phoenix	140.60	0.41	109.20	0.35	76.40	0.27	39.10	0.15
Lacrosse	107.80	0.32	99.40	0.32	105.50	0.37	95.70	0.37
Total	**34,104.84**		**31,407.72**		**28,394.34**		**25,683.49**	
HHI	**3356**		**2795**		**2772**		**2739**	

[a]Original data in euros. Converted to USD using average yearly currency exchange. *Source:* Pacific FX http://fx.sauder.ubc.ca/cgi/fxdata.
[b]FY2005 annualized based on January–September 2005.

Source: Compiled from various National Sporting Goods Association (NSGA) reports.

equipment market, the footwear market is concentrated according the DOJ and FTC merger guidelines. The sharp increase in the HHI in FY2006 is due to a large 10 percent increase in market share for Adidas.

Table 1.9 presents the revenue, market shares, and HHIs for the athletic apparel market from FY2003 to FY2006. This market resembles both the equipment and footwear markets depending on which dimension of the market we are considering. The apparel market resembles the equipment market in terms of size but resembles the footwear market in terms of structure. Total revenues were $3.8 billion in FY2003 and $5.1 billion by FY2006, an increase of 32.5 percent. The HHIs were 2301 in FY2003 and 2275 in FY2004, indicating a concentrated market. The market became far more concentrated in FY2005 and remained that way in FY2006. The HHI increased from 2275 in FY2004 to 5490 in FY2005, which is a very large increase. The main contributor to this increase in concentration is Quiksilver, who captured a greater percentage of the market share in every year and nearly doubled its market share over the four-year period from FY2003 (25.46%) to FY2006 (46.55%).

Demand-Side Estimates

The other side of the sports market is composed of purchases of tickets to spectator sporting events, sports equipment, fees paid for admission to participatory sport, and subscriptions and equipment used to watch and listen to sporting events on some sort of media. In general, these purchases can be made by households, other businesses, and even the government at various levels. For example, households and businesses can buy tickets to spectator sporting events. Individuals, professional sports teams, high school and college sports teams, and amateur sports teams all buy jerseys and other equipment for athletes. So spending on sports participation and spectator sports can come from all parts of the economy. However, we only have access to data on sport related spending by households. We do not know of a source of data on aggregate spending by other businesses and the government on spectator sporting events or sports equipment.

There are a number of sources of data on household spending on sports. Each has its strengths and weaknesses, and none are comprehensive because of the lack of a widely accepted definition of the sports industry. The NSGA conducts an annual survey of consumer purchases of sporting goods.[12] This survey was sent to 80,000 households across the U.S. and was returned by 77 percent of the households contacted. The NSGA survey asks questions about annual spending on many types of sporting goods, including footwear, apparel, and equipment. The U.S. Bureau of Economic Analysis

TABLE 1.9
Revenues, Market Share, and Industry HHI for Apparel Vendors, FY2003–FY2006

Vendor	FY2006 Revenue (in million US$)	FY2006 Market Share (%)	FY2005 Revenue (in million US$)	FY2005 Market Share (%)	FY2004 Revenue (in million US$)	FY2004 Market Share (%)	FY2003 Revenue (in million US$)	FY2003 Market Share (%)
Quiksilver	2,362.30	46.55	1,780.90	32.44	1,266.90	28.06	975.00	25.46
Russell Athletic	n/a		1,435.00	26.14	1,298.20	28.75	1,186.20	30.98
Columbia Sportswear	1,287.70	25.37	1,155.80	21.05	1,095.30	24.26	951.80	24.86
G-III	427.00	8.41	324.10	5.90	214.30	4.75	224.10	5.85
Under Armour	430.70	8.49	281.10	5.12	205.10	4.54	115.40	3.01
Ashworth	209.60	4.13	204.80	3.73	173.10	3.83	149.30	3.90
Volcom	205.30	4.05	160.00	2.91	113.20	2.51	76.30	1.99
Cutter & Buck	131.30	2.59	126.60	2.31	128.40	2.84	131.70	3.44
Sport Haley	21.00	0.41	22.00	0.40	20.80	0.46	19.20	0.50
Total	5,074.90		5,490.30		4,515.30		3,829.00	
HHI	5075		5490		2275		2301	

Source: Compiled from various National Sporting Goods Association (NSGA) reports. http://www.nsga.org.

TABLE 1.10
Consumer Spending on Selected Sports Items, 2005

Item	Total Spending
Sports equipment[a]	16,539,200,000
Sports apparel[a]	10,898,000,000
Sports footwear[a]	15,719,000,000
Admission to spectator sporting events[b]	15,900,000,000

[a]Compiled from various National Sporting Goods Association (NSGA) reports. http://www.nsga.org.
[b]Reported in U.S. Bureau of Economic Analysis, *Survey of Current Business*, August 2006, 86.

publishes estimates of annual consumer spending on admissions to spectator sporting events.[13] This estimate includes spending on admissions to amateur and professional sporting events, including horse and dog racetracks and auto racing.

Table 1.10 shows the estimated consumer spending for several areas in the sports market in 2005 from the NSGA survey and the U.S. Bureau of Economic Analysis.[14] According to the NSGA survey, spending on equipment, footwear, and apparel by participants in sport was $43.2 billion in 2005. This figure does not include consumer spending on fishing equipment, camping gear, and hunting equipment and firearms because these activities are outside the definition of sport used in this chapter. The U.S. Bureau of Economic Analysis reported $15.9 billion was spent on admissions to spectator sports in 2005. Admissions to spectator sports consist of admissions to professional and amateur athletic events and to racetracks. Note that this definition of spectator sports varies in an important way from the definition employed by the U.S. Census Bureau's NAICS codes. Recall the NAICS definition for the spectator sports teams and clubs includes professional or semiprofessional sports teams such as baseball, football, and basketball but does not include amateur athletics like high school and college sports.

Together, this spending on sport accounted for less than 1 percent (0.68%) of the $8.7 trillion of personal consumption expenditures in the United States in 2005. In comparison, this spending is roughly equal to the amount that consumers spent on gas in 2005, and is about one-ninth the size of annual consumer spending on health care.

Table 1.11 presents more detailed data compiled from the NSGA survey of consumer spending on sporting equipment in 2005. The sports represented in Table 1.11 roughly correspond to some of the sports that respondents indicated they participated in the BRFS survey (see Table 1.2). The

TABLE 1.11
Consumer Equipment Purchases by Sport, 2005

Item	Spending (in million US$)
Baseball and softball	372.1
Basketball	309.3
Bowling	183.5
Exercise	5,176.6
Football	95.2
Golf	3,465.5
Skating (hockey and ice skates)	138.5
Racquetball	45.4
Snow skiing	642.7
Soccer balls	66.5
Tennis	397.1
Volleyball and badminton sets	32.1
Waterskis	42.2
Athletic goods team sales	2,567.5

Source: Compiled from various National Sporting Goods Association (NSGA) reports; http://www.nsga.org.

largest expenditures are for exercise equipment ($5.2 billion) and golf equipment ($3.5 billion). These two expenditure categories comprise more than half (52.7%) of total spending on equipment, which was $16.5 billion in 2005. The consumer expenditure data presented in Table 1.11 does not include data for all sports for which the NSGA collected data. For example, we do not show spending on camping equipment or fishing tackle because these activities do not fit the definition of sport used in this chapter. Spending on camping equipment was $1.4 billion in 2005 and spending on fishing tackle was $2.1 billion so spending on equipment for these activities is substantial.[15] After exercise and golf equipment, consumer spending on athletic goods for teams was the next largest category of expenditure at $2.6 billion in 2005.

Estimating Consumer Spending on Sport

The NSGA survey and the U.S. Bureau of Economic Analysis (BEA) are not the only sources of data about consumer spending on sport. While these sources provide important information about consumer spending, they also have limitations. The NSGA survey doesn't require the respondents to consult financial records when reporting their spending, so estimates based on this survey may have recall bias. The BEA estimates are based on National

Income and Product Account estimates and must conform to NAICS industries that do not capture all of the sports industry as defined above.

An alternative source of data on consumer spending on sport is the Consumer Expenditure Survey (CEX), a nationally representative quarterly survey of household spending. Approximately 7,500 households take part in the interview survey each quarter, and the respondents are asked to consult bills and other financial records when responding to hundreds of detailed questions about their household spending and other characteristics. Since the CEX is conducted quarterly, and each household appears in the survey for five consecutive quarters before being replaced, the survey is a rich source of data about consumer spending.

The CEX asks a number of detailed questions about consumer spending on sports. Table 1.12 shows the CEX section and spending item description for all of the sport-related spending variables in the CEX. These spending variables include spending on consumer durables like hunting and exercise equipment, nondurables like clothing and shoes, tickets to spectator sporting events, memberships to fitness clubs and country clubs, and fees for sport participation. We did not exclude spending on consumer durables in this case because, unlike the NGSA data, spending in these categories comprised a relatively small portion of total spending. We group these different sport-spending variables into three categories: spending on sports equipment, spending on spectator sport, and spending on sport participation. The category that each individual CEX spending variable belongs to is shown in column 3 of Table 1.12.

These spending variables, along with the sampling weights in the CEX, can be used to generate national estimates of total annual spending on each of the types of consumer sport spending shown in Table 1.12. If s_j is the spending on CEX item s by household j and w_j is the sampling weight for household j, an estimate of total annual consumer spending on item j can be generated by

$$S = \sum w_j s_j$$

where S is the estimated total annual spending on CEX item s.

As part of the sampling methodology, the BEA publishes sampling weights for each household in the CEX. These sampling weights link the sampled household with the total number of households in the United States with similar characteristics. In other words, each household sampled in the CEX represents a certain number of households in the United States, and the sampling weight reflects this number. If a sampled CEX household spends $100 in a year on tickets to sporting goods, and that sampled household represents fifty households in the U.S. population, then s_j equals $100,

TABLE 1.12
Sport-Related Expenditure Items in the Consumer Expenditure Survey

CEX Section	Item Description	Spending Category	2005 Spending
Appliances and Equipment	General sports equipment	Sports equipment	
	Health and exercise equipment	Sports equipment	
	Hunting and fishing equipment	Sports equipment	
	Winter sports equipment	Sports equipment	
	Water sports equipment	Sports equipment	
	Bicycles	Sports equipment	
	Other sports and recreation equipment	Sports equipment	
Equipment Repair and Service	Sport and recreational equipment	Sports equipment	
Clothing	Active sportswear	Sports equipment	
	Estimated Total Spending on Sports Equipment		$2.294 billion
Subscriptions and Memberships	Season tickets to sporting events	Spectator sport	
Entertainment Expenses	Single admissions to spectator sports	Spectator sport	
	Estimated Total Spending on Spectator Sports		$1.226 billion
Subscriptions and Memberships	Country clubs, health clubs, etc.	Sport participation	
Entertainment Expenses	Fees for participating in sports	Sport participation	
	Estimated Total Spending on Spectator Sports		$3.245 billion

Source: Estimated from data provided in U.S. Bureau of Labor Statistics, Consumer Expenditure Survey, 2005.

w_j equals 50, and their product equals $5,000 in total annual spending. Adding this up for the entire CEX sample produces an estimate of total spending for the entire country.

The fourth column in Table 1.12 shows the annual estimated spending on each of these categories of consumer spending in 2005, the most recent data available in the CEX. Consumer spending on sports equipment was $2.294 billion in 2005, consumer spending on single-game and season tickets to spectator sporting events was $1.226 billion, and consumer spending on memberships to health clubs and fees for sport participation like ski-lift tickets was $3.245 billion. The total estimated consumer spending for all these categories in 2005 was $7.6 billion.

Annual consumer spending on these three categories exhibits some interesting patterns of change in the recent past. Figure 1.1 shows the time path for estimated annual consumer spending on each category in real 2005 dollars over the period 1997–2005. Spending on sport participation shows a downward trend over this period, suggesting that either fewer people are participating in sport, or that participants in sport are spending less each year on sport. Spending on sports equipment shows a similar downward trend, but not as large a decline. Also note that consumer spending on

FIGURE 1.1
Trends in Sport Spending by Category

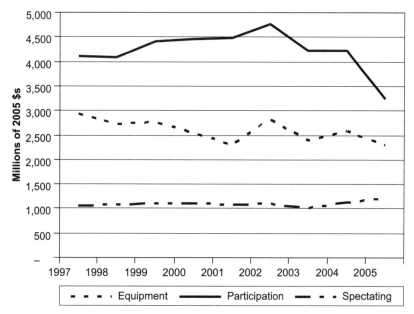

sports equipment responds to the business cycle. The U.S. economy was in a recession in 2001, and spending on sports equipment fell in 2001 and rebounded in 2002. Because many sports equipment purchases are big-ticket items like exercise equipment, skis, boats, and so on, consumer purchases of these items often exhibits a strong cyclical component. Of the three categories of consumer sport spending, only spending on spectator sports increased in real terms over this period, albeit slightly. Also note that consumer spending on spectator sports does not exhibit any cyclical component, as this type of consumer spending did not fall during the recession in the early 2000s.

DISCUSSION AND CONCLUSION

This chapter examined the scope of the sports industry in the United States by examining individual active and inactive participation in sport and estimating the value of economic activity in the sports market from both a supply and demand perspective. While conceptually simple, both aspects of determining the size and scope of the sports market proved to be challenging because of the lack of a commonly accepted definition of the sports industry. The sports industry is somewhat unique in this regard since many industries are clearly defined by the U.S. Census Bureau or other government agency that collects statistical data on economic performance. In addition, determining the amount of inactive participation in sport through attendance at sporting events and viewing and listening to sports on television, radio, and Internet is difficult. Despite the challenges, we developed a working definition of the sports industry for purposes of the chapter and consulted a number of publicly available data sources to develop estimates of the scope of the sports industry.

We define the sports industry as having three principal components: (1) activities involving individual participation in sport; (2) activities involving attendance at spectator sporting events; and (3) activities involving following spectator sporting events on some media. We then examined participation and developed estimates of industry revenues and expenses and consumer expenditures related to these three components.

Our analysis of the NSGA and BRFS surveys indicates that individual participation in sport in the United States is significant. In any year, over 50 percent of the U.S. population reported participating in some sport regularly. Walking is by far the commonly reported exercise. The economic activity associated with participation in sport includes the monetary and time costs incurred to participate in sport. Both of these costs will vary considerably depending on the sport. For example, snow skiing and playing a round of golf are more costly in terms of time, equipment costs, and admission fees than taking a walk or going for a swim. We developed estimates of the monetary costs of participation in sport from industry revenue (supply side) and consumer expenditure (demand side) data. According to data collected by NSGA, revenues for vendors of sporting goods and equipment, footwear and apparel totaled $44.4 billion in 2005. The largest component of the $44.42 billion was for footwear ($31.4 billion), followed by equipment ($7.5 billion), and then by apparel ($5.5 billion). According to Datamonitor, the market value of the sports equipment subindustry was $23.3 billion in 2005. It is likely that Datamonitor's definition of sports equipment is far broader than the equipment sold by the vendors included in the NSGA data. Consumer spending on selected sports item totaled $43.1 billion in 2005 based on NSGA survey data. Estimates of sport-related expenditure items in the CEX indicate consumer spending on sports equipment at $2.3 billion in 2005, significantly less than the NSGA estimates. A plausible explanation for the difference is that the CEX is capturing only household spending while NSGA is capturing household, corporate, and institutional spending. Regardless of market definitions or whether we consider the supply or demand side of the market, sales of and expenditures on sporting goods equipment, footwear, and apparel are significant.

Participation in certain sports, like playing golf and skiing, also require consumer outlays for admission to the venues. The U.S. Census Bureau collects data on sources of revenues according to product lines. One product line captured in these data is admissions. In 2002 revenues from admissions and membership dues to skiing facilities, golf courses and country clubs, fitness and recreation centers, and bowling centers was $15.3 billion or $16.6 billion in 2005 dollars after adjusting for inflation using the Consumer Price Index. The estimate of spending on country clubs, health clubs and fees for participating in sports from the Consumer Expenditure Survey is $3.2 billion in 2005. Taken together, the supply-side estimate of the monetary value of economic activity associated with participating in sports is in the range of $61.0–69.9 billion. The demand-side estimate based NSGA and CEX data is in the range of $32.1–46.4 billion. Turning next to attendance at sporting events, total attendance at a variety of professional and amateur sporting events such as Major League Baseball and NCAA football was just over 277 million in 2005. Like our estimates of the value of economic activity associated with attending sporting events, we come up with a range depending on the data source. The U.S. Census Bureau reported 2002 revenues from admissions to spectator sports, racetracks, and other spectator sports to be $5.8 billion which is $6.3 billion in 2005 dollars. The BEA data indicate that consumer spending on admission to spectator sporting events in 2005 was $15.9 billion. Finally the CEX estimate of spending on season tickets and single-admission tickets to spectator sports in 2005 was $1.2 billion.

Again, the CEX estimates are considerably less than the other sources of data, possibly because the CEX is not capturing corporate spending on admissions to sporting events. Corporate spending is likely a large component of the U.S. Census Bureau data due to corporate spending on premium seating locations and luxury boxes.

The difference between the BEA and Census Bureau numbers may be due to the definition of spectator sports. The BEA definition includes professional and amateur sports while the Census Bureau definition excludes amateur sports. According to NSGA data, 26.7 percent of attendance at sporting events in 2005 was for NCAA football and basketball. While NCAA football and basketball likely comprise a significant portion of total attendance to amateur sports, there are a host of other events not included in these data such as other NCAA sports and high school sporting events. It is quite plausible that spending on amateur athletic events that includes hundreds of events is larger than spending on professional events.

Our sole source of information on the economic value of viewing and listening to sports on television, radio, and the Internet is the U.S. Census Bureau revenue data by product line for subindustries within the sports industry. Revenues derived from radio and television broadcasts totaled $5.2 billion in 2002 or $5.65 billion in 2005 dollars in the spectator sports industry.

What is the bottom line regarding the scope of the sports industry in the United States? A significant number of Americans participate in sports either directly or indirectly and spend a pretty penny doing it. The discussion above identifies a number of data sources that can be used to estimate the economic value of the sports industry in the United States. Recall that we identified three principal components of the sports industry: participation in sport, attending sporting events, and following sporting events through some media. Total estimates of the economic value of these three components can be derived by adding up total revenues earned by businesses, a supply-side approach, or by adding up total expenditures by purchasers, a demand-side approach. Table 1.13 summarizes the estimates reported above and shows four estimates of the economic value of the sports industry in 2005. Table 1.13 disaggregates sport participation into equipment, apparel, footwear, and fees.

From the supply side, we have two estimates. The only difference in these two estimates is the estimated value of sports equipment produced and sold. The NSGA estimates this value in 2005 as $7.5 billion, while Datamonitor estimates it as $16.4 billion. This is a relatively large discrepancy. The difference could stem from either Datamonitor's definition of sports equipment being broader than the NSGA's, Datamonitor surveying a larger sample of firms, or different sampling methodologies. Using the NSGA sports equipment revenue estimate leads to a supply-side estimate of the economic value

TABLE 1.13
Estimated Total Economic Value of Sports Industry, 2005 (In Billions)

		Supply Side		Demand Side	
Component		Estimate 1	Estimate 2	Estimate 3	Estimate 4
Participation	Equipment	7.5[a]	16.4[b]	16.54[a]	2.29[c]
	Footwear	31.4[a]		10.90[a]	
	Apparel	5.5[a]		15.70[a]	
	Fees	16.6[d]		3.25[c]	
	Participation Subtotal	$61.00	$69.90	$46.38	$32.14
Spectating		6.3[d]		15.90[e]	1.22[c]
Mediated		5.65[d]			
Total		$72.95	$81.85	$62.28	$33.36

[a]From NSGA.
[b]From Datamonitor.
[c]From Consumer Expenditure Survey.
[d]From U.S. Census Bureau.
[e]From BEA Survey of Current Business.

of the sports industry of about $73 billion; using the Datamonitor sports equipment revenue estimate leads to a supply-side estimate of the economic value of the sports industry of about $82 billion in 2005.

From the demand side, we also have two estimates. The difference between these two estimates stems from two sources: one, the vastly different estimates of consumer purchases of sports equipment generated by Datamonitor and the CEX that make up spending on sport participation; two, the vastly different estimates of spending on attending spectator sports generated by the BEA *Current Business Survey* and the CEX. In the case of spending on sports equipment, the difference arises because the CEX contains only household spending, while the Datamonitor estimate contains household, business, and institutional spending on sports equipment. The difference between the BEA and CEX estimates of personal spending on attendance at spectator sporting events is difficult to explain.

Based on these two figures, the demand-side estimates range from $33 billion to $62 billion. The demand-side estimates are lower than the supply-side estimates because the demand-side estimates do not capture business and institutional spending on sport.

NOTES

1. Sports Participation in 2005, National Sporting Goods Association, http://www.nsga.org/public/pages/index.cfm?pageid=864.

2. National Center for Health Statistics, Division of Data Services, *Vital Statistics of the United States* (online), http://www.cdc.gov/nchs/products/pubs/pubd/vsus/vsus.htm.

3. U.S. Department of the Treasury, Bureau of Statistics, *Statistical Abstract of the United States* (Washington, D.C.: U.S. G.P.O., 2007), chap. 24.

4. Ibid., 725.

5. Bureau of Economic Analysis, U.S. Department of Commerce, Annual Input-Output Accounts Data, http://www.bea.gov/industry/io_annual.htm.

6. U.S. Census Bureau, *Economic Census 2002*, http://www.census.gov/econ/census02.

7. Datamonitor, *Sports Equipment in the United States: Industry Profile*, Reference code: 0072-0218, November 2006, http://www.datamonitor.com.

8. Ibid., 7.

9. Ibid.

10. Ibid., 10.

11. U.S. Department of Justice and Federal Trade Commission, *Horizontal Merger Guidelines*, 1997 http://www.usdoj.gov/atr/public/guidelines/horiz_book/15.html.

12. Consumer Purchases in 2005, National Sporting Goods Association, http://www.nsga.org/public/pages/index.cfm?pageid=869.

13. Bureau of Economic Analysis, U.S. Department of Commerce, *Survey of Current Business* 86 (August 2006).

14. Ibid., 80.

15. Consumer Purchases in 2005, National Sporting Goods Association, http://www.nsga.org/public/pages/index.cfm?pageid=869.

Two

The Profitability of Sports Teams: International Perspectives

Babatunde Buraimo and Rob Simmons

This chapter reviews the profitability of sports teams in North American major leagues and European soccer.[1] We shall attempt to explain why North American sports clubs tend to be profitable while European soccer teams generally lose money, with some notable exceptions such as Manchester United. Profitability is of concern for sports clubs since their objective might be to make as high a return on investment as possible (profit maximization). Moreover, under the conventional market discipline of capitalism, low profitability will imply lower share prices and risk of takeover. At the level of the league, loss-making teams threaten the integrity of the fixture list, or schedule, and create loss of confidence by fans in the reputation of the league. Broadcasting rights sales and sponsorship and gate revenues would all be reduced as a result.

Driven largely by high and growing broadcast revenues, North American sports teams do generally make positive profits. Tables 2.1 and 2.2 show snapshots of team profits in Major League Baseball (MLB) and National Football League (NFL). The latter has the highest broadcast rights deal in North America, with a total value of $3.735 billion per annum from 2007, spread across all the North American major TV and cable networks. Baseball teams are also generally profitable although the figures are shown after redistribution of revenues from the biggest teams (New York Yankees and Boston Red Sox) to smaller teams. Also, profit figures released by MLB tend to be rather lower than those quoted here from *Forbes*. The arcane practices of conglomerates of baseball clubs in cross-subsidizing other parts of their groups and transferring costs from parent companies to baseball clubs, thus

TABLE 2.1
Operating Profits in Major League Baseball

Team	2000	2005
Arizona Diamondbacks	−7.9	21.8
Atlanta Braves	7.7	27.6
Baltimore Orioles	2.1	2.1
Boston Red Sox	−7.3	−18.5
Chicago Cubs	9.1	7.9
Chicago White Sox	17.8	21.7
Cincinnati Reds	6.9	17.9
Cleveland Indians	4.2	34.6
Colorado Rockies	6.4	16.3
Detroit Tigers	12.1	3.5
Florida Marlins	6.5	−11.9
Houston Astros	22.3	30.2
Kansas City Royals	4.3	20.8
Los Angeles Angels	−8.9	−2.6
Los Angeles Dodgers	−17.4	13.4
Milwaukee Brewers	−1.6	22.4
Minnesota Twins	5.8	7.0
Montreal Expos	−8.1	n/a
New York Mets	21.3	−16.1
New York Yankees	21.9	−50.0
Oakland A's	5.2	16.0
Philadelphia Phillies	−1.1	14.8
Pittsburgh Pirates	2.3	21.9
St. Louis Cardinals	−3.0	7.9
San Diego Padres	−8.0	1.3
San Francisco Giants	27.4	11.2
Seattle Mariners	17.8	7.3
Tampa Bay Devil Rays	−11.3	20.3
Texas Rangers	7.4	24.7
Toronto Blue Jays	−5.9	29.7
Washington Nationals	n/a	27.9

lowering franchise profits, have been extensively discussed by Rod Fort and Andrew Zimbalist.[2] There is an apparent inconsistency between low profit figures and high market values of baseball teams when ownership is traded.

In North America, it seems that teams do not want to appear too profitable. To do so might attract the attention of antitrust regulators who could then pose difficult questions about the various restrictive practices operating in North American sports product and labor markets.

In Europe, it seems soccer teams are fortunate if they make any profit at all, as Table 2.3 shows. Data gathered from Deloitte and Touche financial

TABLE 2.2
Operating Profits in National Football League

Team	2000	2005
Arizona Cardinals	5.1	16.6
Atlanta Falcons	5.0	6.6
Baltimore Ravens	−0.7	27.8
Buffalo Bills	14.5	31.2
Carolina Panthers	30.0	20.7
Chicago Bears	3.3	51.5
Cincinnati Bengals	14.5	20.9
Cleveland Browns	26.3	47.1
Dallas Cowboys	56.4	37.1
Denver Broncos	5.8	26.9
Detroit Lions	−9.7	16.1
Green Bay Packers	9.4	22.3
Houston Texans	n/a	57.6
Indianapolis Colts	−2.4	2.5
Jacksonville Jaguars	21.8	22.5
Kansas City Chiefs	16.6	28.2
Miami Dolphins	6.1	33.4
Minnesota Vikings	13.6	16.3
New England Patriots	−3.7	43.6
New Orleans Saints	−7.6	−4.1
New York Giants	19.2	26.9
New York Jets	17.1	33.1
Oakland Raiders	13.2	9.1
Philadelphia Eagles	6.7	54.2
Pittsburgh Steelers	−9.3	25.5
St. Louis Rams	25.2	33.2
San Diego Chargers	8.9	24.8
San Francisco 49ers	26.1	11.8
Seattle Seahawks	−16.4	5.0
Tampa Bay Buccaneers	35.5	56.9
Tennessee Titans	41.5	48.3
Washington Redskins	76.3	108.4

reports by the authors show that the correlation coefficient between team wage bills and team revenues in the English Premiership over the period 1993 to 2004 is 0.927. Conversely, the correlation coefficient between team revenues and team operating profits is much lower at 0.347. Any increase in team revenues appears to be fully dissipated into team salaries and this result appears to generalize across European soccer. A central question that we address in this chapter is why North American major league clubs are

TABLE 2.3
Operating Profits in the Top Divisions of Five Major European Soccer Leagues

Season	England	France	Germany	Italy	Spain
1995/96	77	5	n/a	−3	−21
1996/97	129	−7	37	8	17
1997/98	143	−46	27	−36	−101
1998/99	104	−70	47	−114	−150
1999/2000	80	36	35	−46	−159
2000/01	121	−41	87	−216	−369
2001/02	125	−98	100	−404	−682
2002/03	185	−61	138	−381	−402
2003/04	223	−102	52	−341	n/a

Source: Deloitte & Touche Annual Review of Football Finance (2003, 2005); Garcia-del-Barrio and Pujol (2007). All magnitudes in millions of euros. Operating profits are profits before net transfer fees, interest, and taxes.

profitable but European soccer clubs are not. Three broad reasons can be discerned:

• A difference in club objectives, with North American teams oriented toward profits while European soccer clubs are essentially not-for-profit organizations; this distinction underlies the so-called North American and European models of sport.[3]

• Different incentives created by the closed-team structure of North American leagues as opposed to the open structure, with promotion and relegation, in European soccer leagues.[4]

• Related to the previous point, close regulation of North American player labor markets as opposed to lack of control in the market for European soccer players.

We pursue these three key points here. The fist section explores some theory that might shed light on determinants of club profitability. The second section looks at the financial crisis in European soccer, triggered by lack of profitability. The next section examines how club profitability is affected by related markets, including the markets for corporate control, for broadcast rights and for player talent.

THEORY

"North American sports teams aim to maximize profits, European soccer clubs are only interested in winning." This pair of propositions underlines the contrast often made by sports economists between the North American and European models of sport. If accepted, these alternative motivations deliver rather different predictions concerning sports team behavior. Other things equal, North American teams should post higher profits than their European counterparts. But in both North America and Europe team owners have established various policies that effectively suppress player salaries and raise club profits. Also, it is in Europe that large soccer clubs have railed against revenue sharing and have sought to retain a larger share of gate receipts for themselves. In North American major leagues, where owners are alleged to have a stronger profit orientation, a wider variety of revenue-sharing devices is offered compared to European soccer. In this section, we focus on the theoretical arguments concerning team behavior under both profit-maximizing and win-maximizing objectives.

A Simple Model

Our theoretical exposition closely follows the work of Stefan Késenne.[5] Team revenues are determined by league win percentage and market size. An extra win has a positive but diminishing impact on revenues. Market size also affects team revenue but this variable is not capable of influence by team owners. Team revenues will be further affected by the quality of the competition and this is summarized by the total amount of talent available in the league as a whole. After the Bosman ruling of 1995, European soccer teams were allowed to field any number of foreign-born European Union (EU) nationals in their allotted sixteen players for a match (eleven plus five substitutes). Work-permit restrictions were also loosened and clubs began to acquire talent in a global search, picking up players from Africa, Asia, Australia, and North America, as well as Europe. It is often argued that this expansive search for talent did indeed result in higher-quality players in European soccer leagues. It is also argued by some of a more protectionist disposition that domestic talent became "crowded out" by this global search, but that is not the point of discussion here.

For analytical purposes, it is convenient to assume a competitive player labor market such that the unit cost of talent is fixed. It is also convenient to assume that relative playing strength of a team maps into team win percentage. Such a relationship cannot be overly deterministic; if it were, then the league title could simply be awarded to the team with the highest payroll without playing any games. Also, a competition with such determinism would be perceived by fans and viewers as boring; part of the appeal of team sports is that a lowly ranked team can beat a more powerful opponent "on any given Sunday" to cite the NFL cliché. This feature of uncertainty will be abstracted from here.

Given this structure the profits of any team will depend on:

- The proportion of its revenue that is retained by the club, that is, not shared with other teams

- The revenue of the team
- The average club revenue for league weighted by the sharing of these revenues
- The unit cost of talent
- The total amount of talent hired by the team.

The idea of talent is somewhat nebulous as it refers to "quality" or "skill" rather than number of players.

A League with a Fixed Supply of Talent

If there is a fixed supply of talent, then it can readily be shown that the distribution of talent will be unaffected by league revenue-sharing rules or by restrictions on player mobility and contracts such as North American–style player drafts and restrictions on free agency. This is the *invariance proposition* first postulated by Simon Rottenberg and demonstrated more formally by Rod Fort and James Quirk.[6] Under this theoretical prediction, league rules that share revenues or restrict player mobility serve to raise team profits and lower player salaries. But league outcomes, in terms of sporting performance, will be unaffected.

With a fixed supply of talent, adding one more unit of talent in one team must reduce the level of talent across all other teams. In this type of league, revenue sharing will drive down the competitive level of player earnings. For most teams (those that have player expenditures not "too large") this translates into higher profits. Such teams therefore have an incentive to install revenue-sharing policies such as sharing of TV revenues or gate receipts. If clubs have team payrolls that are higher than the league average, then, Késenne shows, these teams will suffer *lower* profits as a consequence of revenue sharing. Hence these teams will oppose revenue sharing. It then becomes apparent why we see persistence of revenue sharing in the North American major leagues in the form of sharing of gate receipts as in NFL and general sharing of TV and merchandise revenues. The major North American leagues are organized such that teams from large cities coexist with teams from smaller cities, yet the big-city teams do not emerge as excessively dominant. To make sure championship dominance does not occur, various measures are imposed such as a hard salary cap in the NFL and a luxury tax in MLB, whereby the New York Yankees and Boston Red Sox effectively agree to a transfer of revenues from themselves to the rest of the league. In MLB the New York Yankees do indeed have a much bigger payroll than the league average and probably suffer reduced profits when revenue-sharing measures are toughened. However, the Yankees and Red Sox lack a credible threat to form a rival league and so must accept lower profits and find other ways to augment revenues. Of course, even if some clubs suffer lower profits from greater revenue sharing, the league as a whole will still have increased profits as player costs will fall with unchanged total revenue.

A League with a Flexible Supply of Talent

In professional soccer, the supply of talent is more elastic as teams search for players on a global market. This is not so true for smaller sports such as Rugby League, where available talent is more localized to those countries and regions that tend to play the sport (primarily northern England and Australia). If teams still try to maximize profits, but face a flexible supply of talent, then the extra (marginal) revenue from one more win is a function of the hiring strategy of all the other teams in the league. This introduces strategic behavior into the theory. Késenne shows that, as before, low-payroll teams will obtain higher profits from increased revenue sharing, despite lower aggregate quality of talent across the league. Large-payroll teams gain from reduced player costs. But these clubs suffer large adverse revenue effects from the reduction in total quality of talent. In this case the profits of big teams rise or fall if revenues are shared more equally.

Win Maximization

Peter Sloane is generally credited with being the originator of the "utility maximizing" model of sports teams.[7] In this model, teams maximize utility that is determined by both winning (or "success") and profits. Teams must also satisfy a break-even or maximum loss constraint. Késenne has adapted and formalized this model to posit a maximum win level subject to a zero profit constraint.[8] In his version, clubs just break even so revenues equal costs. But the model is equally applicable to a league where clubs have fixed losses. There are (at least) two concerns with this approach. First, in practice the loss that a club can sustain will depend on club size. Bigger teams (in terms of market size) will be able to secure larger bank overdrafts than smaller clubs. In this sense the sustainable loss allowed by creditors will vary across clubs. Second, we need to consider the longer-term dynamic consequences of a sequence of club financial deficits. In most business sectors, sustained losses lead to either takeover or bankruptcy. In European soccer in particular, most teams are in closed private ownership with no market for corporate control. The standard market discipline of lower share prices inducing takeover as value of assets falls is no longer binding. Moreover, creditors, especially commercial banks, are reluctant to call in bad debt for fear of bad publicity. In the Scottish Premier League, all clubs have overdrafts with the Bank of Scotland but the bank will be most unlikely to call in an overdraft although it will insist on particular limits.[9] With this kind of creditor-community-club relationship installed, losses can be and are sustained over long periods. Of course, observation of persistent losses is not in itself evidence in favor of a win-maximizing objective as the losses may simply be the lowest attainable.

In Késenne's theory, clubs again take the unit cost of talent as competitively given. Total revenues are set equal to total cost. If revenues are shared more equally, then the unit cost of talent is forced downward. But revenues and costs must be balanced by construction and so the impact on profits has to be neutral.

For the reasons advanced above, the notion of a given and immutable break-even condition for all clubs seems too strict, although useful for deriving some theoretical propositions. In practice, teams that might be suspected of win-maximizing behavior have adopted behavior that is actually consistent with a profit-maximizing objective. Take the case of the English Premier League, formed in 1992 after a power struggle in which five "big" English clubs had threatened to break way from the English Football League. Prior to 1992, there were ninety-two English Football League clubs organized in a four-division hierarchy, with promotion and relegation between divisions. Gate-revenue sharing was abolished in England at the end of the 1982/83 season, largely to appease the demands of the bigger top-division clubs.[10] As sales of TV broadcasting rights became more valuable to teams, the largest clubs demanded a higher share of the TV revenues for themselves. The particular clubs most vocal in this breakaway threat were Arsenal, Everton, Liverpool, Manchester United, and Tottenham. Fifteen years on, a list of top four clubs by market size would exclude Everton and Tottenham and include Chelsea, suggesting that "size" of club is not a fixed or given characteristic. In the end the top division of the Football League was transformed into the new Premier League and a more lucrative broadcasting deal was struck with BSkyB, which is a partner of Fox TV in North America.

What this story shows is the drive of some teams to *reduce* revenue sharing, increase own revenues, and raise profits. Moreover, Manchester United in particular experienced rising profits over the 1990s but whether this is a result of increased brand recognition (in Asia especially) or reduced revenue sharing is a moot point. To some extent, despite the ambiguity of the theory, reduced revenue sharing can lead to higher profits for larger teams. In contrast, in North America it can be argued that the larger market teams have been less resistant to moves to increase revenue sharing. In making this comparison it should not be forgotten that loss of divisional and other forms of status do lead to sharp reductions of revenue in European soccer and this is a further important incentive to resist revenue sharing.

In Europe, the Union of European Football Associations (UEFA) Champions' League is an additional competition with revenue streams that exceed domestic competitions. Entry to this supranational league is by virtue of winning a domestic league or being placed sufficiently high in league standings to merit qualification under the number of places allocated by UEFA. Since revenue losses from failing to qualify for the Champions' League are so substantial, it is in bigger clubs' interests to resist a toughening of revenue sharing. In such circumstances, it is hardly surprising that a collusive group would be formed (the G14 group of clubs), which tries to protect big club interests vis-à-vis UEFA. The aim of this group is to sustain qualification into the Champions' League on a regular basis for its members, initially fourteen but now eighteen. The group has lobbying power in that it has the threat to break away and form a closed European League if negotiations over Champions' League prize money, sponsorship, and (especially) TV broadcasting receipts became sufficiently unfavorable to these clubs.

FINANCIAL CRISIS IN EUROPEAN SOCCER

In March 2004 a group of sports economists met in Rimini, Italy, to debate the existence of a "financial crisis" in European soccer leagues. Where such a crisis could be diagnosed, likely causes and remedies were discussed. The findings of the Rimini Group were published in the *Journal of Sports Economics* in February 2006.

A persistent lack of profitability is dangerous for sports leagues for two key reasons. First, a bankrupt club may be unable to fulfill its fixtures in a season. This causes substantial damage to a league's credibility and reputation and could discourage fans, TV companies, and sponsors from continuing their support both for individual clubs and for the sport as a whole. Second, when one club folds others may follow in a domino effect. Financial contagion may result, as often occurs when investors become disappointed with company performance.

The European soccer leagues with the most spectacular losses in recent times are Italy's Serie A and Spain's La Liga, as shown in Table 2.3. It is Italian soccer that has the most unstable structure. In 2002 Fiorentina was declared bankrupt and was relegated to Serie B, though it did return to Serie A with promotion under new ownership. Financial fragility has been manifested in sluggish revenue growth, especially from gate receipts, and spiraling salaries and transfer fees for players.[11] In 2005 the tax authorities demanded payment of taxes held back by clubs and in 2007 several clubs were found guilty of manipulating the allocation of referees to fixtures so as (allegedly) to favor the chances of these winning. The penalties awarded to clubs by the Italian Football Association included relegation of Juventus to Serie B and stripping of their most recent two titles plus points deduction for the 2006/07 season for AC Milan, Reggiana, and Fiorentina. AC Milan and Juventus were also barred from competing in the UEFA Champions' League. The appearance of Juventus in Serie B may have generated a financial windfall for the smaller teams in that division, but the lower quality of contest in Serie A must have exacerbated the delicate balance sheets of the clubs in an already loss-making league.

In contrast, Spanish clubs have continued to thrive despite large losses for La Liga as a whole. Guido Ascari and Phillipe Gagnepain report high growth of broadcasting revenues.[12]

The concern for Spanish football is that extra revenue appears to have been dissipated more than fully into player salaries and transfer fees, with Barcelona and Real Madrid competing aggressively to bring star players from outside Spain (such as Zidane, Ronaldo, and Beckham as the "galacticos" at Real Madrid). Nevertheless, Barcelona and Real Madrid could sustain high ratios of wage bill to turnover and team payrolls three times the league average by virtue of its closed supporter–businessmen ownership structure supported by directors with deep pockets and local authorities willing to underwrite the clubs' debts. Whereas in North America local authorities heavily subsidize sports stadia, it seems that in Spain they effectively subsidize the team's wage bill. The motive for the unusually large deficits incurred by Barcelona and Real Madrid is that such high expenditures on players were needed in order to win the UEFA Champions' League and Barcelona did indeed do just that by beating Arsenal in the 2006 final.

The aggressive search for player talent by big Italian and Spanish clubs has been criticized by those clubs that have operated more prudently. Manchester United and Bayern Munich have somewhat lower wage-bill-to-turnover ratios than Inter Milan and Barcelona. The former clubs have been vocal in demanding self-regulation of wage-bill-to-turnover ratios to a voluntary ratio of no more than 0.7. Not surprisingly, Manchester United and Bayern Munich have figures below this limit and would benefit in terms of Champions' League competitiveness from any cutbacks that Barcelona and Real Madrid would have to make.

Financial Crisis in English Soccer

The English soccer leagues comprise ninety-two clubs with twenty in the Premier League and seventy-two in the Football League. The time-series pattern of revenues, wage bill, and operating profits is displayed for each division in Figures 2.1 to 2.3. Strong features of the graph plots are widening

FIGURE 2.1
Revenue by Division in English League Soccer

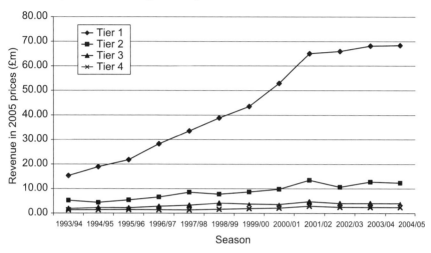

Source: Deloitte & Touche Annual Review of Football Finance (various years).

disparities of revenue growth by division, the tendency for revenue growth and growth of wage bill to covary, and the lack of profitability in all divisions below the Premiership.

FIGURE 2.2
Seasonal Wages by Division in English League Soccer

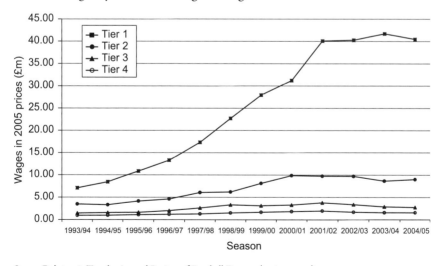

Source: Deloitte & Touche Annual Review of Football Finance (various years).

FIGURE 2.3

Ratio of Wages to Revenue by Division in English League Soccer

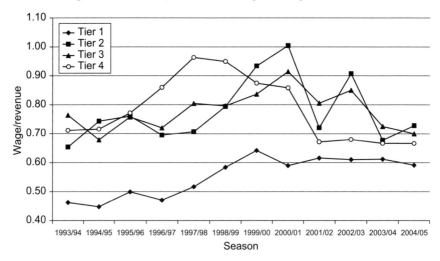

Source: Deloitte & Touche Annual Review of Football Finance (various years).

England has the largest soccer league in Europe, but surprisingly very few clubs have folded due to financial deficits. The last club to close due to debt problems was Accrington Stanley in 1962. Under English corporate law, a

FIGURE 2.4

Pre-Tax Profits for the FA Premier League and the Football League's Championship Division

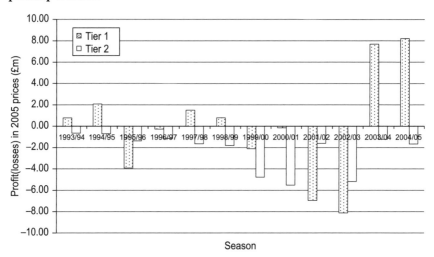

Source: Deloitte & Touche Annual Review of Football Finance (various years).

FIGURE 2.5
Pre-Tax Profits for League One and League Two of the Football League

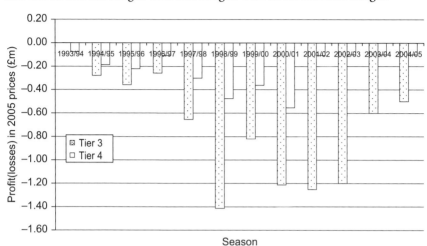

Source: Deloitte & Touche Annual Review of Football Finance (various years).

company can declare itself insolvent and go into "administration." This is the UK counterpart to Chapter 11 bankruptcy, with the key difference that a firm of accountants takes over the management of the company (the old management is released) and either sells off any remaining assets or sells the company "as a going concern." Babatunde Buraimo, Rob Simmons, and Stefan Szymanski report twenty cases of clubs going into administration between 2001 and 2005.[13] All of these clubs were from the English Football League, that is, not in the Premiership. In most cases the move into administration was triggered not by banks calling in overdrafts but by Inland Revenue or Customs and Excise calling in unpaid income tax or sales tax payments due to them. In no case did a club exit the Football League, although Wimbledon did move location (unusually for a soccer team) to become Milton Keynes Dons. Some of the accumulated debt was quite substantial. Bradford City and Ipswich had debts of £36 and £35m, respectively, while Leicester City posted debt of £30m.

Typically, clubs that go into administration are sold to new owners who buy at a low purchase price but agree to take on the debt. Ipswich Town offers an example where the previous owners retained control but left administration with a package of cost-cutting measures. Leicester City, in contrast, was sold to a consortium of owners headed by former player and sports TV presenter Gary Lineker.

Of the clubs that went into administration, the largest debts were incurred by teams from the Championship, the tier just below the Premiership. In the 2001/02 season, the Championship teams suffered a financial blow when ITV Digital went bankrupt and failed to pay the full value of their TV contract. Clubs had committed themselves to inflexible and expensive long-term player contracts in an attempt to gain promotion to the Premiership and share in the much larger revenues from its more lucrative TV contract with BSkyB. Each season the top two clubs from the Championship are promoted automatically to the Premiership while clubs placed three through six compete in an end-of-season playoff competition for a further place in the Premiership. In recent seasons, it appears that at least one promoted club was demoted the following season or the one after. But even so, the club still benefits financially from promotion as gate revenues, sponsorship, merchandise sales (which are retained entirely by the club), and especially TV broadcast fees are significantly higher with elevated status. Moreover, the TV contract between the Premiership and BSkyB provides for "parachute payments" where demoted teams receive a share of Premiership broadcast income for up to two seasons following relegation.

The ITV Digital fiasco was not entirely unpredictable. Television ratings for Championship games were remarkably low (in some cases just a few thousand viewers), which was a reflection of a thin subscriber base and also low quality of games. Yet, clubs engaged in a rat race, trying to buy promotion with large increases in payroll spent on players of moderate quality, given that the best players were already in the Premiership.

Stefan Szymanski has pointed out, with numerous coauthors such as Thomas Hoehn, Babatunde Buraimo and Rob Simmons, and Andy Zimbalist, the folly and futility of the attempts by small- or medium-market teams to break into the Premiership by extravagant expenditure on player contracts.[14] The implication seems to be that clubs with small or moderate markets should know their place and accept that long tenure in the Premiership is not for them. Babatunde Buraimo, David Forrest, and Rob Simmons developed a formal econometric model of English League standings over the seasons 1997/98 through 2003/04. Using measures of market size derived from Census of Population data, they found that market size is a fundamental determinant of league standings. Teams in larger markets finish higher up the league rankings, on average. This occurs despite an open structure of promotion and relegation.[15]

However, promotion and relegation create great excitement for European soccer fans. Even the threat of relegation can create a contest of a certain macabre quality, one that is gripping and important to the fans involved. A closed-league structure for domestic European Leagues, with North American–style conferences and playoffs, was advocated on economic welfare grounds by

Szymanski and Hoehn. Essentially, hermetically sealed large clubs would derive higher profits and fans would become more interested in what would allegedly be a superior brand of soccer. Such a structure is unlikely to find favor with fans or governing bodies at the present time, although the potential for the G14 clubs to break away and form a rival league to the UEFA Champions' League does remain a serious threat.

Fortunately, the financially weak clubs in the Football League learned their lessons after the ITV Digital fiasco and player contracts became shorter in length and more performance-related, so that if a club was demoted it would automatically incur lower salary payments consistent with lower status. But there remained a free-rider incentive problem in that a club could spend extravagantly and proceed to administration while other clubs practiced financial prudence. A club that went into self-declared bankruptcy could then secure higher status through promotion. This was alleged to be the case for Leicester City in the 2002/03 season. Leicester, it was alleged, deliberately overspent on player contracts in an attempt to gain promotion from the Championship while in administration retaining the players it had acquired. Actually, Leicester failed to achieve promotion but Championship rivals were not impressed and made complaints to the Football League.

The English Football League now has an incentive system in the form of points deduction to deter clubs from entering administration. In the 2004/05 season, Wrexham of League One (the third tier of English football) was docked ten points for entering administration, with a debt of £2.6m and £800,000 owed to the Inland Revenue. Partly (but not entirely) as a result, the club was demoted to the fourth tier at the end of the season. The Football League sees the points penalty, plus tighter regulations on corporate governance including a "fit and proper persons" test for club directors, as essential for financial stability.

Buraimo, Simmons, and Szymanski point out that smaller teams in English soccer face the greatest risk of bankruptcy as they become squeezed by a combination of low gate revenues, lack of TV exposure, and high player costs. A common feature of entry into administration over 2001 to 2005 appears to be low gate-attendance/ground-capacity ratios.

One much cited case of financial failure in the English Premier League is that of Leeds United. In the 2000/01 season, Leeds appeared in a Champions' League semifinal. Leeds lacked a strong youth training program as adopted by other successful clubs such as Arsenal, Liverpool, and Manchester United. In an attempt to make further progress in both the Premiership and European competitions, Leeds undertook expensive acquisition of new player contracts that turned out to be unsuccessful, so much so that the team was relegated in 2003/04. Once relegated, players who had been bought via high transfer fees were sold on to other clubs in a "fire sale." In some cases, Leeds agreed to continue paying part of the salary costs of players even though they had left. Add to this some considerable turnover of managers and coaching staff and one has a graphic picture of financial and sporting instability. In 2006/07 the club faced further woe as it reached the relegation zone in the Championship. Leeds is now held up as an example of team mismanagement (on and off the pitch) and financial ineptitude. Fortunately, Leeds appears to be a spectacular and special case of financial failure in the top echelons of English soccer.

IMPACTS OF PARTICULAR SPORTS MARKETS ON TEAM PROFITABILITY

In this section we examine the impacts on team profitability from three particular sports markets: corporate control, broadcasting rights, and players. Each market generates impacts on team profitability. Our focus is on English soccer but references will be made to other European soccer leagues, especially the Bundesliga.

The Market for Corporate Control

In England, the Football Association imposed its Rule 34, which barred payments to club directors and placed a ceiling on dividend payouts. Clubs were mainly established as limited liability companies but with a few businessmen owning a majority of shares. These tended to operate soccer clubs largely on a not-for-profit basis, almost as a hobby.

In the 1980s clubs began to be listed on the English stock exchange with Tottenham Hotspur and Millwall leading the way, followed by England's most profitable team, Manchester United, in 1991. The formation of the Premier League led to increased expectations of revenue and profit growth from the new broadcasting deal with BSkyB. Manchester United posted a rapid growth of its share price and this led to a demonstration effect inducing other clubs toward stock market flotation. A further sixteen English clubs obtained stock market listing between 1995 and 1997. A strong motive for flotation was the acquisition of external finance for projects including stadium development (Manchester United) or acquisition of player registrations in the transfer market (Aston Villa, Newcastle, and Tottenham).

The flotation of several large Premier League clubs attracted the attention of various leisure and media corporations, most notably BSkyB, which anticipated benefits from ownership of one or more teams. With ownership BSkyB could considerably reduce the uncertainty surrounding the auction process for sales of broadcasting rights and sustain its position as monopoly broadcaster of English soccer in perpetuity. In 1999 BSkyB made a takeover bid for Manchester United that was referred to the UK antitrust regulator of the time, the Monopolies and Mergers Commission. In a celebrated court case, the commission found the takeover to be against the "public interest" and the move was blocked. Consequently, media corporations were restricted to a 10 percent ownership of English soccer clubs.[16] Hence, the North American business model for sports team ownership, where media conglomerates play an important role, could not be applied to English, or indeed European, soccer. Nevertheless, there are recent cases of English club takeover by American businessmen who also hold ownership of North American sports franchises. The Glazer family (Tampa Bay Buccaneers) bought control of Manchester United, Randy Lerner (Cleveland Browns) took control of Aston Villa, and George Gillett (Montreal Canadiens) and Tom Hicks (Texas Rangers, Dallas Stars) gained joint control of Liverpool. This appears to be part of a general drift toward foreign acquisition of English Premiership soccer clubs.

An interesting question arises as to whether the wave of stock market flotation in the 1990s led to a change in clubs' orientation toward a stronger profit motive. Stephanie Leach addresses this issue in her Ph.D. thesis.[17] On a descriptive level, she finds that in general the profitability of English clubs fell after flotation. The listed clubs had an average loss of £2.1m per club in the five years before flotation. After flotation, these clubs posted average losses of £32.1m per club. Only Manchester United reported consistent and large profits after flotation. Moreover, clubs' market values also declined after flotation. This is consistent with rational expectations of profitability and share prices. Table 2.4 reports operating profit figures for six teams listed on the English stock market.[18]

Leach then undertakes an econometric analysis of the financial and sporting performance of English clubs, focusing on league position and team revenues. Postflotation, teams experienced falling profits but improved performance. A simple explanation for this is that clubs spent the proceeds of flotation on transfer fees and higher player salaries. However, this in itself does not support a simple switch between utility-maximizing and profit-maximizing behavior.

With hindsight, the move to stock-market flotation looks like a fad, and an idiosyncratic English one at that. Stock-market flotation was not vigorously pursued in the rest of Europe, with some notable exceptions (Borussia Dortmund in Germany). Several clubs delisted due to financial difficulty (Nottingham Forest, Leeds, and Queens Park Rangers, who were all relegated at some time since 1996). Most spectacularly, two of England's biggest clubs reverted to private ownership as Roman Abramovich took control at

TABLE 2.4
Operating Profits of Six Publicly Quoted English Soccer Clubs

Season	Manchester United	Aston Villa	Leeds	Newcastle	Southampton	Tottenham
1995/96	15.4	−0.5	−7.1	−26.8	−0.3	8.3
1996/97	26.5	−0.7	−10.8	9.5	−0.2	0.9
1997/98	17.9	6.8	−1.8	−2.6	0.1	−1.0
1998/99	1.8	−2.4	3.0	−8.4	1.8	−3.5
1999/2000	24.5	0.7	−18.5	−9.0	−3.6	−9.1
2000/01	13.1	−6.6	−18.1	−3.6	0.3	7.3
2001/02	17.3	−3.5	−33.4	3.8	−1.0	2.3

Note: In this table, operating profits are shown after computation of net transfer fees but before interest and taxes.

Chelsea and the Glazer family bought and then delisted Manchester United. For Chelsea and Manchester United it may well be the case, as Leach notes, that utility of ownership was larger under private compared to public ownership.

The Market for Broadcast Rights

North American major-league sports have thrived on growing broadcast revenues. The NFL stands out in this regard, with multiple contracts to the full set of U.S. major TV and cable networks earning a total value of $3.74 billion over the period 2006 to 2011. Not surprisingly, since the regular season has just eight home games, broadcast revenues for NFL franchises easily dominate gate receipts in club balance sheets. The convention in North America is for broadcast revenues to be shared equally among teams. Team profitability is clearly dependent on healthy broadcasting revenues. Following record low ratings for the 2006 World Series between Detroit and St. Louis, Major League Baseball has expressed concern that future growth of broadcast revenues may not be sufficient to sustain present rates of profitability.

In contrast to North America, European soccer leagues tend to sell broadcast rights to a single TV company by a sealed-bid auction. In England, this has led to monopoly dominance of the soccer and, indeed, whole sports broadcasting sector by BSkyB. BSkyB had a business model in which sports broadcasting would lead the way for customer subscription packages in which other TV programs (mainly U.S. imports, movies and news and only a modest amount of domestically produced content) would form part of a lucrative bundle.[19] When soccer fans began to watch live Premiership soccer games in pubs and clubs, BSkyB was quick to raise subscriptions for communal viewing.

Across the rest of Europe, however, leagues have struggled to adapt to the new pay-per-view and cable or satellite platforms that grew in the 1990s. Several broadcasters merged or became bankrupt after 2000. The demise of ITV Digital in England in 2002 has already been noted. In Spain Sogecable and Via Digital merged in 2001, leading to greater concentration of sports provision among the fewer remaining companies. In Germany, the Kirch Group, at the time the major broadcaster of Bundesliga games, became insolvent in 2002. Bernd Frick and Joachim Prinz point out that buoyant attendance demand in the top Bundesliga division has not been matched by growth of broadcast revenues, at least compared to England.[20] They report German sales of broadcast rights as "cheap," in turn related to the reluctance of German TV and cable to fully engage with live soccer broadcasting.

Most European soccer leagues practice collective selling of broadcast rights. Unlike in North America, revenues are not necessarily equally shared. In England, there are three components to the TV revenue distribution. First, each Premiership club receives an equal, fixed share of total revenue. Second, each club (whether home or visitor) receives a fee for each live broadcast. Third, there is a convex schedule of prize money based on end-of-season standings. Thus, big clubs like Manchester United and Chelsea will receive much greater broadcast revenues than smaller clubs, both because of higher prize money won and because these teams will be shown more frequently over the season. A peculiar feature of English soccer broadcasting is that not all games are shown live. This point was noted by the European Union Competition Commission as a possible restriction of trade. Even after lengthy negotiations between the English Premier League and European Union Competition Commission authorities, the new TV deal for 2007 has an increased number of Premier League games shown (up to 166 from 112 out of a potential 380) and one extra minority broadcaster (Setanta with rights to Monday night soccer). BSkyB still retains its dominant status.

The European Union Competition Commission made the argument that individual selling of broadcast rights by teams might generate greater competition in the sports broadcasting rights. The Premier League's response was that collective selling would raise total league profits and permit effective redistribution of broadcast revenues to smaller clubs (while preserving incentives to invest in playing talent through the convex prize formula). David Forrest, Stefan Szymanski, and Rob Simmons present a theoretical model in which individual selling of broadcast rights would raise profits for individual clubs, largely because more games would be shown.[21] They also show that broadcasting extra games would not imply reduced gate revenues and would raise revenues for clubs. The restriction on number of telecast games seems unwarranted. However, the authors show that coordination costs may prevent the Premiership clubs from agreement on a package with an increased number of games.

Some experience of individual selling of TV rights comes from Italy. However, the results are not appealing. In 1999 a combination of legal reform and tougher Italian competition policy authority stance toward restrictive practices in soccer meant that clubs were encouraged to form individual broadcasting deals directly with TV companies. Over the 1999/2000 and 2000/01 seasons, TV broadcast revenues rose by more than double and in 2000/01 pay-TV channels alone paid 550m Euros for broadcast rights.[22] But this growth in revenue stalled in 2002/03 as TV companies passed sluggish subscription growth on to lower rights fees. Moreover, smaller clubs complained that the distribution of TV broadcast revenues was widening and successfully demanded greater redistribution.

In European soccer, TV broadcast revenue has been on a rising trend over the last ten to fifteen years. Even minority sports have benefited. For example, BSkyB's coverage of the English rugby league, coupled with an astute switch of season away from winter to summer to reduce competition from soccer, has led to the Super League transforming aggregate losses into profits. But rising TV broadcast revenues do not appear to have translated into rising profitability. The next subsection investigates the player labor market to see if rising player salaries are a large part of the explanation for this apparent paradox.

The Market for Players

At first glance, rising player salaries should be more of a problem for North American major leagues than for European soccer. Players in North America are highly unionized and the players' unions exert substantial bargaining power. Sometimes collective bargaining breaks down resulting in a strike or lockout. The NHL lost its entire 2005/06 season due to a salary dispute between team owners and the players' union. Baseball and American football have each endured strikes or lockouts over the last twenty years. In contrast, European soccer players tend to belong (if at all) to unions that have little influence over player salaries. Of course, North American player salaries are not usually bound by union-negotiated rates; these rates form lower bounds and individual bargaining between player and owner will settle the final salary package.[23] In Europe, though, unions do not even negotiate minimum salary levels although they may influence pension plans and insurance for injury.

However, North American major leagues are more regulated than European soccer leagues. First, players are drafted in MLB, NBA, NFL, and NHL. Second, all major leagues have restrictions on free agency. Full free agency is only achieved late in most players' careers, after four seasons in NFL or six in MLB. European soccer has no draft and free agency exists for all players over twenty-one. However, one key difference is that European soccer operates a system of trades of within-contract players for cash rather than for players or draft picks as in North America.

A fundamental reason for low and falling profitability of European soccer clubs is often alleged to be a chronic failure to control player costs in the form of transfer fees and player salaries. This argument surfaces regularly in the contributions of the Rimini Group. For example, Baroncelli and Lago describe "soaring" player costs in Italy while Frick and Prinz point to "extraordinary high salaries" paid to players of FC Schalke and (publicly quoted) Borussia Dortmund in the Bundesliga.

There is no doubt that player salary costs and transfer fees grew substantially in top European soccer leagues since 1995. The graph plot for the English Premiership in Figure 2.2 is by no means atypical for Europe. It should be noted that transfer fees are now treated in club balance sheets as intangible fixed assets to be depreciated over the life of a contract (normally three years for soccer players in the top divisions). Both Spain and England are net importers of player talent from the rest of Europe and indeed worldwide. The high rate of growth of expenditures of players needs to be reconciled with some simple economics. First, rational clubs ought to be able to foresee and control player salaries. Failure to do so implies either some underlying incentives to perform "irrationally" and/or some inefficiency in use of player and coaching inputs to achieve sporting performance. Second, in a competitive market players get paid the going rate. After all, soccer players are generally very mobile and moral hazard or "hidden action" problems are overcome by continuous monitoring of condition and performance. Auctions for player talent are usually restricted to just two or three clubs at most, despite the attempts of some agents to engineer competitive bidding to help their clients. Hence, the winners' curse of excessive salaries should be just a curiosity. Third, growth in player salaries is ultimately determined by growing demand for talent that is only sustainable if there is in turn growing audience demand (from TV viewers as well as fans at the gate). Fourth, it is not clear why rising broadcast revenues and rising player salaries should combine to deliver *lower* profitability.

Incentives to overpay soccer players can be found in the promotion and relegation system operated in all European soccer leagues. The desperate attempt to gain promotion, with its large rewards, leads to an arms race between clubs as they seek to gain competitive advantage to just beat their rivals for the promotion places. The arms race is exacerbated by playoff systems that give mediocre mid-table teams the chance of promotion from a late push, which might take them to sixth place. At top division level, a similar set of incentives applies for Champions' League qualification. In England, the fourth-placed Premiership team qualifies for the Champions' League. These incentive-based impacts on player salaries have been discussed in detail by Ascari and Gagnepain.[24] Also, Buraimo, Simmons, and Szymanski point out that the clubs in financial distress in England tend to come from divisions below the Premiership where high growth in player costs has coincided with lack of TV exposure and sluggish gate revenues.

Although the notion of a competitive market for soccer players has some appeal, we should recall that the number of firms (clubs) is relatively small and that some players (especially goal-scorers) have scarce ability. Hence the market for players can be regarded as "thin." In such a structure clubs should in principle have some buyer (monopsony) power. Salaries would then fall below marginal revenue product (what an extra unit of talent generates in additional revenue).

Players and teams try to extract economic surpluses over and above their respective fall-back positions. For players the next best salary is usually in a blue-collar occupation and even lower division players will comfortably exceed the reservation wage that will induce them to become footballers. What emerges is a bilateral monopoly with (individual) bargaining between players (via agents) and teams. There is plenty of anecdotal evidence that club directors and CEOs are sometimes weak in negotiations with player agents. But there is also evidence of growing managerial expertise and acumen as more business skills have been introduced to soccer.

Pedro Garcia-del-Barrio and Francesc Pujol elaborate a theoretical explanation as to why soccer clubs do not earn the expected surpluses from bilateral monopoly negotiations.[25] Thinking of, and empirically testing for, Spanish soccer, although their argument should generalize, part of the player labor market is characterized by buyer power. This is the market for "ordinary" players who are plentiful and elastic in supply. But teams also hire "superstars" who have rare abilities. These outstanding players are the ones who make critical differences between winning and losing games and between league standings. These few players are in winner-take-all markets. Teams spend their surpluses from the ordinary players on superstars who then extract all the available rents. The consequence is that big clubs (the only ones who can afford superstars) find their profits lessened by high payments to superstars.

This "hidden monopsony rent" story seems well suited to Barcelona, Real Madrid, and Inter Milan. It is less helpful to explain the persistent profitability of Manchester United, unless one thinks of that team as one without super-stars. But then Manchester United did hire one of the most famous current superstars, David Beckham, for a number of seasons. Moreover, it is the smaller clubs that have fallen into financial crisis in England, not the bigger clubs (with the notable counterexample of Leeds United.

If large losses are ultimately attributable to "bad management," it is in-cumbent on analysts to uncover precisely what this means. One approach is to focus on the extent of technical inefficiency in soccer clubs. This involves construction of a production frontier showing sporting performance as a function of player inputs. Then departures from the frontier are due partly to stochastic elements (luck) and partly to inefficiency in use of inputs. Sto-chastic frontier techniques have been used in papers to separate out the ran-dom luck element and identify the extent and causes of inefficiency. Both Leo Kahane for NHL and Bernd Frick and Rob Simmons for the Bun-desliga show that head-coach characteristics are important in determining how close a team is to the production frontier.[26] In particular, Frick and Sim-mons find that teams that hold on to their head coaches (i.e., do not fire them too readily) and teams that have longer tenure in the top division, such as Bayern Munich and Werder Bremen, have lower inefficiency scores. Moreover, they also uncover evidence to suggest that head coaches tend to be underpaid relative to their abilities.

Of course, advice to soccer clubs to retain their head coach when per-formance has recently been poor is unlikely to be heeded when the threat of relegation is high and fans are disaffected. Clubs will be more concerned about Type II error (the error of thinking a head coach is good when he is actually bad) as opposed to Type I error (the error of thinking a head coach is bad when he is actually good) as the former is potentially more costly with relegation. But instability of club coaching and player staff will tend to be associated with lower profitability.

CONCLUSIONS

This chapter has highlighted the sharp contrast between generally high profitability of North American major-league franchises and poor or even negative profitability of European soccer clubs. In sports, expenditure on player salaries should translate into player and team performance. Evidence from the four North American major leagues and European soccer leagues suggests this is a valid proposition.[27] The NFL has the weakest correlation between team payroll and team performance, not surprising given the scope of labor and product market intervention practiced in that league. Team performances should then translate into team revenues. Again this is generally valid though again the NFL is an exception. But whereas in North America team revenues convert into team profitability, this connection does not exist in European soccer.

The lack of profitability of European soccer clubs can be explained on both sides of the balance sheet. Revenue opportunities, especially in terms of concessions, merchandise sales, and sponsorship, are not exploited as cleverly as in North America. However, greater commercial expertise is gradually being introduced into European soccer and this situation will surely change. On the costs side, evidence points to high growth of player salaries across European soccer leagues. This is at least partly due to rat-race effects induced by promotion and relegation systems. Such systems are popular with fans and audiences so rather than abolish them, leagues should reinforce their attempts to construct offsetting incentives. The recent introduction of points penalties for clubs that declare themselves bankrupt is a step in the right direction. Further penalties could be introduced for precise standards of overspending, although application of a salary cap for top divisions of European soccer face insurmountable obstacles in the form of monitoring and compliance problems.

NOTES

1. Notation differs across the Atlantic. We shall adopt the notation of "operating profit" to refer to profits before tax, dividends and interest payments. This is equivalent to "net income" in North American terminology.

2. Rod Fort, "The Value of Major League Baseball Ownership," *International Journal of Sport Finance* 1 (2006): 9–20. Andrew Zimbalist, *May the Best Team Win* (Washington, D.C.: Brookings, 2003).

3. See Wladimir Andreff and Paul Staudohar, "The Evolving European Model of Professional Sport Finance," *Journal of Sports Economics* 1 (2000): 257–276, and Peter Sloane, "The European Model of Sport," in *Handbook on the Economics of Sport,* ed. Wladimir Andreff and Stefan Szymanski (Cheltenham: Edward Elgar, 2006).

4. See Umberto Lago, Rob Simmons, and Stefan Szymanski, "The Financial Crisis in European Football: An Introduction," *Journal of Sports Economics* 7 (2006): 3–12.

5. Stefan Késenne, "Revenue Sharing and Owner Profits in Professional Team Sports," *Journal of Sports Economics* 8 (2007): 519–529.

6. Simon Rottenberg, "The Baseball Players' Labor Market," *Journal of Political Economy* 64 (1956): 242–258; Rod Fort and James Quirk, "Cross-subsidization, Incentives and Outcomes in Professional Sports Leagues," *Journal of Economic Literature* 33 (1995): 1265–1299.

7. Peter Sloane, "The Economics of Professional Football: The Football Club as a Utility Maximiser," *Scottish Journal of Political Economy* 18 (1971): 121–146.

8. Stefan Késenne, "Player Market Regulation and Competitive Balance in a Win Maximizing Scenario," in *Competition Policy in Professional Sports: Europe after the*

Bosman Case, ed. C. Jeanrenaud and S. Késenne (Antwerp: Standaard Editions, 1999), 117–131.

9. Stephen Morrow, "Scottish Football: It's a Funny Old Business," *Journal of Sports Economics* 7 (2006): 90–95.

10. Stephen Dobson and John Goddard, *The Economics of Football* (Cambridge: Cambridge University Press, 2001).

11. Alessandro Baroncelli and Umberto Lago, "Italian Football," *Journal of Sports Economics* 7 (2006): 13–28.

12. Guido Ascari and Philippe Gagnepain, "Spanish Football," *Journal of Sports Economics* 7 (2006): 76–89.

13. Babatunde Buraimo, Rob Simmons, and Stefan Szymanski, "English Football," *Journal of Sports Economics* 7 (2006): 29–46.

14. Thomas Hoehn and Stefan Szymanski, "The Americanisation of European Football," *Economic Policy* 28 (1999): 207–240; Umberto Lago, Rob Simmons, and Stefan Szymanski, "The Financial Crisis in European Football: An Introduction," *Journal of Sports Economics* 7 (2006): 3–12; Stefan Szymanski and Andrew Zimbalist, *National Pastime: How Americans Play Baseball and the Rest of the World Plays Soccer* (Washington, D.C.: Brookings, 2005).

15. Babatunde Buraimo, David Forrest, and Rob Simmons, "Freedom of Entry, Market Size, and Competitive Outcome," *Southern Economic Journal* 74 (2005): 204–213.

16. See Simon Lee, "The BSkyB Bid for Manchester United PLC," and Jonathan Michie and Christine Oughton, "Football and Broadcasting and the MMC Case," in *The Business of Football: A Game of Two Halves?*, ed. S. Hamil, J. Michie, and C. Oughton (Edinburgh: Mainstream, 1999).

17. Stephanie Leach, "Financial Viability and Competitive Balance in English Football," Ph.D. thesis, Imperial College, London, 2006.

18. For further details and analysis see John Gannon, Kevin Evans, and John Goddard, "The Stock Market Effects of the Sale of Live Broadcasting Rights for English Premiership Football: An Event Study," *Journal of Sports Economics* 7 (2006): 168–186.

19. For an analysis of BSkyB audience for Premiership soccer see David Forrest, Rob Simmons, and Babatunde Buraimo, "Outcome Uncertainty and the Couch Potato Audience," *Scottish Journal of Political Economy* 42 (2005): 641–661. For a general perspective on European sports broadcasting see the contributions in Claude Jeanrenaud and Stefan Késenne, *The Economics of Sport and the Media* (Cheltenham: Edward Elgar, 2006).

20. Bernd Frick and Joachim Prinz, "Crisis? What Crisis? Football in Germany," *Journal of Sports Economics* 7 (2006): 60–75.

21. David Forrest, Rob Simmons, and Stefan Szymanski, "Broadcasting, Attendance, and the Inefficiency of Cartels," *Review of Industrial Organization* 24 (2004): 243–265.

22. Baroncelli and Lago, "Italian Football."

23. Michael Leeds and Peter von Allmen, *The Economics of Sports*, 2nd ed. (Boston: Addison Wesley, 2004).

24. Guido Ascari and Philippe Gagnepain, "Evaluating Rent Dissipation in the Spanish Football Industry," *Journal of Sports Economics* 8 (2007): 468–490.

25. Pedro Garcia-del-Burrio and Francesc Pujol, "Hidden Monopsony Rents in Winner-Take-All Markets: Sport and Economic Contribution of Spanish Football Players," *Managerial and Decision Economics* 28 (2007): 57–70.

26. Leo Kahane, "Production Efficiency and Discriminatory Hiring Practices in the National Hockey League: A Stochastic Frontier Approach," *Review of Industrial Organization* 27 (2005): 47–71; Bernd Frick and Rob Simmons, "The Impact of Managerial Quality on Organizational Performance: Evidence from German Soccer," mimeo, Lancaster University.

27. Rob Simmons and David Forrest, "Buying Success: Team Salaries and Performance in North American and European Sports Leagues," in *International Sports Economics Comparisons*, ed. R. Fort and J. Fizel (Westport, Conn.: Praeger, 2004).

Three

Perspectives on the Sports Industry in China

Adam Antoniewicz

The Romance of the Three Kingdoms, one of China's most influential works of literature, states in its opening stanza: "The Empire, long divided, must unite; long united, must divide. Thus it has ever been."[1] The history of China, unlike that of the United States, does not follow a linear progression; it follows a cyclical path. China rose to become the world's most developed country around the time of the Dark and Middle Ages in Europe. Four crucial technological inventions emerged from China during this period: gunpowder, the compass, printing techniques, and papermaking. However, in the last stages of the final imperial dynasty, the Qing, China started a precipitous fall which continued until the late 1970s when Deng Xiaoping declared: "To get rich is glorious."[2] China is now poised to become the next big superpower and is "set to overtake the United States as the biggest economy globally by 2050," according to a recent PricewaterhouseCoopers report.[3] This may come as a surprise to most of the world, but to the Chinese it is equivalent to Manifest Destiny.

The sports industry, one of several key developing areas in China, is aiding the country's continuing rise to power. Sport is, arguably, the most visible arena for China to demonstrate its status as a growing superpower. The cyclical development of China's economic and political past is reflected in its sports as well, and one must examine all three together to gain a full understanding of the sports industry. Key trends in China's political and economic development illuminate the enormous challenges and opportuni-

TABLE 3.1
Seminal Moments in China's Sports History

Event	
Ping-pong diplomacy (1971)	"Let us accept the fact that our organization was used as a medium for the expression of Chinese determination to demonstrate its friendly intentions in a world upon which it had turned its back for six years," President of ITTF H. Roy Evans said.[a] Ping-pong diplomacy signaled to the world that China was back from its self-imposed isolation of the Cultural Revolution. China also realized the power that sports wields in the world as an international "ice breaker" as well as a means to demonstrate strength.
Olympics (1984)	The 1984 Olympics is the moment where China presented itself to the world on the sports stage. China was the first Communist country to break with the Soviet boycott, which signaled a change in policy consistent to its economic policies trumping its ideological policies in the early 1980s. China's performance at the 1984 Games helped it realize that sports can become a tool to promote China's rise as an international power. Meanwhile, the nationalist tendencies spawning from the success at the Games was a convenient means for the government to bind Chinese together through the reform process.
Establishment of the Chinese Football Association (1994)	The Chinese Football Association was the first experiment in a commercial sports league in China. In 1994 the CFA started with teams being sponsored by major companies in the cities they represented. The launch of commercial opportunities in the sports industry started with the founding of the CFA, and a floodgate of domestic leagues were created in its wake as well as international entities bringing their events to China.
2008 Olympics	The 2008 Olympics will be China's biggest moment in sports history. It will be China's opportunity to showcase its history, culture, and dynamic society as well as demonstrate its power as a global sports powerhouse. The combination of political, economic, and sports ramifications will combine to bring China proudly onto the world stage.

[a]http://www.usatt.org.

ties in the Chinese sports industry. Table 3.1 shows some of the key events in China's sports history. However, any understanding of the foundation of the modern sports industry in China must begin with the founding of the People's Republic of China in October 1949.

1949–1978: ERA OF MAO

When Mao Zedong proclaimed the founding of the People's Republic of China on top of the Gate of Heavenly Peace (Tiananmen) in late 1949, his first aim was to level the playing field of 2,000 years of feudal society and eliminate the land ownership system in order to free peasants from generations of accumulated debts. This goal was largely achieved by collectivization and nationalization of all industries under the protection of the state. Economic gains weren't immediately evident, as gross domestic product (GDP) grew 6.7 percent annually from 1950 to 1980, according to figures from the International Monetary Fund (IMF). While a large percentage of those gains were from a doubling of the population, there was a small surge in productivity growth in the 1970s. The gains during this period were largely intangible; women gained a more equal standing with their male counterparts when Mao declared: "Women hold up half the sky." Overriding gender concerns was the perception that all achievement by the people was due to the benevolence of the state and all glory of accomplishment was for the state.

This pattern was echoed in sports, where all sports heroes were treated as tools of the state seeking glory for the motherland. One of the most highly visible examples of this was the ping-pong diplomacy between China and the United States. A delegation of U.S. ping-pong players went to China for an exhibition match in 1971. One of the participating players, Zhuang Zedong, was exalted as a hero sportsman because he showed the world that the Chinese could compete on the world sports stage. It was the first sign of a burgeoning global sports potential that China would unleash in in the form of sports schools after the Cultural Revolution wound down in the mid-1970s.

China's sports schools were based on a Soviet model that originated in the Sino-Soviet technological exchange in the 1950s, when Soviet engineers roamed China trying to build and implement new technology to bring China into the twentieth century. One of the products of this exchange was the development of athletes through an elite selection system. Sports schools select the most athletically gifted elementary school students, based on body type, coordination, and growth projections, to stock the schools with "most likely to succeed" athletes. These students are chosen at an early age by different methods, such as X-raying "a youngster's wrist, which the Chinese believe hold some obscure genetic key to a child's future growth."[4] Students selected enroll in a sports academy and combine their academic studies with eight to ten rigorous hours of training a day to develop into world-class athletes. The goal is to identify a small group of young athletes with high potential and invest heavily to help them compete as Olympians. As China opened up to the world in the late 1970s, the quest to prove itself as an international power manifested itself in the drive for Olympic medals.

1979–1990: THE RISE OF DENG

Deng Xiaoping, China's once banned but rehabilitated leader, rose to power after Mao's death in 1976. Deng's first task was to raise the standard of living for all Chinese and bring China back onto the world stage. The seminal moment was the National Party Congress in December 1978, where "the attainment of economic goals would be the measure of the success or failure of policies and individual leadership; in other words, economics, not politics, was in command."[5] Deng's revolution moved quickly to bring China's economy up to a level consistent with its natural resources and human potential by modernizing the economic system and decentralizing economic decisions from national to local leaders. This experimental rise of locally held power created a disparity in income among local officials, entrepreneurs, and the working class. Because this threatened to derail many of the reforms, the central government focused on tools to maintain support for the reforms and create internal harmony. Sports became one of these tools. "Government regards sport media positively, since, through it, the population has an outlet to channel its discontent onto sport instead of on critical social issues such as unemployment."[6]

The sports industry also underwent reform but trailed other sectors by several years. As part of these reforms, sports officials gained more freedom to try new programs. However, the sports ministry was still a political body and its leaders were judged by political measures. The measure of success for the sports ministry, unlike most commercial industries, was not economic but political: gold medals. The Chinese Olympic team strived to catch up to the world in the rapidly changing environment following the 1978 National Party Congress reform announcements. The central government realized that "sports can be one instrument of pride and identity for its people, one signal to the outside world that China is advancing."[7]

The first opportunity to showcase Chinese sports abilities on a world stage came with the 1984 Los Angeles Olympics. However, those games were threatened by a Soviet-led Communist boycott. The need to promote China's progress both internally to its citizens and externally to the world overrode the Soviets' protests. Peter Ueberroth, the head of the Los Angeles Olympic Committee, negotiated directly with China to secure its participation, which ultimately led other Communist countries to abandon the boycott. This act of defiance not only revived the modern Olympics, as the 1984 Games was the first sponsor-focused Olympics, but also shocked the

Chinese into believing in their own potential when they won fifteen gold medals in the first games China had participated in since 1952.

The 1984 Olympic gold medal winners, including Xu Haifeng, Li Ning, and Lang Ping, immediately became state heroes, bringing glory to the Chinese people. In addition to the athletes, coaches and officials gained recognition and political status by producing champions, such as Yuan Weimin, the coach of the 1984 gold medal women's volleyball team, who subsequently rose to the top spot in the Chinese Sports Administration in the 1990s. While entrepreneurs and political officials became rich in the 1980s, sports officials sought gold medals to increase their political status. This led to a move toward regionalization in the sports industry, where sports bureaucrats in different provinces and cities focused on cultivating talent and teams to promote their own political careers by bringing glory to the state. All of this came to a standstill in June 1989, when a student protest at Beijing's Tiananmen Square resonated throughout the political system of China.

1990–2001: THE ROARING NINETIES

The Tiananmen incident illuminated to the central government that reform wasn't benefiting all its citizens. Deng Xiaoping, although retired from his official title as chairman after Tiananmen, still wielded significant influence in the country. In 1992 he made a swing into southern China to invigorate the economy, where commerce was buzzing due to its close proximity to Hong Kong. He instituted the first Special Economic Zones (SEZs), where experiments with foreign investment lead to unprecedented gains in economic activity. Jiang Zemin, the country's new chairman, continued reforms by pushing forward major developments in technological and scientific industries, as well as launching the country's first space program. China's GDP grew at almost 10 percent per annum, according to IMF figures, as market reforms brought China to the world economic stage.

The sports industry mirrored these developments by seeking similar market reforms and setting up its own version of SEZ: commercial sports leagues. Just as sports officials realized in the 1980s that political promotion came with international recognition for local athletes, in the 1990s they realized that banking on local athletess to win a gold medal isn't the only path to glory. With increased market reforms happening in all industries around China, sports officials realized that sports have a commercial side as well. The first experiment came through a partnership between the Chinese Football Association (CFA) and the sports agency IMG in which "IMG signed a five-year, US$8 million guarantee as exclusive agent for CFA's advertising rights and international television rights for both the [Chinese Football] league and the [Chinese] FA Cup."[8] Richard Avory, a sports executive from IMG, is "widely credited with the commercial success behind the CFA vision."[9] The CFA's first professional commercial football (soccer) league was launched in 1994 to much fanfare in response to Chinese citizens' rising incomes and an increased demand for entertainment. Fans flocked to stadiums in twelve major cities around China. The inaugural season of the CFA featured Marlboro as the naming rights sponsor.[10] As Avory noted, "It was an incredibly exciting period to have the first professional soccer league in China, the first companies to advertise at events, the first time tickets were sold for a football event and the first showcase for young Chinese stars."[11] Several other professional leagues soon followed, including the Chinese Basketball Association, Chinese Volleyball Association, and table tennis. This was the first opportunity for sports bureaus to directly profit from the success of their development of athletes.

China's new leagues ushered in the era of the team athlete. Sports officials still sought China's next gold medal winners at their sports schools, but they also fought to build a successful regional professional team. The rise of Dalian's football club, which won seven of the first ten CFA league championships, showed other provinces that a concentration of talent and coaching can produce glory for China as well as reap economic gains for the clubs. The success of Dalian drove more fans to watch its matches at stadiums and on TV, generating excess cash that was subsequently plowed back into developing players and the coffers of the sports bureau. The Chinese populace took to regional heroes and fervently supported their local teams. The economic changes in the country led to regional struggles for economic success and manifested itself in the average sports fan's interest shifting from state heroes to team heroes.

Meanwhile, foreign corporations and sports properties saw the potential for profit in the 1990s' sports industry reforms. Some properties, such as the National Basketball Association (NBA) and the Italian Football Federation, had been trying to build their presence prior to the start of the 1990s through TV. But only limited demand for international sports properties developed. The 1990s brought commercial gains for regional sports bureaus, and foreign outfits wanted a piece of the action. Major companies that used sports to connect with consumers in the United States or Europe wanted to follow the same formula in China. Motorola, Coca-Cola, British-American Tobacco, Nike, and Adidas all rushed to sponsor teams in the newly minted sports leagues. Their early enthusiasm waned as leagues failed to live up to the lofty commercial standards of international companies, and many canceled sponsorships after short-lived honeymoons. Domestic leagues, run by local and national sports officials who had almost no commercial experience, were often poorly run and didn't cater to the needs of the fans, media, or sponsors. Lack of professionalism and the creeping influence of corruption in the leagues, which largely arose from gambling, led to declining attendance and a poor commercial product. By 2001 it was estimated that "the average annual loss per club is, therefore, around RMB19,000,000 (almost US$ 2.3M)."[12] International sports properties didn't fare much better as China's Sports Administration protected its turf and made successful imported events economically unviable. The market reforms of the 1990s benefited most Chinese citizens and industries, but it only directly benefited a small group of sports officials in major provinces. Without continued reforms, the industry remained largely closed off to foreign sports properties. This trend changed radically in 2001, as a result of two momentous developments: the International Olympics Committee awarded Beijing the 2008 Summer Olympic Games, and China was invited to join the World Trade Organization (WTO).

2001–2008: WTO TO THE OLYMPIC GAMES

On December 11, 2001, after fifteen years of negotiation over the terms of the General Agreement on Tariffs and Trade (GATT), the People's Republic of China joined the WTO. The concessions from the Chinese government to gain entry would play out over the subsequent five years in almost all major industries. Since joining the WTO, the Chinese economy has experienced unprecedented GDP growth of almost 13 percent per year. According to the IMF, most of the growth has occurred in the manufacturing sector. The rapid growth of China's manufacturing productivity, fueled by its reservoir of cheap labor, has led to a massive trade imbalance with the United States. Analysts project the trade imbalance between the nations to reach $233 billion in 2007.[13] Most major industries have seen significant reform, and international competitors have entered the domestic market, pushing former state monopolies into competition for Chinese customers. Growing prosperity has led to a rapidly expanding middle class, particularly in major cities along the eastern seaboard. Some experts estimate the middle class will grow to 200 million in 2008. Higher disposable incomes will allow Chinese consumers to enjoy a broad range of luxury products.[14] The sports industry was not one of the key industries specifically identified in the WTO conditions, but due to the increasing disposable income it has been one of the major beneficiaries of the secondary effects of WTO membership. The spirit of reform and improving market conditions led to increased international involvement in the domestic sports market. This is due not only to the improving market conditions, but also to the largest showcase of China's global status, the awarding of the 2008 Beijing Olympic Games.

The awarding of the Olympic Games was a seminal event for China's central government as well as its sports industry, because it was the first chance for China to showcase its progress to the world. The government has latched on to this opportunity to increase tourism, promote business ties, and demonstrate the superiority of China by striving to win the gold medal count in 2008. It will be the moment when the Chinese Communist Party can proudly proclaim that it has come full circle from previous decline; a moment that all Chinese have sensed as destiny due to its cyclical dynastic history over the past 5,000 years.

In its quest to put on the "greatest Games ever" as stated by Beijing mayor Liu Qi in 2003, the government has pledged over $20 billion in infrastructure projects in Beijing to highlight that it has joined the global community at a world-class level.[15] The government has encouraged hosting of international events to "test" China's readiness before the Games. The impact has been transformational. Until the early 2000s, China had hosted only two major international sporting events, the Asian Games in 1990 and the World University Games in 2001. Shortly after receiving the bid to host the 2008 Games, China began to invest in the development of its sports infrastructure. Numerous facilities were created, including a state-of-the-art motor sports race track in Shanghai, a new tennis center in Beijing, and a spectacular sports complex in Nanjing. The response from major sports properties around the globe was immediate. Over the last several years, China has hosted the ATP Tennis Masters Cup, a Formula One race, the FIFA Women's World Cup, and numerous exhibition tours such as the Real Madrid tour and NBA exhibition games. All of these events brought some of the world's premier sports properties to the Chinese, which has increased expectations of the Chinese sports consumer in Beijing and Shanghai.

While competition from international sports properties has increased remarkably, the Chinese domestic leagues have suffered tremendously from competition scandals, inferior quality of play, and poor league operations that lack a consumer focus. The CFA has seen fan attendance drop by more than 50 percent. This decline stems from increased competition without significant reform of the sports ministry and their young professional leagues. This phenomenon mirrors the perils of the SOEs (state-owned enterprises) that have failed to reform their operations in the face of rising international competition.

The domestic sports industry is caught between the two major events of the new millennium, WTO and the Beijing 2008 Games. The increased competition due to the WTO reforms is counterbalanced by the immense political pressure to perform during the Beijing Games. The sports industry is directly responsible for the gold medal count during the 2008 Games. If there's anything short of first place in the gold medal count, then the sports ministry and all the officials will suffer politically. Ministry officials have been unwilling to reform the system, because they want to continue to manage according to the methods that took China from fifteen gold medals in 1984 to thirty-two gold medals in the 2004 Games. Faced with two-pronged pressure of increased competition and pressure to perform in the gold medal race, politically appointed sports officials have overwhelmingly chosen to keep the industry on track to win the gold medal race. The result has been the demise of the domestic professional leagues.

In the shadow of these developments, the sports industry has seen a shift from team heroes to individual heroes. With an increasing number of international sports properties bringing the highest level of sports entertainment to China, the Chinese consumer has shifted allegiance from regional sports teams to international teams such as Real Madrid, the Houston Rockets, and Team Ferrari. These teams feature individual stars including David Beckham, Ronaldo, Michael Schumacher, and China's own Yao Ming. In conjunction with these individual stars, individual athletes such as Liu Xiang, the 2004 Olympic 110-meter hurdle gold medalist, have risen to inspire a new generation of Chinese. Companies such as Nike and Adidas continue to fuel the cult of the hero-athlete and young Chinese have flocked to purchase anything with the logos of these modern-day heroes.

TRENDS IN THE SPORTS INDUSTRY

Three major trends emerge from China's sports-development history over the past thirty years: constant reform, politics, and the rising disparity between haves and have-nots. While these trends are most evident in China's political and economic history, they are strongly correlated with the sports industry's development. These trends will continue into the near future in all major industries in China.

Constant Reform

"Constant reform" sums up development in Chinese sports over the past thirty years. While many Western politicians come from legal or financial backgrounds, China's leaders are comprised of scientists and engineers. This is evident in the scientific-method "trials" of reform policies. The use of various policy trials to test opening markets since the 1978 Party Congress is commonplace and many have been revoked after unfavorable consequences arose.

As policies changed quickly during the 1980s and 1990s, economically driven entities from all industries adapted to the new requirements. The sports industry created their own SEZs in the 1990s in the form of the first commercial sports leagues. Companies such as IMG and Marlboro moved in to take advantage of these new policies. Additional reform policies developed over the next ten years will continue to change the sports landscape. The key for any sports company or property is to keep a close eye on sports policy because it will change quickly.

National policy drives decision-making at the higher levels of government in China and, subsequently, policy for the municipal sports bureaus are affected as national policies "trickle down" through the system. A close watch of national policies can help predict potential changes or opportunities in the sports industry.

Government-policy changes need to be balanced with insights into Chinese consumer behavior. Consumers are often at the leading edge of reform and markets can develop before policy changes have been implemented. This was evidenced by the early success of the Heineken Open tennis tournament in Shanghai during the late 1990s and early 2000s. Due to the increasing demand for world-class entertainment, tennis entrepreneurs worked hard to convince the local government to bring a tennis event to Shanghai. This event was run according to international standards, and the local consumers flocked to see the newest sports property in Shanghai. Due to the initial success of the event and the increased profile of Shanghai, the municipal government started heavily supporting sports events, which led to Shanghai receiving the 2002 Masters Cup Tennis Championships. Entrepreneurs' success in various industries have led to policy review at the highest levels of government, and an incorporation of a double-edged approach of careful attention to national policy changes and consumer insight can lead to opportunities in the sports industry in the long-term.

Politics

"Politics, not commerce" is perhaps the best way to describe the role of the Sports Administration in China's government. Sports in China are almost entirely controlled by the government. All senior Sports Administration officials are political appointees. China's sport goals are politically motivated and based on the policy of the central government. The State General Administration of Sports is not a ministry, but exists just below the ministry level as an organization controlled by the State Council. The State General

Administration of Sports is a national body, but it also has local branches, commonly referred to as the sports bureaus, which are run through provinces and cities. They report both to local government and the national Sports Administration. This system resembles the structure of major multinational corporations with both a geographic responsibility and a function responsibility. In China's political hierarchy, most sports officials take their direction from policies passed down from above, and are largely risk averse when it comes to initiating reform.

For the Sports Administration, the success measures are clear: gold medals. The primary objective of the Sports Administration is to develop medal-winning athletes for the Olympics, world championships, Asian Games, and China's National Games. All relationships with outside entities are viewed through the lens of this objective. If the opportunity doesn't help the local sports bureau to produce medal-winning athletes, then a secondary objective comes into play: revenue generation for the bureau (to help build coffers to meet the primary objective). However, revenue generation will not be given much weight if it is in direct conflict with higher ministry policies or is deemed politically sensitive. Outside organizations with success in the sports industry have successfully partnered with the Sports Administration by positioning their services as directly benefiting China's race for gold medals or providing substantial revenue to the coffers of the sports bureaus.

The ultimate goal of both the China Sports Administration officials and local sports bureau officials is to preserve their careers. Any activity or opportunity presented to officials that could jeopardize their careers usually is rejected. For international sports properties or companies attempting to enter the Chinese market, a careful consideration of sports officials' political goals is vital to achieving long-term success. The Sports Administration or local sports bureaus will not disappear as a political body, so political concerns will remain paramount when engaging in the sports industry in China. A careful balance of commercial interests with political concerns is the ideal formula for long-term success.

Rising Inequality

The increasing gap between the rising upper and middle classes and the stagnant lower class is a major factor affecting sport opportunities in China. The growing inequality affects all levels of government and should be an important component of any long-term strategy involving sport in China. The development of the Chinese economy has expanded from SEZ on the east coast to the interior. Since the nation's economic model is built on becoming the "workhouse of the world," favorable taxes and access to convenient transportation have kept much of China's wealth concentrated along the coastline. Factories, shipping companies, and freight forwarding have built the east coast into an economic powerhouse where GDP per capita is around $1,875 compared with $406 in China's rural areas.[16]

This regional disparity in income has had other consequences in China. The poorer interior provinces have experienced mass migrations of educated workers to the major cities of the east. Attempts to bring sports opportunities to the interior or less-developed regions of China will be met with great interest by local and national sport leaders. A number of policies have been enacted to encourage economic development in all major industries in the interior. While the sports industry hasn't been the target of specific policies in the interior, there's a high possibility that sport-specific policy initiatives might be passed in the future.

A majority of the international sporting events held in China target one of the Tier One cities (Beijing, Shanghai, Guangzhou) due to the higher standard of living in these cities. However, many second- and third-tier cities are approaching the level of development of the eastern seaboard and are eager to promote sporting events in their region, similar to Shanghai's municipal government in the late 1990s. Table 3.2 shows the Tier One and Tier Two cities in China, along with their estimated populations in 2005. International sports properties could gain tremendous political goodwill and operate in favorable conditions by hosting events in second- or third-tier cities. Municipal governments would likely provide economic incentives to help build the reputation of their cities, similar to the Beijing and Shanghai governments in the 1990s. Taking advantage of this trend would lead to long-term success for any outside property or organization seeking to enter the Chinese market.

CHALLENGES TO THE SPORTS INDUSTRY

Trends in the development of sports in China are important building blocks to consider when doing business in China. A careful consideration of the effect of these trends when formulating an entry or growth strategy is crucial to long-term success. However, in addition to the trends, there are three major challenges facing organizations hoping to conduct business in China: the conflicting objectives of the Sports Administration, the legal system, and the lack of a sports playing tradition.

Conflicting Objectives

As mentioned above, the primary objective of the Sports Administration is to produce gold medals. Revenue generation is a consideration only in

TABLE 3.2
Tier 1 and Tier 2 Cities in China

First-Tier Cities	2005 Population	Second-Tier Cities	2005 Population
Beijing	7,741,274	Changchun	2,423,015
Guangzhou	5,056,025	Changsha	1,599,169
Shanghai	10,840,516	Chengdu	2,588,577
		Chongqing	4,865,499
		Dalian	2,263,923
		Fuzhou	1,301,961
		Guiyang	1,416,119
		Haerbin	2,758,136
		Hangzhou	2,635,655
		Hefei	1,254,625
		Hohhot	888,245
		Jinan	2,164,229
		Kunming	1,774,124
		Lanzhou	1,649,169
		Lhasa	141,188
		Nanchang	1,461,190
		Nanjing	3,266,404
		Nanning	1,092,933
		Qingdao	2,084,974
		Shenyang	4,111,624
		Shenzhen	1,333,466
		Shijiazhuan	1,987,484
		Taiyuan	2,067,551
		Tianjin	5,083,657
		Urumqi	1,438,031
		Wuhan	5,147,431
		Xi'an	2,878,939
		Xining	675,011
		Zhengzhou	1,964,179

Source: Adapted from Nielsen media reports and various media sources.

that it can increase the capability to achieve the primary objective. The State General Administration of Sport and its affiliated local sports bureaus receive an annual budget appropriation from the central government. Any additional financial support must come from other sources. Increasingly, sports administrators have looked favorably on forming partnerships with private firms or commercial leagues (e.g., Heineken, the NBA) to augment their limited budget resources. The challenge for foreign sports organizations, particularly in non-Olympic sports, is to provide a solution that benefits one or both of the Sports Administration's objectives.

Obviously, for non-Olympic sports only one of the Sports Administration's objectives, producing increased revenue, is relevant. These twin objectives are perceived as mutually exclusive, especially for non-Olympic sports that are at a distinct disadvantage in the Chinese sport system. Non-Olympic sports have to develop a compelling argument why they benefit a China sports system that is focused on gold medals. Consequently, non-Olympic sports properties must be positioned to enhance revenue-generating opportunities.

One international sports property that balanced this approach well is the National Basketball Association (NBA). Basketball is an Olympic sport, and the NBA approached the Chinese sports authorities with a balanced offering of Team USA versus Team China games and NBA preseason games in China. This package allowed sports authorities to claim support for the Olympics by supplying international competition for the national team. The prestige of hosting an NBA preseason game also adds to each municipal government's international prestige. By balancing the offering and partnering with the Chinese Basketball Association, Team USA Basketball, and the local municipal governments, the NBA crafted a win-win strategy for all parties involved.

The National Football League took a slightly different track. American football is not an Olympic sport and is played by less than 1 percent of the population in China. The NFL adopted a grassroots strategy to build interest in the sport from the ground up. In addition to this strategy, the NFL wanted to promote the sport commercially by hosting a preseason game in Beijing. In order to balance the interests of the Sports Administration, the NFL proposed a strategy to benefit the primary objective: making the 2008 Olympics the greatest ever. The NFL, as the most-watched sports property in the United States, proposed that a preseason game could serve as a "postcard" to Americans considering going to China for the 2008 Olympics. Ultimately the game was postponed for numerous reasons, but the NFL's attempt at supporting the Beijing Olympics has not been lost on sports officials. When the first preseason game is finally held in Beijing, the NFL will have a larger grassroots base built to complement the professional product on the field.

The NFL, based on ten years of experience building a loyal fan base in Europe through NFL Europe, decided to reevaluate their development strategy in China. China, a country with a 1.3 billion people (400 million youth), had less than 0.001 percent youth participation in American football. The approach to the development of football in China had to be completely different from Europe due to a complete lack of exposure to the sport, low sports participation, and the politically based Chinese sports system. As a result, the NFL adopted a grassroots participation strategy. This long-term approach is intended to build interest in football by introducing the sport to children at an age early enough to induce a long-term commitment. This strategy will take ten to fifteen years to bear fruit, but comes with a much lower level of investment. The ultimate goal of the "bottom-up" approach is to reach the top of the player development pyramid and find, as then-Commissioner Paul Tagliabue noted, "Yao Fling," the first Chinese player for the NFL.

A strong base of grassroots players coupled with a national hero in the sport could lead to marketing success and increased popularity of the NFL in China. This strategy is similar to the explosion in the popularity of the NBA generated by Yao Ming's entry into the league. However, the NBA already had an extremely large Chinese player base (approximately 300 million basketball players according to the NBA), a professional league (the Chinese Basketball Association), and televised games since 1987. However, Yao Ming converted casual fans to avid fans, which sources claim has led to marketing partnership sales approaching US$30 million in 2006. The NFL, although significantly behind the NBA at the grassroots level, has committed resources to gain ground in the youth market.

The NFL launched its grassroots efforts in 2003 with a national flag football league in sixty schools at the junior high school level. The competition was in partnership with the Education Ministry, which had been charged with increasing the physical activity of school children to battle obesity and high stress levels among students studying for college entrance exams. A partnership with the NFL was seen as a method to increase sports participation and allow youth to learn key teamwork skills that have been lacking in the education system. The program grew from sixty schools to more than four times that number by 2007.

The long-term vision of the NFL program is to develop professional football players from the vast talent pool in China while building a fan base with experience playing the game at a young age. The benefits of this early investment won't be visible until at least 2015, but the connection to football will be a deep one that can stay with the consumer for a lifetime. Based on research from local sports agency ZOU Marketing, the strength of affiliation with sports in China is profoundly linked to participation in that sport. Finally, the NFL wanted to be positioned as a sport purely, as opposed to a fashion, in the key youth demographic. Studying previous efforts at developing the NFL internationally shows that licensed products revenue can grow quickly from fashion-focused marketing (e.g., product placement with singers and actors), but can also lose popularity just as quickly. The NFL wanted to ground its brand in sports through participation and build a foundation before attempting to extend its brand through other methods.

Along with building a strong foundation of players and fans, the NFL is launching a second development effort by hosting preseason games in China. The first China Bowl is an effort to promote the NFL at a national level to average consumers with an interest in sport. The curiosity surrounding a new sport, similar to that experienced by Formula One in 2002, helps build marketing partnerships and consumer awareness, and solidify brand loyalty for NFL early adopters in the market. The China Bowl allows the NFL to tell the story and showcase the entertainment of the league and the game of football, which should ultimately lead to increased interest in the grassroots development of the game.

A big part of the NFL's success was partnerships with both local and international organizations. The NFL's first agency agreement was with ZOU Marketing, a sports branding agency with a long ties to Nike, who advised against an immediate national entry into China. According to one previous Nike director, Nike's China business took more than ten years to break even. China's massive market is regionally diverse, and building brand awareness can be an expensive undertaking. So a long-term investment plan is absolutely imperative. The NFL adopted this strategy to avoid the "boom and bust" scenario of only playing preseason games in China. The "boom and bust" scenario describes a circus-like situation where marketing and interest coalesce around an event (like the circus) at an extremely intense level—but only when the event is in town. As soon as the event leaves, awareness and interest drop to almost zero. ZOU advised the NFL to refine its marketing strategy to maintain a consistent level of engagement year-round or at least seasonally. The NFL needed to invest in the development of the sport, similar to Nike's strategy in the 1990s, where a low-level, consistent message of sports development at the grassroots level increased Nike's market share and revenues as China's sports market grew. ZOU played a key role in crafting the NFL's entry into China in a manner similar to Nike's early efforts.

A second key strategy was the development of role-specific partnerships for various functional duties. The NFL hired a digital/Internet agency, a fantasy football partner, a broadcasting partner, and a research agency to parcel out all functional aspects of their business. China-based agencies with local knowledge and international perspectives helped ground the NFL's vision in China. Local relationships with the conglomeration of agencies and the Education Ministry kept all strategic initiatives focused on long-term results while minimizing investment. A common mistake among international companies trying to enter the Chinese market is to work with global agencies that lack local knowledge and enter the market at the national level. The Rugby Federation encountered this problem in 2000 when they decided to invest US$1.0 million annually through the Sports Administration to develop grassroots participation. Five years after the initial investment, the number of rugby players in China was far less than expected. Most of the investment went toward overhead payments to the Sports Administration rather than specifically to building grassroots participation programs.

Formula One offers another effective approach for succeeding in China. Formula One gained access to the Chinese market by working with key officials in Shanghai city government. Recognizing its limitation as a non-Olympic sport, Formula One emphasized its ability to enhance economic development and to raise the international profile of Shanghai. High-level officials in the municipal government pushed Formula One through the local sports bureau as a higher priority goal. The traditional hierarchy of the system worked to the advantage of Formula One, because they were able to bypass the local sports bureau to appeal to the benefit of Shanghai's highest leaders.

Working with state-controlled media poses some unique challenges for commercial sports properties and events in China. China Central Television, commonly abbreviated as CCTV, is the major television broadcaster in the PRC. Organizationally, it falls under the central government's State Administration of Radio, Film and Television. As a state-controlled agency it does not have any editorial independence. However, CCTV offers a wide range of programming, including certain U.S. shows such as *CSI: New York* and *Lost*, across 16 national channels. One of the CCTV's national channels, CCTV-5, is dedicated to sports programming. Because television is state-controlled, a principal objective of the medium is to disseminate information, whether government policies or international news, throughout China. Unlike in most western nations, the commercial success of programs isn't the ultimate deciding factor for content on television in China. Therefore, it is challenging for new programming to get placement on local TV. Also, due to the strict government control of content, and the lack of a commercial focus for TV stations, broadcast rights for sports properties are often extremely low. "China is one of the few sports markets in the world, if not the only major market, mainly funded by sponsorship revenues and not television or other media rights."[17] For example, CCTV-5 paid US$25 million in rights fees for the 2002 and 2006 FIFA World Cup.[18] CCTV received over RMB 1.0B (roughly US$125 million) in advertising revenues alone during the 2006 World Cup.[19] The monopoly power of state-run television allows for price controls on the rights fees paid for sporting events. As long as artificially low pricing for sporting events is common, then sporting events will have a difficult time growing in China.

Legal System

The legal system is a major impediment for international sports properties trying to enter China. Unlike the English common-law tradition, China has no history of a formal written legal code. The modern Chinese legal system was written in the early 1980s and is loosely constructed to allow large variations in interpretation. The legal system has been evolving to better protect companies and individuals, but ultimately the law is interpreted by a handful of judges who are charged with maintaining social harmony (the ultimate objective of all Chinese dynasties). According to the legal code, disputes will be decided based on the best outcome for Chinese society, no matter how attorneys might interpret them. Sports properties that have come into conflict with government bodies will have a difficult time protecting their interests in this system. Successful sports businesses have relied upon strong local business savvy combined with a solid position of being a win-win proposition for the local sports bureau as well as the Chinese people. Success in the sports business in China comes through a strong relationship with local and regional government coupled with mutually beneficial goals between the entity and the government partner. If a contract is used to force the actions of one party, then compromises are rarely reached. Early corporate partners with the domestic leagues in the mid-1990s realized this issue very quickly. The grandiose promises of the commercial benefits of domestic leagues were rarely met, and subsequent legal disputes led to the departure of several top sponsors of those leagues. However, successful sports properties such the Heineken Open tennis tournament worked closely with the local government to demonstrate the value of meeting all agreed-upon legal points of the contract to create a strong partnership.

China is improving rapidly in the legal arena as its WTO requirements have been fully implemented. Intellectual property rights are being increasingly enforced for international and domestic companies that have built up valuable brands and trademarks. China's legal system is rapidly reforming to offer greater protection for these companies and, subsequently, encouraging the world's top brands to enter China. Despite substantial reform in the legal system, China still remains far behind other developed countries in legal protection and this will remain a major challenge for companies looking to enter the Chinese market.

Sports Participation Traditions

China has a long academic tradition that spans back to the Han Dynasty, which started in 206 BC with the implementation of imperial exams. This system is rooted in the firm belief that the highest social class is the intelligentsia, where government officials were chosen from the highest scores on national exams. This academic tradition is continued today through China's *Gao Kao*, the college entrance exam. Parents' belief that their child's success is linked directly to what college the child attends is firmly established. Entrance exams have started moving to lower schools, and currently there are high school and middle school entrance exams that put children on the path to schools that will better prepare them for the college entrance exam. Most high school students' time is spent in preparation for these exams; weekends, nights, and summer breaks are often spent with tutors as well as in English or special subject study sessions. Sports and free time are often one of the first sacrifices made to their academic duties.

The government created the Sports Administration at a level below several major ministries such as Education and Culture. The regulation of sports has been primarily to promote the glory of the state through sports victories. Top athletes are segregated from the general populace at a young age to train in specialized sports schools. Athletes don't "rise to the top" from grassroots or community sports competitions, but are trained and conditioned to perform at a high level from an early age. Therefore, widespread sports participation is not a tradition in schools or in communities. Elementary and middle-school students receive general physical education and some basic skills training, but a developed competitive sports system is lacking for average students. Sports participation at the youth level primarily takes the form of classes or unorganized play after school.

Despite recent success in the Olympics, China does not have a strong tradition of community sports. Many of China's children have played some sports—mostly ping-pong, badminton, or basketball—with their family or friends, but a competitive foundation for youth sports is entirely contained within the Sports Administration system. Whereas Australia and the United States have extensive community-based sports systems, China has focused its effort on the development of elite state-run sports programs to achieve its national goal of developing gold medal–winning athletes. According to statistics from the China National Sports Foundation, "There are approximately 20,000 registered Chinese athletes. . . . China has over 600,000 sports venues of various types throughout the country, and the total number of participants in sports activities is currently more than 100 million."[20] The percentage of sports participants among the general population is around 7 percent, and only .02 percent are registered athletes. Until sports is perceived as an acceptable path to success and the Sports Administration receives substantially higher funding for programs, competitive sports will remain an almost exclusive opportunity for elite state-sponsored athletes.

However, some sports properties have succeeded in grassroots sports participation by positioning their product as contributing to society's goals.

Under China's one-child policy, many children today are growing up without a brother or sister to share experiences. The natural concept of teamwork is also not fostered within the academic framework that stresses individual performance on exams. The Education Ministry is aware of this growing issue and is trying to take steps to improve the situation. Some successful sports properties have provided their services under the heading of "teaching teamwork." Team-based sports opportunities are giving many children today the brother or sister they lacked and is fostering the notion of using teamwork to achieve goals.

OPPORTUNITIES FOR SPORT

Despite the numerous challenges facing sports organizations in China, the opportunities are almost boundless in a country that is in a constant state of trying to improve the life of its citizens. Sports properties, companies, and entities that desire to enter China have several opportunities. A critical consideration for foreign firms hoping to succeed in China is focusing on the welfare of the Chinese people. Connecting new initiatives to enhancing the social, physical, or economic welfare of the state and its people is crucial to gaining government support. To truly gain a long-term partnership in China's system, laying out the direct benefits to the Sports Administration, Chinese citizens, or other government agencies must be the primary concern. Once this concern is addressed, partnerships are easier to forge.

Due to the limited access to community sports and the increasing pressure of academic success for China's youth, developing grassroots events is an excellent opportunity to address a pressing social need as well as a market desire. With rising income levels and an increasing youth-obesity problem in large cities, the opportunity to provide healthy activities for youth will be increasingly attractive to the general populace and government officials. Teaching the fundamentals of teamwork to achieve goals is a prime concern of the Education Ministry. Grassroots activities in areas with a strong fan base—basketball, football (soccer), and volleyball—are well positioned to connect to interested consumer groups and achieve the goal of providing team sports for all ages. Nontraditional grassroots sports are another area that could be expanded. Chinese officials in both the Education Ministry and the Sports Administration are open to novel sports opportunities if the tangible benefits to society are clear. It is important to position a sport first and foremost as a societal benefit rather than strictly as a commercial opportunity. China's growing affluence has created increased demand for travel and entertainment. China experienced a rapid increase in demand for overseas travel from 2000 to 2005. Disney, after opening Disneyworld Hong

Kong, has pledged to open Disneyworld Shanghai in the next ten years. The Olympics and the World Expo are two major entertainment gatherings in China's two largest cities, Beijing and Shanghai. China's return to its traditional glory has increased its appetite for the world's best entertainment properties. The Broadway show *The Lion King*, the Rolling Stones, and the Three Tenors were all enthusiastically received by Chinese consumers. A number of western sports properties have also attempted to exploit China's growing entertainment appetite. The NBA, the Association for Tennis Professionals, and Formula One have all staged successful events. The standard for entertainment in China has risen as more international acts have appeared. The average Chinese consumer in one of the major cities expects either a new entertainment experience or international-quality entertainment. A variation of this opportunity also exists in China's interior. While Beijing, Shanghai, and Guangzhou have hosted some of the top sports events in the world, many of the interior cities have yet to experience these top-level events. Chengdu, Chongqing, Wuhan, Nanjing, and Changsha are cities that have expanded their entertainment offerings but are hoping to receive something world class to enhance their stature. Sports properties should consider these large, second-tier cities attractive locations for the production of sports and cultural opportunities. Companies pursuing this approach will find strong support from the central government, which has pledged to commit more resources to developing the interior cities of the China. China's sports history has closely paralleled its political and economic development. With the Chinese economy growing at more than 9 percent per year over the past twenty years, the opportunities in the sports industry are at one of the most advantageous points in recent history. A political environment encouraging growth, an economy growing more rapidly than any other country in the world, and a nation poised to win the 2008 Olympics gold medal count is a powerful combination to launch China's sports industry into the twenty-first century. Companies that are ahead of the surge will engender goodwill with political officials as well as the Chinese populace that will create long-term benefits for those entities willing to invest early in China's success.

The Chinese word for crisis, *wei ji*, is the combination of two characters: danger and opportunity. In all dangerous situations there are opportunities, similar to the Western notion of "nothing ventured, nothing gained." China is a difficult market that requires a subtle approach attuned to the changing political conditions and flexible enough to maximize the opportunities inherent in each new policy. The sports industry offers many of these opportunities for companies or organizations willing to take a chance on the Chinese market. However, it takes a larger view of the unique political and economic circumstances in China to put the sports industry in context. Only with a more holistic perspective can companies achieve long-term success in China, but with this outlook international organizations can turn what originally was a dangerous crisis into a major growth opportunity.

NOTES

1. Luo Guanzhong. *Three Kingdoms,* 4th ed., trans. Moss Roberts (Beijing: Foreign Languages Press, 2003).

2. Tim Healy and David Hsieh, "To Get Rich Is Glorious," *Asiaweek* (March 7, 1997), http://www.asiaweek.com/asiaweek/97/0307/cs5.html.

3. Zhang Fengming, "China to Be Biggest Economy by 2050," *China Daily,* http://www.chinadaily.com.cn/china/2006-05/22/content_596360.htm (accessed 15 November 2007).

4. E. M. Swift, "Sleeker, Stronger," *Sports Illustrated* 69, no. 7 (August 15, 1988): 51.

5. "The People's Republic of China," University of Maryland, http://www-chaos.umd.edu/history/prc.html (accessed November 15, 2007).

6. Chris Ashton, *China: Opportunities in the Business of Sport* (Franklin Lakes, N.J.: SportBusiness Group Limited, 2002).

7. Swift, "Sleeker, Stronger," 44.

8. Ashton, *China,* 73.

9. Ibid., 75.

10. James Roy, "Sporting Chance," *Eurobiz Magazine,* http://www.sinomedia.net/eurobiz/v200602/market0602.html (accessed 15 November 2007).

11. Ashton, *China,* 67.

12. Ibid., 75.

13. "Why China Will Not Cave to Pressure over Trade Imbalance," Power and Internet News Report, http://pinr.com/report.php (accessed June 27, 2007).

14. Ashton, *China,* 31.

15. "Liu Qi's Speech for Beijing 2008 Emblem Unveiling," *People's Daily,* http://english.peopledaily.com.cn/200308/03/eng20030803_121617.shtml (accessed November 15, 2007).

16. "The Organizational Structure of the State Council," China.org, http://www.china.org.cn/english/kuaixun/64784.htm (accessed November 15, 2007); "Per Capita Income in Yangtze River Delta Tops US$1,875," China.org, http://www.china.org.cn/english/BAT/161574.htm (accessed November 15, 2007).

17. Ashton, *China,* 138.

18. Alkman Granitsas, "China Sees Dawn of Big-Money Sports TV—CCTV Books Record Ad Revenue Ahead of National Soccer Team's Foray into World Cup," *Wall Street Journal,* Eastern ed. (May 31, 2002), B.4 (accessed November 19, 2007, from ABI/INFORM Global database).

19. *Oriental Morning Post,* July 22, 2006.

20. Buy USA Information, "Sporting Goods Market in China," http://www.buyusainfo.net/docs/x_3734998.pdf (accessed November 19, 2007).

Four

Mega-Events: The Effect of the World's Biggest Sporting Events on Local, Regional, and National Economies

Victor A. Matheson

Sports boosters often claim that major sporting events, so-called mega-events, inject large sums of money into the cities lucky enough to host them. Promoters envision hoards of wealthy sports fans descending on a city's hotels, restaurants, and businesses and showering them with fistfuls of dollars. For example, the National Football League (NFL) typically claims an economic impact from the Super Bowl of around $300 to $400 million, Major League Baseball (MLB) attaches a $75 million benefit to the All-Star Game and up to almost $250 million for the World Series, and the estimated effect of the National Collegiate Athletic Association (NCAA) Men's Basketball Final Four ranges from $30 million to $110 million.[1] Multiday events such as the Summer or Winter Olympics or soccer's World Cup produce even larger figures. See Table 4.1 for a list of published economic impact estimates for a variety of large sporting events.

Of course, leagues, team owners, and event organizers have a strong incentive to provide economic impact numbers that are as large as possible in order to justify heavy public subsidies. The NFL and MLB use the Super Bowl and baseball's All-Star Game as carrots to prompt otherwise reluctant city officials and taxpayers to provide lavish funding for new stadiums to the great financial benefit of the existing owners. For example, in baseball, of the fifteen new major-league stadiums built between 1970 and 1997, thirteen were selected by MLB to host an All-Star Game within five years of their construction.[2] Similarly, during a visit to the Dallas–Fort Worth area just before a crucial vote on public funding for a new stadium in Arlington, Texas, NFL Commissioner Paul Tagliabue suggested that the construction

TABLE 4.1

Examples of Mega-Event *Ex Ante* Economic Impact Studies

Event	Year	Sport	Impact	Author
Super Bowl (Atlanta)	1994	Football	$166 million 2,736 jobs	Jeffrey Humphreys, Georgia State University[a]
Super Bowl (Miami)	1999	Football	$393 million	Kathleen Davis, Sports Management Research Institute[b]
Super Bowl (San Diego)	2003	Football	$367 million	Marketing Information Masters, Inc.[c]
MLB All-Star Game	1999	Baseball	$75 million	Bud Selig, MLB[d]
MLB World Series	2000	Baseball	$250 million	Comptroller of New York City[e]
NCAA Men's Final Four (St. Louis)	2001	Basketball	$110 million	St. Louis Convention and Visitor's Bureau[f]
U.S. Open	2001	Tennis	$420 million	Sports Management Research Institute[g]
World Cup (Japan)	2002	Soccer	$24.8 billion	Dentsu Institute for Human Studies[h]
World Cup (South Korea)	2002	Soccer	$8.9 billion	Dentsu Institute for Human Studies[h]
World Cup	2006 /2010	Soccer	$6 billion 129,000 jobs	South Africa Football Association[i]
Summer Olympics (Atlanta)	1996	Multiple	$5.1 billion 77,000 jobs	Jeffrey Humphreys and M. K. Plummer[j]
Winter Olympics (Vancouver, British Columbia)	2010	Multiple	Can$10.7 billion 244,000 jobs	B.C. Ministry of Competition, Science and Enterprise and InterVISTAS Consulting[k]

[a]Jeffrey Humphreys, "The Economic Impact of Hosting Super Bowl XXVIII on Georgia," *Georgia Business and Economic Conditions* 54, no. 3 (May–June 1994).

[b]National Football League, "Super Bowl XXXIII Generates $396 Million for South Florida," *NFL Report* 58, no. 7 (1999).

[c]National Football League, "Super Bowl XXXVII Generates $367 Million Economic Impact on San Diego County," http://www.nfl.com/news/story/6371262, May 14, 2003 (accessed October 15, 2006).

[d]Bud Selig, J. Harrington, and J. Healey, "New Ballpark Press Briefing: July 12, 1999," www.asapsports.com/baseball/1999allstar/071299BS.html (accessed August 29, 2000).

[e]Dan Ackman, "In Money Terms, the Subway Series Strikes Out," *Forbes Magazine*, October 21, 2000.

[f]T. Anderson, "St. Louis Ready to Raise NCAA Flag if Atlanta Can't," *St. Louis Business Journal*, January 19, 2001.

[g]U.S. Tennis Association, "2000 U.S. Open Nets Record $420 Million in Economic Benefits for New York," www.usta.com/pagesup/news12494.html (accessed January 9, 2002).

[h]Jonathan Finer, "The Grand Illusion," *Far Eastern Economic Review* 7 (March 2002): 32–36.

[i]South Africa Football Association, "World Cup Bid Details," www.safa.ord.za/html/bid_det.htm (accessed January 9, 2002).

[j]Jeffrey Humphreys and M. K. Plummer, "The Economic Impact on the State of Georgia of Hosting the 1996 Summer Olympic Games" (Athens: Selig Center for Economic Growth, University of Georgia, 1995).

[k]InterVISTAS Consulting, "The Economic Impact of the 2010 Winter Olympics and Paralympic Games: An Update" (British Columbia Ministry of Competition, Science and Enterprise, November 20, 2002).

of a new stadium would lead to the opportunity for the metro area to host the Super Bowl in the next decade. Since the NFL touts economic benefits from hosting the Super Bowl of $300 to $400 million, an amount that meets or exceeds the proposed $325-million public subsidy for the stadium, in effect, Commissioner Tagliabue was saying that combined with a Super Bowl, Arlington would be getting a new stadium for free.

With an event like the Olympics, the huge cost of hosting the event to the standards now required by the International Olympic Committee (IOC), as well as providing adequate security, almost necessitates an infusion of taxpayer money. For example, while on paper the 2002 Winter Olympics in Salt Lake City made a profit, the cost figures did not include millions of dollars of additional security provided by the U.S. Department of Defense at no cost to the local organizing committee. For the 2004 Summer Games, the government in Athens spent $1.5 billion on security alone. These figures illustrate why organizers often rely on lofty reports that promise huge monetary windfalls to host cities. Since many economic-impact studies are commissioned by owners, leagues, or event organizers, which stand to directly benefit from the public subsidies such reports are designed to elicit, one must question whether such studies can be believed.

EX ANTE ECONOMIC MODELING AND ITS DEFICIENCIES

A typical predictive, or *ex ante,* economic-impact study of the type used by event promoters estimates the number of visitors an event is expected to draw, the number of days each spectator is expected to stay, and the amount each visitor will spend each day. Combining these figures, an estimate of the "direct economic impact" is obtained. This direct impact is then subjected to a multiplier, usually around 2, to account for the initial round of spending recirculating through the economy. This additional spending is known as "indirect economic impact." Thus, the total economic impact is double the size of the initial spending.

For example, in assessing the impact of Super Bowl XXVIII on the city of Atlanta and the state of Georgia, Jeffrey Humphreys estimated that the event created 2,736 jobs and had an impact of $166 million on the Georgia economy.[3] Of the $166 million, Humphreys estimated direct and indirect economic impact of $76 and $90 million, respectively. The direct impact was derived from estimating the number of "visitor days" (306,680) and multiplying that statistic by the average estimated per diem expenditures per visitor ($252). The indirect or induced economic impact was estimated using the Regional Input-Output Multiplier System (RIMS II) model developed by the Bureau of Economic Analysis. More recent NFL estimates of the economic impact of the Super Bowl arrive at a figure roughly double that of Humphrey's 1994 study, in part due to general inflation in the economy, but mostly as a result of increases in the assumed number of visitors and the daily spending attributable to each of them.

While such an estimation method is relatively straightforward, academic economists have been quick to point out the failings of such *ex ante* studies as they often rely on poor methodology and also suffer from several theoretical problems. First, many booster estimates are wildly optimistic about the number of potential guests and their spending habits. In March 2005 Denver tourism officials predicted 100,000 visitors for the National Basketball Association (NBA) All-Star Game. Considering that the Pepsi Center, the game's venue, only holds 20,000 fans, and that Denver has only about 6,000 hotel rooms, it is not clear exactly how such an influx of basketball fans would be even be possible, much less probable.

Similarly, in other cases, the size of the estimates themselves strain credulity. The Sports Management Research Institute estimated the direct economic benefits of the U.S. Open Tennis tournament in Flushing Meadows, New York, at $420 million for the tristate area, more than any other sports or entertainment event in any city in the United States. This sum represents 3 percent of the total annual direct economic impact of tourism for New York.[4] It is simply impossible to believe that one in thirty tourists to New York City in any given year are visiting the city solely to attend the U.S. Open. The projected $6-billion impact of the World Cup proposed for South Africa in 2006 suggested that soccer games and their ancillary activities would have represented over 4 percent of the entire gross domestic product of the country in that year.[5] Along the same lines, a study by the Dentsu Institute for Human Studies estimated a $24.8-billion impact from the 2002 World Cup for Japan and an $8.9-billion impact for South Korea.[6] As a percentage of total national income, these figures represent 0.6 and 2.2 percent of the total Japanese and South Korean economies, respectively.

In other cases, the variation in estimated benefits alone is enough to question the validity of the studies. A series of studies of the NBA All-Star game produced numbers ranging from a $3-million windfall for the 1992 game in Orlando to a $35-million bonanza for the game three years earlier in Houston.[7] Similarly, the 1997 NCAA Women's Basketball Final Four was estimated to have an economic impact of $7 million on the local economy of Cincinnati, but the same event was predicted to produce a $32-million impact on the San Jose economy just two years later.[8] The five- or tenfold disparity in the estimated impact for the same annual event serves to illustrate the ad hoc nature of these studies. In some cases, economic impact figures appear to be completely fabricated. While city or league officials may suggest a certain monetary figure from a particular event, when they are pressed on the details, the "missing study" syndrome arises.[9]

Sports boosters also often cite civic pride or national exposure as a primary benefit of mega-events and of sports in general. In many cases, it is undoubtedly true that mega-events bring intangible psychological value to the communities that host them. The 1995 Rugby World Cup in South Africa represented an opportunity for the country to announce its re-emergence as a full member of not only the world's sporting community but also its political community. The picture of South African president Nelson Mandela wearing the jersey of the white South African captain Francois Pienaar while presenting him with the championship trophy was a powerful image to the world indicating that South Africa had emerged from its years of racial oppression and serving to unify the country.[10] Similarly, Ray Nagin, the mayor of New Orleans, pointed to the return of the NFL to the city in September 2006 as an important symbol to the rest of the country that the city was fully on the road to recovery from Hurricane Katrina, which had devastated the city the year previously.

Obviously, measuring such benefits is fraught with difficulty, and academic studies are mixed on the subject. Most researchers find no correlation between economic growth and the presence of new sports facilities, franchises, or events, suggesting that the intangible value of these events tends not to translate into any measurable benefits to the host cities.[11] On the other hand Coates and Humphreys did find that cities that win the Super Bowl (not the host cities) tend to experience a statistically significant increase in their per capita incomes following the game, a result they attribute to higher productivity due to a happier labor force.[12] In other words, it is certainly possible that something intangible (happiness) can produce something tangible (productivity and real income). Coates and Humphreys' claim of higher per capita personal incomes in winning cities, however, has been at least in part refuted by Victor Matheson.[13]

At least one study by Gerald Carlino and Edward Coulson has found that rental housing prices are higher in cities with professional sports teams, indicating a higher willingness of buyers to pay for housing in cities with these amenities, and this idea could, in theory, be applied to cities that host mega-events as well.[14] Dennis Coates, Brad Humphreys, and Andrew Zimbalist, however, have suggested that Carlino and Coulson's results are highly susceptible to the model specification used in estimating the results.[15] It is also clearly true that cities with professional teams, since they are generally larger metropolitan areas, also can offer many other cultural attractions besides professional sports in comparison to smaller cities, which may also contribute to the higher willingness to pay for housing in these cities.

Of course, the use of sporting events to provide entertainment for the masses has been around for centuries. The term "bread and circuses" dates from the first-century Roman empire, where extravagant games were held in conjunction with giveaways of subsidized food in order to pacify the citizenry and reduce urban unrest.

The other major intangible benefit of mega-events claimed by sports boosters is that of national and international exposure. Sports fans may enjoy their visit to the city and return later, raising future tourist revenues for the area. Corporate visitors, it is claimed, may relocate manufacturing facilities and company headquarters to the city. Television viewers might decide to take a trip to the host city at some time in the future based on what they see during the broadcast of the mega-event. Finally, hosting a major event might raise perception of the city so that it becomes a "major-league" or "world-class" city and travel destination. All of these claims are potentially true, although little empirical research has conclusively demonstrated any long-run connections between hosting mega-events and future tourism demand. There are not even any anecdotal examples of companies moving corporate operations to a city based on the hosting of a sporting event.

While intangible benefits to mega-events certainly exist, two caveats must be mentioned. First, the presence of a mega-event may bring with it intangible costs as well as benefits. For example, the publicity associated with a sporting event may not always place a city in a positive light. Following the riots that occurred during the NBA finals in Detroit in the early 1990s, the city's national image basked in the glow of car fires and burning buildings rather than the goodwill associated with an NBA championship, and the bribery scandal that surrounded the 2002 Winter Olympics in Salt Lake City certainly didn't enhance the city's reputation. Similarly, the international reputations of Munich and Atlanta were tarnished by the terrorist events that occurred during the Olympic Games held in their respective cities.

In addition, if the lion's share of the benefits of an event is intangible, this is a significant cause for concern since this type of benefit is most likely to be based upon assumption and guesswork. While sports boosters often suggest that the exposure a city receives during a mega-event is invaluable to the area, in the words of University of Chicago economist Allen Sanderson, "Anytime anybody uses the word 'invaluable,' they are usually too lazy to measure it or they don't want to know the answer."

Even when *ex ante* studies are done carefully and in a considered manner, they suffer from three primary theoretical deficiencies: the substitution effect, crowding out, and leakages. The substitution effect occurs when consumers spend money at a mega-event rather than on other goods and services in the local economy. A local resident who goes to an All-Star Game when it is in town is spending money at the game that likely would have been spent locally elsewhere in the absence of the game. Therefore, the local consumer's spending on a sporting event is not new economic activity, but rather a reshuffling of local spending. For this reason, most economists advocate that spending by local residents be excluded from any economic impact estimates.

Even including only out-of-region visitors in impact studies may still result in inflated estimates if a large portion of the nonlocal fans at a game are "casual visitors," that is out-of-town guests who go to a sporting event, but are visiting the host city for reasons other than the sporting event itself. For example, a college professor at an academic conference may buy a ticket to a local game, and therefore the ticket would be counted as a direct economic impact of the sports contest. The professor, however, would have come to the city and spent money on hotels and restaurants in the absence of the sporting match, and again the money spent at the game substitutes for money that would have spent elsewhere in the local economy.

Similarly, *ex ante* estimates may be biased upwards if event guests engage in "time-switching," which occurs when a traveler rearranges a planned visit to a city to coincide with a mega-event. One example of time-switching is someone who has always wanted to visit Hawaii who plans a trip during the NFL's Pro Bowl. While the Pro Bowl did influence the tourist's decision about *when* to come, it did not affect the decision *whether* to come. Therefore total tourism spending in Hawaii is unchanged; the Pro Bowl simply affects the timing of such spending.

In the case of mega-events, the amount of new spending that is new to the economy is thought to be quite large in comparison to the total amount of spending, since these "premier" events are thought to attract large audiences from outside the local economy, many of whom come specifically for the event. Whereas 5 to 20 percent of fans at a typical MLB game are visitors from outside the local metropolitan area, the percentage of visitors at an event like an All-Star Game or the Super Bowl is thought to be much higher.[16] High prices charged by hotels and other businesses in the hospitality industry also tend to dissuade casual visitors during mega-events.

A second source of bias is "crowding out," which is the congestion caused by a mega-event that dissuades regular recreational and business visitors from coming to a city during that time. Many large sporting events are staged in communities that are already popular tourist destinations. If hotels and restaurants in the host city normally tend to be at or near capacity throughout the time period during which the competition takes place, the contest may simply supplant rather than supplement the regular tourist economy. In other words, the economic impact of a mega-event may be large in a gross

sense but the net impact may be small. Scores of examples of this phenomenon exist. As a case in point, during the 2002 World Cup in South Korea,
the number of European visitors to the country was higher than normal,
but this increase was offset by a similar-sized decrease in number of regular
tourists and business travelers from Japan who avoided South Korea due to
World Cup hassles. The total number of foreign visitors to South Korea
during the World Cup in 2002 was estimated at 460,000, a figure identical
to the number of foreign visitors during the same period in the previous
year.[17]

A third source of bias comes from leakages. While money may be spent
in local economies during mega-events, this spending may not wind up in
the pockets of local residents. The taxes used to subsidize these events, however, are paid for by local taxpayers. The economic multipliers used in *ex
ante* analyses are calculated using complex input-output tables for specific
industries grounded in interindustry relationships within regions based upon
an economic area's normal production patterns. During mega-events, however, the economy within a region may be anything but normal, and therefore, these same interindustry relationships may not hold. Since there is no
reason to believe that the usual economic multipliers are the same during
mega-events, any economic analyses based upon these multipliers may, therefore, be highly inaccurate.[18]

In fact, there is substantial reason to believe that during mega-events
these multipliers are highly overstated, which overestimates the true impact
of these events on the local economy. Hotels, for example, routinely raise
their prices during mega-events to three or four times their normal rates.
The wages paid to a hotel's workers, however, remain unchanged, and
indeed workers may be simply expected to work harder during times of high
demand without any additional monetary compensation. As a hotel's revenue increases without a corresponding increase in costs, the return to capital
(as a percentage of revenues) rises while the return to labor falls. Capital
income is far less likely to stay within the area in which it is earned than
labor income, and therefore one might expect a fall in the multiplier effect
during mega-events due to these increased leakages.[19]

Most league-sponsored economic impact studies not only potentially exaggerate the benefit-side of the cost-benefit equation but also often completely ignore the costs of hosting such an event. Most leagues and event
organizers require sparkling new stadiums and arenas before awarding the
privilege of hosting a mega-event to a city. The NBA and MLB as well as
the National Hockey League and Major League Soccer use their All-Star
games to showcase new facilities and explicitly use the promise of hosting
these events as an enticement to cities to build new stadiums and arenas.

This is not a uniquely American phenomenon. Both the Summer and Winter Olympics routinely entail major construction projects as a condition of winning the bid. The Federation Internationale de Football Association (FIFA), soccer's world-governing body, extracts similar promises of new stadiums from its host countries. Germany spent over 1.4 billion euros building or rehabilitating twelve stadiums for the 2006 FIFA World Cup of which at least 35 percent was provided by local, state, and federal taxpayers.[20]

It is a common error in cost-benefit analysis for the costs of infrastructure improvements to be counted as a benefit and not a cost. While construction expenditures for sports infrastructure undoubtedly have stimulative effects on the economy, the opportunity cost of capital must also be considered. Public expenditures on sports infrastructure and event operations necessarily entail reductions in other government services, an expansion of government borrowing, or an increase in taxation, all of which produce a drag on the local economy.[21] At best public expenditures on sports-related construction or operation have zero net impact on the economy as the employment benefits of the project are matched by employment losses associated with higher taxes or spending cuts elsewhere in the system.

At worst, the spending on sports projects represents true costs. If specialized materials, labor, or technology must be obtained from outside the local economy, these expenditures result in an outflow of money away from the city. Furthermore, due to the distortions caused by the tax system, all funds raised by a local government to pay for stadium construction result in some level of dead-weight loss that can easily exceed $0.25 for every dollar spent. Finally, even if all monies spent on construction stay in the local economy, there is nothing to suggest that stadium building is the best use of government funds and that the return on sports infrastructure exceeds the return on the next-best alternative. In many cases, sports venues are often highly specialized facilities that have only limited use following an event. For example, what does one do with a world-class, 10,000-seat swimming facility once the Olympics are over? Indeed, unless a compelling case can be made that a local community is in dire need of fiscal stimulus and that no other projects exist that would provide a comparable return, infrastructure spending must be considered a cost and not a benefit.

Besides the infrastructure costs associated with hosting these games, sporting events and the crowds associated with them require government expenditures on public safety, sanitation, and public transportation, and the larger the event the larger the potential costs. The variable costs borne by the host city are at least $1.5 million for the Super Bowl,[22] and Greece spent over $1.5 billion on security alone for the 2004 Summer Olympics. In addition, noneconomic costs such as "traffic congestion, vandalism, environmental degradation, disruption of residents' lifestyle, and so on are rarely reported."[23] Following championship matches, for example, informal celebrations all too frequently degenerate into riots, resulting in violence and the destruction of property, which negatively affect productive activity in the short-run. The failure to account for the public costs associated with athletic contests serves to give an upwards bias to the reported net impact of these events.

While *ex ante* estimates often do a credible job in determining the economic activity that occurs as a result of a mega-event and may also address the issue of the substitution effect by excluding spending by local residents, they generally do a poor job of accounting for crowding-out and almost never acknowledge the problems associated with the application of incorrect multipliers. Of course, one solution to the criticisms of *ex ante* economic analysis is to simply perform better cost-benefit analysis that fully accounts for the costs involved and more thoroughly addresses the issues of appropriate multipliers, opportunity costs, and the substitution effects of mega-events.

Larry Dwyer, Peter Forsyth, and Ray Spurr estimate the economic impact of the Quantas Australian Grand Prix automobile race using both standard input-output analysis and a more sophisticated computable general equilibrium (CGE) model that better accounts for the theoretical deficiencies discussed previously. By the standard input-output analysis, the race increased real output by $112 million for the state of New South Wales and $120.1 million for the country as a whole while the CGE model presented much more modest figures of $56.7 million and $24.5 million for the state and country, respectively.[24]

EX POST STUDIES OF MEGA-EVENTS

While Dwyer, Forsyth, and Spurr advocate the use of CGE over simple input-output-based models in generating economic impact estimates, they concede that any type of *ex ante* approach requires making many heroic assumptions about the state of the economy and the response of host cities to mega-events. For this reason, other scholars have performed *ex post* studies of regions that have hosted large sporting events to examine whether the advertised *ex ante* estimates conform to *ex post* observations of the economic impact mega-events exert on their host cities. These *ex post* analyses generally confirm the criticisms of economic impact studies discussed previously, finding that *ex ante* studies routinely exaggerate the benefit of mega-events often by up to a factor of 10.

Ex post analyses of mega-events are performed by examining the economic performance of a host region during a mega-event and comparing this performance to similar regions at the same time which did not host the event. Alternatively, one can compare a city's economy during a mega-event to the same city before and/or after the event. Scholars most commonly use personal income, per capita personal income, employment, and taxable sales or sales tax collections in their studies, although economic variables such as hotel occupancy rates and prices, and airport arrivals and departures have also been used to attempt to measure the economic impact of mega-events on host economies.

The primary difficulty facing practitioners of *ex post* economic impact analysis is that even significant economic events may be hard to isolate within the large, diverse metropolitan economies in which they take place. For example, even if the Super Bowl does result in a $400-million boost to the host city, this is less than 0.1 percent of the annual personal income of a metropolitan area like Los Angeles, a frequent Super Bowl host. Any income gains as a result of the game may be obscured by normal fluctuations in the region's economy. If the event can be isolated within space and time, however, any potential impact is more likely to be identified. For example, while the presence of the World Series might have a large effect on neighborhood businesses, the overall effect on a state or country's economy will be minuscule and hard to identify. Furthermore, these same economic effects may be large for the time period immediately surrounding the event, but over the course of an entire year the impact during this perhaps week-long period is not likely to show up as an important change. Therefore, the use of quarterly or monthly data is superior to annual data, and city, county, or metropolitan area data is preferred to state or national figures. In addition, if one can examine multiple events, or the same event over a number of years, patterns that are not be evident when observing an individual event may be revealed.

While the earliest studies of the economic impact of professional sports concentrated on the presence of professional franchises and the construction of new playing facilities, more recently work has begun to focus on the economic impact of mega-events on local economies.[25] See Table 4.2 for a summary of multiple *ex post* mega-event impact studies.

Robert Baade and Victor Matheson examine annual city-wide employment data during MLB's All-Star Game and find that employment growth in host cities between 1973 and 1997 was 0.38 percent lower than expected compared to other cities.[26] A similar examination of the 1996 Summer Olympics in Atlanta by the same authors found employment growth of between 3,500 and 42,000 jobs, a fraction of 77,000 new jobs claimed in *ex ante* studies.[27] An examination of metropolitan area-wide personal income during thirty NCAA Men's Final Four Basketball tournaments

TABLE 4.2
Examples of Mega-Event *Ex Post* Economic Impact Studies

Event	Years	Variable	Impact	Author
MLB All-Star Game	1973–97	Employment	Down 0.38%	Robert Baade and Victor Matheson[a]
Super Bowl	1973–99	Employment	537 jobs	Robert Baade and Victor Matheson[b]
Summer Olympics (Atlanta)	1996	Employment	293,000 jobs	Julie Hotchkiss, Robert Moore and Stephanie Zobay[c]
Summer Olympics (Atlanta)	1996	Employment	3,500–42,000 jobs	Robert Baade and Victor Matheson[d]
Super Bowl	1970–2001	Personal Income	$91.9 million	Robert Baade and Victor Matheson[e]
MLB playoffs and World Series	1972–2000	Personal Income	$6.8 million/game	Robert Baade and Victor Matheson[f]
NCAA Men's BB Final Four	1970–99	Personal Income	Down $44.2–$6.4 million	Robert Baade and Victor Matheson[g]
World Cup	1994	Personal Income	Down $4 billion	Robert Baade and Victor Matheson[h]
Multiple Events	1969–97	Personal Income/capita	Not statistically significant	Dennis Coates and Brad Humphreys[i]
Daytona 500	1997–99	Taxable Sales	$32–$49 million	Robert Baade and Victor Matheson[j]
Super Bowl	1985–95	Taxable Sales	No effect	Phil Porter[k]
Multiple Events (Florida)	1980–2005	Taxable Sales	Down $34.4 million (avg.)	Robert Baade, Rob Baumann, and Victor Matheson[l]
Multiple Events (Texas)	1991–2005	Gross Sales	Varied—positive and negative	Dennis Coates[m]
Multiple Events (Texas)	1990–2006	Sales Tax Revenue	Varied—positive and negative	Dennis Coates and Craig Depken II[n]
NHL regular-season games	1990–1999	Hotel Occupancy	Slight increase	Marc Lavoie and Gabriel Rodriguez[o]

[a]Robert Baade and Victor Matheson, "Home Run or Wild Pitch? Assessing the Economic Impact of Major League Baseball's All-Star Game," *Journal of Sports Economics* 2, no. 4 (2001): 307–327.

[b]Robert Baade and Victor Matheson, "An Assessment of the Economic Impact of the American Football Championship, the Super Bowl, on Host Communities," *Reflets et Perspectives* 34, nos. 2–3 (2000): 35–46.

[c]Julie Hotchkiss, Robert E. Moore, and Stephanie M. Zobay, "Impact of the 1996 Summer Olympic Games on Employment and Wages in Georgia," *Southern Economic Journal* 69, no. 3 (2003): 691–704.

[d]Robert Baade and Victor Matheson, "Bidding for the Olympics: Fool's Gold?" in *Transatlantic Sport: The Comparative Economics of North American and European Sports*, ed. Carlos Pestanos Barros, Muradali Ibrahimo, and Stefan Szymanski (London: Edward Elgar, 2002), 127–151.

[e]Robert Baade and Victor Matheson, "Padding Required: Assessing the Economic Impact of the Super Bowl," *European Sports Management Quarterly* 6, no. 4 (December 2006).

[f]Robert Baade and Victor Matheson, "A Fall Classic? The Economic Impact of the World Series," *International Journal of Sport Management and Marketing* (forthcoming).

[g]Robert Baade and Victor Matheson, "An Economic Slam Dunk or March Madness? Assessing the Economic Impact of the NCAA Basketball Tournament," in *Economics of College Sports*, ed. John Fizel and Rodney Fort (Westport, Conn.: Praeger, 2004), 111–133.

[h]Robert Baade and Victor Matheson, "The Quest for the Cup: Assessing the Economic Impact of the World Cup," *Regional Studies* 38, no. 4 (2004): 341–352.

[i]Dennis Coates and Brad Humphreys, "The Economic Impact of Post-Season Play in Professional Sports," *Journal of Sports Economics* 3, no. 3 (2002): 291–299.

[j]Robert Baade and Victor Matheson, "High Octane? Grading the Economic Impact of the Daytona 500," *Marquette Sports Law Journal* 10, no. 2 (Spring 2000): 401–415.

[k]Phil Porter, "Mega-Sports Events as Municipal Investments: A Critique of Impact Analysis," in *Sports Economics: Current Research*, ed. John Fizel, Elizabeth Gustafson, and Larry Hadley (Westport, Conn.: Praeger, 1999).

[l]Robert Baade, Robert Baumann, and Victor Matheson, "Selling the Big Game: Measuring the Economic Impact of Mega-Events Through Taxable Sales," *College of the Holy Cross Working Paper Series*, no. 05-10 (2005).

[m]Dennis Coates, "Tax Benefits of Hosting the Super Bowl and MLB All-Star Game," *International Journal of Sport Finance* (forthcoming).

[n]Dennis Coates and Craig Depken, II, "Mega-Events: Is the Texas-Baylor Game to Waco What the Super Bowl Is to Houston?," *International Association of Sports Economists*, Working Paper no. 06-06 (2006).

[o]Marc Lavoie and Gabriel Rodríguez, "The Economic Impact of Professional Teams on Monthly Hotel Occupancy Rates of Canadian Cities: A Box-Jenkins Approach," *Journal of Sports Economics* 6, no. 3 (2005): 314–324.

found that, on average, personal incomes were lower in host cities during tournament years.[28] A similar study of the 1994 World Cup in the United States found that personal income in host cities was $4 billion lower than predicted, a direct contradiction to *ex ante* estimates of a $4 billion windfall.[29] Coates and Humphreys examine the effect of postseason play in all four major U.S. sports on per capita personal incomes and find in all cases that hosting playoff games has a statistically insignificant impact on per capita incomes.[30] Finally, Baade and Matheson examined thirty-two Super Bowls held between 1970 and 2001 and found that the average increase in personal incomes in host cities was $91.9 million, roughly one-quarter of the figures routinely touted by the NFL, and that an increase in personal incomes due to the game of greater than $300 million could be ruled out at the 5 percent significance level.[31]

Taxable sales or sales tax collections have also frequently been used to assess the economic impact of sporting events. These measures are ideally suited to measuring the economic impact of large sporting events for several reasons. First, there is often a direct connection between sales tax collections and sporting events or facilities. Boosters often include large sums for visitor spending in their *ex ante* estimates of the economic impact of a event, and numerous publicly funded sports facilities have also been financed directly from sales taxes collections or through specific increases in the sales tax rate, making an examination of taxable sales especially relevant.[32] In addition, taxable sales are a good indicator of economic well-being as they represent approximately 40 percent of overall economic activity. Finally, the previously mentioned studies of mega-events have used personal income, per capita income, or employment data to estimate the *ex post* economic impact of sports. These data are generally available only annually and at the county or metropolitan area level, and therefore these studies suffer from the limitations mentioned previously. Taxable sales data, however, are often published either monthly or quarterly and can cover areas down to the city level or smaller. Therefore, these data can be analyzed to identify activities that are much smaller in scale and duration.

Phil Porter provides a detailed analysis of taxable sales with respect to mega-events, using regression analysis to determine that the economic impact of the Super Bowl was statistically insignificant, that is not measurably different from zero. After reviewing short-term data on sales receipts for several Super Bowls, Porter concluded:

> Investigator bias, data measurement error, changing production relationships, diminishing returns to both scale and variable inputs, and capacity constraints anywhere along the chain of sales relations lead to lower multipliers.

Crowding out and price increases by input suppliers in response to higher levels of demand and the tendency of suppliers to lower prices to stimulate sales when demand is weak lead to overestimates of net new sales due to the event. These characteristics alone would suggest that the estimated impact of the mega-sporting event will be lower than the impact analysis predicts. When there are perfect complements to the event, like hotel rooms for visitors, with capacity constraints [benefits are] reduced to zero.

Other studies relying on taxable sales have also been made. Baade and Matheson challenged an NFL claim of a $670-million boost in South Florida's taxable sales due to the 1999 Super Bowl and arrived at a figure of a mere $37-million increase.[33] Baade and Matheson also examined taxable sales in California to determine the effect of MLB's All-Star Game on local economies. They found that the three California cities that hosted All-Star Games between 1985 and 1997 suffered an average drop in taxable sales of roughly $30 million in the quarter in which the game took place.[34]

Other more recent studies have examined multiple events in Florida and Texas using taxable sales and gross sales/sales tax collections, respectively.[35] As in previous papers, the authors find no consistently positive statistically significant relationship between mega-events and either retail sales or sales tax collections.

Only one *ex post* mega-event analysis has identified significant economic benefits from a mega-event. Julie Hotchkiss, Robert Moore, and Stephanie Zobay, in a retrospective study of the 1996 Atlanta Olympics, estimated that the Games resulted in an increase in employment of 293,000 jobs in areas that hosted events, a figure that exceeded even the optimistic projections of the event organizers.[36] A more careful look at their results, however, points at the difficulty of identifying mega-events in the grand scheme of overall metropolitan area economic development. The authors found that employment growth in Atlanta and the surrounding area was a mere 0.2 percent higher than would have otherwise been expected over the time period from 1991 through 1996. If this higher growth over the entire period is attributed solely to the presence of the Olympics, then indeed job growth was 293,000 jobs higher than would have otherwise been observed. Even slight changes in large economies over long time periods, however, can result in eye-popping numbers. While it is certainly possible that the Summer Olympics were responsible for these employment gains, the study also serves as a cautionary tale against extrapolating small changes over large areas and time periods.

POLICY RECOMMENDATIONS AND CONCLUSIONS

While sports boosters routinely claim large benefits from hosting mega-events, the overwhelming majority of independent academic studies of these events have shown that their economic impact appears to be limited. While the gross impact of these huge games and tournaments is undoubted large, attracting tens or hundreds of thousands of live spectators as well as television audiences that can reach the billions, the net impact of mega-events on real economic variables such as taxable sales, employment, personal income, and per capita personal income in host cities is negligible. There are ways, however, that host cities can work to maximize the net benefits that accrue to the area.

First, by limiting the amount of new infrastructure built to accommodate an event, costs can be substantially reduced significantly, increasing the probability that an event will result in positive net benefits. The local government of Montreal built multiple new facilities for the 1976 Summer Olympics, including the grandiose Olympic Stadium, and wound up with debts totaling $1.2 billion. These debts were not paid off until thirty years after the Games. In contrast, the 1984 Los Angeles Olympic Committee exclusively used existing sports venues around the city, spent less than $1 billion in total to put on the Games, and ended up with a profit of over $200 million.[37]

Second, while academic economists are nearly universal in their criticism that specialized sports infrastructure does little to promote economic growth, mega-events often spur spending on nonsports-related infrastructure that may provide for future economic development. Only a fraction of Beijing's $22 billion in infrastructure improvements planned for the 2008 Summer Olympics will be spent on sports facilities, for example. A mega-event may prompt otherwise reluctant public officials into making needed improvements in general infrastructure.

On the other side of the coin, there is, of course, no reason to believe that general infrastructure improvements necessarily increase economic growth. Even infrastructure that is not directly sports related may go unused after the completion of the event, or may be a second-best use of scarce investment capital.[38] Furthermore, the separation between what is "sports" infrastructure and what is "general" infrastructure is not always clear. The new Wembley Stadium in London was originally slated to cost around $500 million. In addition, over $150 million in "general" infrastructure improvements were proposed at the same time, including new roads and a completely renovated Underground station. Without the presence of Wembley Stadium, however, no new roads or subway station would be required. Therefore, from a objective standpoint, the entire $650-million price tag should be considered specialized sports infrastructure, and an analysis of the expenditure would likely lead to a negative appraisal of its economic benefit.[39]

A third item that local officials should keep in mind is that there are several reasons to believe that hosting a series of smaller events may result in higher net benefits than a strategy that encourages large, but infrequent mega-events. First, crowding out is much less likely to occur during a small event than during a mega-event. It is difficult to believe that large numbers of travelers will fundamentally change their travel plans due to a relatively minor event such as a local marathon or amateur track and field event, and therefore these events may get all of the benefits of increased visitor spending without the costs of displaced visitors. Second, since smaller events are less likely to cause deviations from normal business patterns, the multipliers applied for these events are also much more likely to represent an accurate estimate of indirect spending. Third, while security measures cannot be ignored for these smaller events, the security costs and the local inconveniences caused by toughened security measures will be orders of magnitude lower than for mega-events. Fourth, lower-profile events are less likely to place additional demands on local organizers such as state-of-the-art facilities and first-class accommodations for athletes and organizers raising the costs of the hosting. Finally, mega-events simply require larger (and consequently more expensive) sporting facilities that are likely to be little used in future. Quite simply put, mega-events cause overinvestment in rarely used sports facilities.[40]

The most important piece of advice that a local government can take regarding mega-events, however, is simply to view with caution any economic impact estimates provided by entities with a incentive to provide inflated benefit figures. While most sports boosters claim that mega-events provide host cites with large economic returns, these same boosters present these figures as justification for receiving substantial public subsidies for hosting the games. The vast majority of independent academic studies of mega-events show the benefits to be a fraction of those claimed by event organizers.

NOTES

1. National Football League, "Super Bowl XXXIII Generates $396 Million for South Florida," *NFL Report* 58, no. 7 (1999); Bud Selig, "New Ballpark Press Briefing: July 12, 1999," www.asapsports.com/baseball/1999allstar/071299BS.html (accessed August 29, 2000); Dan Ackman, "In Money Terms, the Subway Series Strikes Out," *Forbes Magazine*, October 21, 2000; T. Anderson, "St. Louis Ready to Raise NCAA Flag If Atlanta Can't," *St. Louis Business Journal* (January 19, 2001); M. Mensheha, "Home-Court Edge: Final Four Promises to Be Economic Slam Dunk," *San Antonio Business Journal* (March 27, 1998).

2. Robert Baade and Victor Matheson, "Home Run or Wild Pitch? Assessing the Economic Impact of Major League Baseball's All-Star Game," *Journal of Sports Economics* 2, no. 4 (2001): 307–327.

3. Jeffrey Humphreys, "The Economic Impact of Hosting Super Bowl XXVIII on Georgia," *Georgia Business and Economic Conditions*, 54, no. 3 (May–June 1994).

4. United States Tennis Association, "2000 U.S. Open Nets Record $420 Million in Economic Benefits for New York," www.usta.com/pagesup/news12494.html (accessed January 9, 2002).

5. South Africa Football Association, "World Cup Bid Details," www.safa.ord.za/html/bid_det.htm (accessed January 9, 2002).

6. Jonathan Finer, "The Grand Illusion," *Far Eastern Economic Review* 7 (March 2002): 32–36.

7. J. Houck, "High-stake Courtship," *FoxSportsBiz.com*, January 21, 2000, www.foxsports.com/business/trends/z000120allstar1.sml (accessed September 14, 2000).

8. Knight Ridder News Service, "Final Four's Financial Impact Hard to Gauge," *Enquirer Sports Coverage*, March 25, 1999, enquirer.com/editions/1999/03/25/spt_final_fours.html (accessed August 30, 2001).

9. Patrick Anderson, *Business Economics and Finance with MATLAB, GIS and Simulation Models* (New York: Chapman & Hall/CRC, 2004), 131.

10. Robert Baade and Victor Matheson, "Mega-Sporting Events in Developing Countries: Playing the Way to Prosperity?" *South African Journal of Economics* 72, no. 5 (December 2004): 1084–1095.

11. Robert Baade, "Professional Sports as a Catalyst for Metropolitan Economic Development," *Journal of Urban Affairs* 18, no. 1 (1996): 1–17; Dennis Coates and Brad Humphreys, "The Growth Effects of Sports Franchises, Stadia, and Arenas," *Journal of Policy Analysis and Management* 14, no. 4 (1999): 601–624; Phil Porter, "Mega-Sports Events as Municipal Investments: A Critique of Impact Analysis," in *Sports Economics: Current Research*, ed. John Fizel, Elizabeth Gustafson, and Larry Hadley (Westport, CT: Praeger, 1999), 61–74.

12. Dennis Coates and Brad Humphreys, "The Economic Impact of Post-Season Play in Professional Sports," *Journal of Sports Economics* 3, no. 3 (2002): 291–299.

13. Victor Matheson, "Contrary Evidence on the Economic Impact of the Super Bowl on the Victorious City," *Journal of Sports Economics* 6, no. 4 (2005): 420–428.

14. Gerald Carlino and N. Edward Coulson, "Compensating Differentials and the Social Benefits of the NFL," *Journal of Urban Economics* 56, no. 1 (2004): 25–50.

15. Dennis Coates, Brad Humphreys, and Andrew Zimbalist, "Compensating Differentials and the Social Benefits of the NFL: A Comment," *Journal of Urban Economics* 60, no. 1 (2006): 124–131.

16. John Siegfried and Andrew Zimbalist, "The Economics of Sports Facilities and Their Communities," *Journal of Economic Perspectives* 14, no. 3 (2000): 95–114.

17. M. Golovnina, "S. Korean Tourism Sector in Blues Despite World Cup," *Forbes.com*, http://www.forbes.com/newswire/2002/06/19/rtr636036.html, posted June 19, 2002 (accessed June 20, 2002).

18. Victor Matheson, "Economic Multipliers and Mega-Event Analysis," College of the Holy Cross Working Paper Series, no. 04-02 (2004).

19. Ibid.

20. Robert Baade, Victor Matheson, and Mimi Nikolova, "A Tale of Two Stadiums: Comparing the Economic Impact of Chicago's Wrigley Field and U.S. Cellular Field," *Geographische Rundschau International Edition* 3, no. 2 (April 2007).

21. Siegfried and Zimbalist, "Economics of Sports Facilities."

22. Dennis Coates, "Tax Benefits of Hosting the Super Bowl and MLB All-Star Game," *International Journal of Sport Finance* (forthcoming).

23. Soonhwan Lee, "A Review of Economic Impact Study on Sport Events," *The Sport Journal* 4, no. 2 (2001).

24. Larry Dwyer, Peter Forsyth, and Ray Spurr, "Estimating the Impacts of Special Events on an Economy," *Journal of Travel Research* 43 (May 2005): 1–9.

25. Robert Baade and Richard Dye, "The Impact of Stadiums and Professional Sports on Metropolitan Area Development," *Growth and Change* 21, no. 2 (1990): 1–14; Coates and Humphreys, "Growth Effects of Sports Franchises."

26. Baade and Matheson, "Home Run or Wild Pitch?"

27. Robert Baade and Victor Matheson, "Bidding for the Olympics: Fool's Gold?" in *Transatlantic Sport: The Comparative Economics of North American and European Sports*, ed. Carlos Pestanos Barros, Muradali Ibrahimo, and Stefan Szymanski (London: Edward Elgar, 2002), 127–151.

28. Robert Baade and Victor Matheson, "An Economic Slam Dunk or March Madness? Assessing the Economic Impact of the NCAA Basketball Tournament," in *Economics of College Sports*, ed John Fizel and Rodney Fort (Westport, Conn.: Praeger, 2004), 111–133.

29. Robert Baade and Victor Matheson, "The Quest for the Cup: Assessing the Economic Impact of the World Cup," *Regional Studies* 38, no. 4 (2004): 341–352.

30. Coates and Humphreys, "Economic Impact of Post-Season Play."

31. Robert Baade and Victor Matheson, "Padding Required: Assessing the Economic Impact of the Super Bowl," *European Sports Management Quarterly* 6, no. 4 (December 2006).

32. Robert Baade and Victor Matheson, "Have Public Finance Principles Been Shut Out in Financing New Stadiums for the NFL?" *Public Finance and Management* 6, no. 3 (Summer 2006): 284–320.

33. Robert Baade and Victor Matheson, "An Assessment of the Economic Impact of the American Football Championship, the Super Bowl, on Host Communities," *Reflets et Perspectives* 34, nos. 2–3 (2000): 35–46.

34. Baade and Matheson, "Home Run or Wild Pitch?"

35. Robert Baade, Robert Baumann, and Victor Matheson, "Selling the Big Game: Measuring the Economic Impact of Mega-Events Through Taxable Sales," College of the Holy Cross Working Paper Series, no. 05-10 (2005); Coates, "Tax Benefits"; Dennis Coates and Craig Depken II, "Mega-Events: Is the Texas-Baylor Game to Waco What the Super Bowl Is to Houston?" International Association of Sports Economists, Working Paper no. 06-06 (2006).

36. Julie Hotchkiss, Robert E. Moore, and Stephanie M. Zobay, "Impact of the 1996 Summer Olympic Games on Employment and Wages in Georgia," *Southern Economic Journal* 69, no. 3 (2003): 691–704.

37. Holger Preuss, *Economics of the Olympic Games* (Cheltenham: Edward Elgar, 2004).

38. Baade and Matheson, "Mega-Sporting Events in Developing Countries."

39. Ibid.

40. Victor Matheson, "Is Smaller Better? A Comment on 'Comparative Economic Impact Analyses' by Michael Mondello and Patrick Rishe," *Economic Development Quarterly* 20, no. 2 (May 2006): 192–195.

Five

The Financing and Economic Impact of the Olympic Games

Brad R. Humphreys and Andrew Zimbalist

The Olympic Games are among the largest and most visible athletic events in the world. Every two years, the world's best athletes from hundreds of countries come together to compete in lavish new venues in front of thousands of spectators. Hundreds of millions of sports fans worldwide watch the Games on television.

The "Olympic Movement," which the International Olympic Committee (IOC) defines as "all those who agree to be guided by the Olympic Charter and who recognize the authority of the International Olympic Committee," is the driving force behind the Olympic Games. The stated goal of the Olympic Movement is to help build a better world. While Pierre de Coubertin, who founded the modern Olympics in the nineteenth century, may have had altruistic, idealistic notions of pure amateur competition, unsullied by financial motivations in mind, the Olympic Games have become a big business. The participants are effectively professional athletes; the organizers are highly compensated, professional bureaucrats; hosting the Games involves huge construction and renovation projects that take decades to complete, and these expenditures are usually justified by claims of extraordinary economic benefits that will accrue to the host city or region as a direct result of hosting the Games.

In this chapter, we examine the financing of the Olympic Games, the sordid details of how the awarding of the Games became a high-stakes contest to see which country could shower the IOC with the most gifts and perks, and the economic impact of the games. We focus primarily on the evolution of the financing of the Olympic Games over the past thirty five years, and the assessment of the economic impact of the Games.

FINANCING THE OLYMPICS

The modern Olympic Games began in 1896, but it was not until 1976 that a watershed event shook up the financing model for the Games and set the Olympics on its current economic course. In that year, the city of Montreal hosted the summer Games. Montreal incurred a debt of $2.8 billion, which was finally paid off in 2005.[1] Annual debt service created a large budgetary hole for the city for three decades.

By the end of the Montreal Games, the 1980 Games had already been set for Moscow, but no city wanted to bid for the right to host the 1984 Games.[2] After some scrambling, Los Angeles agreed to host the Games, but only on the condition that it took on no financial obligation. With no alternative, the IOC accepted this condition and Los Angeles was awarded the 1984 summer Games on July 1, 1978.

The year 1978 also marked the first significant relaxation of Olympic amateur rules under then–IOC president Lord Killanin. In that year, Rule 26 of the Olympic Charter was modified so that athletes were allowed openly to earn money from endorsements, if the money went to their national sports federation or their country's National Olympic Committee (NOC). The receiving organization was then permitted to pay the athlete's expenses, including "pocket money." "Broken-time" payments for time away from the athlete's regular job were also authorized if the athlete had a regular job. But the rule continued to declare that professional athletes were ineligible.

During the 1980-2001 reign of IOC president Juan Antonio Samaranch, the complete professionalization and commercialization of the Olympics were promoted by further liberalizing the amateur regulations. In 1982 the amateur rules were revised to permit payments into a trust fund that provided expenses during the athlete's active career—and substantial sums thereafter. Eventually, decisions about accepting professionals were left to the International Federation (IF) of each sport. The new professional era was heralded during the 1992 Games in Barcelona, when the United States sent its dream team of NBA stars which, unlike their more recent incarnations, went on to win the gold medal. Nominally, for the 2004 Games in Athens, boxing was the only sport that did not accept professionals, but even this distinction is dubious, because the NOCs of many countries gave their boxing medalists cash prizes.

These changes also led to increased commercialization and increased TV and sponsorship money, which, in turn, led to corruption and scandal within the IOC. Samaranch set a new tone for the IOC when he began his reign in 1980. He insisted on being referred to as "His Excellency" and to be treated as a head of state. Before he took over in 1980, the 112 IOC representatives had to pay their own way to cities bidding for the Games. Within a year they were getting not one but two first-class tickets, plus all expenses paid for as well as lavish entertainment. Samaranch himself always insisted on limousine service and the best suite in the best hotel in any city. In Lausanne, Switzerland, IOC headquarters, he had the IOC rent him a massive penthouse suite at the Palace Hotel for $500,000 a year.

IOC representatives who voted on the host city followed Samaranch's lead and payoffs grew by leaps and bounds. Outrageous tales of the excesses abounded. One surrounds the selection of Nagano, Japan, to host the 1998 Winter Games. The son of Samaranch's close adviser Artur Takacs was a lobbyist for Nagano's organizing committee, for which he was paid a salary of $363,000, plus a bonus if Nagano won the Games. A consortium of Japanese businessmen promised $20 million for the construction of an Olympic Museum in Lausanne if Nagano got the Games, which, not surprisingly, it did. Salt Lake City lost out, but the city learned a lesson.

The previous Winter Games were in Albertville, France. Most observers believed that Falun, Sweden, had a better bid. Samaranch, however, prevailed upon the IOC members, the large majority of whom he appointed, to select Albertville for 1992; that way Paris would be effectively eliminated from competition for the 1992 Summer Games, which instead went to his hometown Barcelona.

Gifts to IOC members ranged from free first-class trips, to college entrance and tuition, room and board for children, rent-free apartments, free shopping expeditions, sexual favors, and tens of thousands of dollars in cash. All this fun came to a head with revelations around the Salt Lake bid for the 2002 Games. Since then, the IOC has supposedly reformed itself, *inter alia,* by reducing the number of voters and by officially declaring an outright ban on gifts.

Meanwhile, the modest financial success of the 1984 Games in Los Angeles led to a new era of international competition among cities to host the Games. The relative success of Los Angeles, however, was *sui generis*. Los Angeles had very little construction expense and the chair of the Los Angeles Organizing Committee for the Olympic Games (OCOG), Peter Ueberroth, was able to raise substantial sums by selling sponsorships to corporations. LAOCOG generated a small surplus (just over $300 million) and reset the Olympic financial model for less public and more private financing.

Nonetheless, other host cities found it impossible to procure the same proportion of private support and, instead, relied upon large public expenditures. Several billion dollars of public monies were committed in Seoul

(1988), Barcelona (1992), Sydney (2000), and Athens (2004). In some cases, the local OCOG ran a modest surplus (20% of any surplus must be shared with the IOC), but the local government laid out billions of dollars to help finance the activities of the OCOG.[3] In the case of Athens, for instance, the public investment exceeded $10 billion—some of this public investment resulted in improved, more modern infrastructure for the city, but some of it resulted in white elephants. Many facilities built especially for the Games go un- or underutilized after the sixteen- or seventeen-day period of the Olympic competition itself, while requiring tens of millions of dollars annually to maintain and occupying increasingly scarce real estate. Public investment for Beijing (2008) is expected to well exceed $30 billion.

Salt Lake Olympiad chief and former governor of Massachusetts Mitt Romney questioned whether U.S. cities should enter bids to host the Olympic Games, stating that they were increasingly driven by "giganticism" with the addition of new sports and more frills. Romney said: "It's a fair question to ask, 'Is it worth it or not?' My own position is that the Games make sense, not as a money-making enterprise, but as a statement for peace."[4]

PRESENT-DAY FINANCIAL ARRANGEMENTS

The IOC presents the financing of the Olympic Games in terms of its own organizations: the local organizing committee (OCOG), the NOC, the IFs, and itself. The OCOG budget is not the same as the budgetary impact on the local city that hosts the games. The local city, its state government, and its national government may provide billions of dollars of subsidies to the OCOG, and the OCOG may report a surplus.[5] This surplus has little meaning regarding the budgetary impact on public bodies from hosting the Games. Moreover, it is common practice for the OCOG budget to consist entirely (or almost entirely) of operating, as opposed to capital, expenditures.[6] Nonetheless, to the extent that the OCOG receives funding from the IOC or from private sources, the lower will be the financing burden that falls on the local, state, and national governments that host the Games. What follows, then, is a discussion of how the IOC distributes the revenue that is collected from the staging of each Olympic Games.

Table 5.1 presents the total revenue that accrues to the IOC or any of its constituent organizations during each quadrennial Olympic cycle, consisting of one Winter and one Summer Game. It shows a healthy revenue growth in each of the major categories, with television revenues the largest single source of revenue by a factor of 3. The Olympic Partner (TOP) program consists of eleven companies that hold exclusive category sponsorships as the official Olympic company.

TABLE 5.1
Olympic Movement Revenue (In Millions US$)

Source	1993–1996	1997–2000	2001–2004
Broadcasting	1,251	1,845	2,230
Worldwide sponsorship	279	579	663
Domestic sponsorship	534	655	796
Ticketing	451	625	411
Licensing	115	66	87
TOTAL	2,630	3,770	4,187

Source: Adapted from IOC, *2006 Olympic Marketing Fact File*, www.olympic.org, 16.

TOP program revenues go 50 percent to the local OCOGs, 40 percent to the NOCs, and 10 percent to the IOC.[7] Broadcast revenue goes 49 percent to the OCOG and 51 percent to the IOC, which, in turn, distributes the lion's share of this revenue to the NOCs and IFs. Prior to 2004, the OCOGs received 60 percent of broadcast revenue. Beginning in 2012, it has been determined that OCOGs will receive a fixed number, rather than a fixed percentage, as broadcast revenues continue to rise.[8] Overall, the IOC retains 8 percent of Olympic revenue; the remaining 92 percent is shared by the OCOGs, NOCs, and IFs.

Table 5.2 depicts the astronomical growth in television broadcasting revenue for the Summer and Winter Games since 1960. Not surprisingly, the

TABLE 5.2
Past Broadcast Revenue (In Millions US$)

Summer		Winter	
Olympic Games	Broadcast Revenue	Olympic Games	Broadcast Revenue
1960 Rome	1.178	1960 Squaw Valley	.050
1964 Tokyo	1.578	1964 Innsbruck	.937
1968 Mexico City	9.750	1968 Grenoble	2.613
1972 Munich	17.792	1972 Sapporo	8.475
1976 Montreal	34.862	1976 Innsbruck	11.627
1980 Moscow	87.984	1980 Lake Placid	20.726
1984 Los Angeles	286.914	1984 Sarajevo	102.682
1988 Seoul	402.595	1988 Calgary	324.897
1992 Barcelona	636.060	1992 Albertville	291.928
1996 Atlanta	898.267	1994 Lillehammer	352.911
2000 Sydney	1,331.550	1998 Nagano	513.485
2004 Athens	1,494.028	2002 Salt Lake	736.135

Source: Adapted from IOC, *2006 Marketing Fact File*, 46.

largest share of broadcast revenue comes from the United States. For instance, for the 2004 Athens Games, the IOC contract with NBC yielded $793.5 million, or 53.1 percent of the total. Following the U.S. rights fee were Europe ($394 million), Japan ($155 million), Australia ($50.5 million), Canada ($37 million), and South Korea ($15.5 million). All told, there were eighty rights holders televising the Athens Games to 220 countries and two billion potential viewers worldwide. Ten thousand media personnel were on hand to cover the Games.[9]

OCOGs do not cover all their expenses from the above sources. For instance, the Nagano OCOG in 1998 had revenues of $990 million, of which approximately $435 million came from the IOC. Similarly, the Salt Lake OCOG had revenues of $1.348 billion, of which approximately $570 million came from the IOC.[10]

RESULTS

Economic theory would suggest that any expected local economic benefit would be bid away as cities compete with each other to host the Games. More precisely, with perfect information the city with the highest expected gain could win the Games by bidding $1 more than the expected gain to the second-highest city. Such an outcome could yield a small benefit to the winning city, but this would require perfect information and an open-market bidding process. In fact, the bidding process is not done in dollar amounts, but comes rather in the form of providing facilities and guaranteeing financing and security.[11] In the post-9/11 world, security costs are far from trivial. Total security costs in Athens in 2004 came to $1.4 billion, with 40,000 security people; Beijing in 2008 is projected to have over 80,000 security personnel working the Games.

It is also widely acknowledged that the bidding process is laden with political considerations. Moreover, the bidding cities are more likely to be motivated by gains to particular private interests within the city (developers, construction companies, hotels, investment bankers, architects, real estate companies, and so on) than by a clear sense that the city as a whole will benefit economically.

In contrast, the IOC views its principal role as promoting sport, not economic development. It requires buildings and infrastructure to be financed with non-Olympic money.[12]

Accordingly, even though a local OCOG may break even or have a small surplus, the greatest likelihood is that the city itself (and state and national governments) experiences a fiscal deficit from the Games.[13] On the one hand, the only tax revenue that would accrue to host governmental bodies would be from incremental sales and income resulting from hosting the Olympic Games. The evidence on this score is not encouraging. On the other hand, hosting governmental bodies, together with any private support, must pay for facility construction, upgrade, and infrastructural improvements necessitated by the Games. It must also pay for the opening and award ceremonies, transportation of the athletes to the various venues, entertainment, a telecommunications/broadcasting center, and security, among other things.

The initial publicized budgets of the OCOGs invariably understate both the ultimate cost to the OCOG and, to a much greater degree, the total cost of staging the Games. The former escalates for several reasons. First, construction costs inflate significantly and land values increase with growing scarcity during the ten-year cycle of Olympic host selection and preparation. Second, the early proponents of hosting the Games in a particular city find it in their interest to underrepresent the true costs as they seek public endorsement. Third, as the would-be host city enters into competition with other bidders, there is a natural tendency to match their competitors' proposals and to add bells and whistles to their plan. The latter escalates because it includes infrastructure and facility costs while the publicized OCOG budget includes only operating costs. The infrastructure and facility costs usually form the largest component of total expenses and often do so by a substantial margin.

Thus, Athens initially projected that its Games would cost $1.6 billion, but they ended up costing closer to $16 billion (including facility and infrastructure costs). Beijing projected costs of $1.6 billion, but current estimates are that they will cost between $30 billion and $40 billion.[14] London expected its 2012 Games to cost under $5 billion, but they are now projected to cost $19 billion.[15] In a world where total revenue from the Games is in the neighborhood of $4 to $5 billion for the Summer Olympics and roughly half that for the Winter Games, costs above these levels mean that someone has to pay.[16] While private companies often contribute a share of the capital costs (beyond the purchase of sponsorships), host governmental bodies usually pick up a substantial part of the tag. Moreover, as we have seen, not all the money generated at the Games stays in the host city to pay for the Games; rather, close to half the money goes to support the activities of the IFs, the NOCs, and the IOC itself.[17]

Thus, while the Sydney OCOG in 2000 reported that it broke even, the Australian state auditor estimated that the Games' true long-term cost was $2.2 billion.[18] In part, this was because it is now costing $30 million a year to operate the 90,000-seat Olympic Stadium.[19] Similarly, the 1992 Olympics in Barcelona generated a reported surplus of $3 million for the local organizing committee, but it created a debt of $4 billion for the central Spanish government and $2.1 billion for the city and provincial governments.[20]

For all of the foregoing reasons, if there is to be an economic benefit from hosting the Olympic Games, it is unlikely in the extreme to come in the form of improving the budgets of local governments. This raises the question of whether there are broader, longer-term, or less tangible economic gains that accrue from hosting the Olympic Games, and it is to this question that we now turn.

HOW DO THE OLYMPIC GAMES AFFECT THE ECONOMY?

In general, sporting events produce two types of economic benefits: direct and indirect. Direct economic benefits include net spending by tourists who travel from out of town to attend the event, spending on capital and infrastructure construction related to the event, long-run benefits—for example, lower transportation costs attributable to an improved road or rail network—generated by this infrastructure, and the effect of hosting a sporting event on local security markets, primarily stock markets. Indirect benefits include possible advertising effects that make the host city or country more visible as a potential tourist destination or business location in the future, and increases in civic pride, local sense of community, and the perceived stature of the host city or country relative to other cities or countries. The Olympic Games are much like other sporting events, except that the Games involve many more participants, officials, and fans, involve more infrastructure construction, induce many more visitors from out of town, and have a much higher profile than most other sporting events.

Because of the larger size and profile of the Olympic Games, they have a greater potential to generate economic benefits than smaller sports events. However, the criticisms about overstatement of economic benefits made about smaller sporting events also apply to the Olympic Games, as we will soon see.

Among the direct economic benefits generated by the Olympic Games, tourist spending is probably the most prominent. From Table 5.3, an average of 5.1 million tickets was sold for the past six Summer Olympic Games, including almost six million tickets to the 1984 Games in Los Angeles. The Winter Games are considerably smaller, averaging 1.3 million tickets over the past five Winter Olympics. Even though selling five million tickets does not mean that there are five million spectators, and many of the tickets are sold to local residents, especially for the Summer Games, which typically take place in large metropolitan areas, a sporting event of this size and scope has the potential to attract a significant number of visitors from outside the

TABLE 5.3
Ticket Sales and Revenues

Games	Tickets Sold	% Capacity	Revenue to OCOG (95% total)
1984 Los Angeles	5.700 million	83%	US$156,000,000
1988 Calgary	1.600	78%	$32,000,000
1988 Seoul	3.300	75%	$36,000,000
1992 Albertville	0.900	75%	$32,000,000
1992 Barcelona	3.000	80%	$79,000,000
1994 Lillehammer	1.200	87%	$26,000,000
1996 Atlanta	8.300	82%	$425,000,000
1998 Nagano	1.300	89%	$74,000,000
2000 Sydney	6.700	88%	$551,000,000
2002 Salt Lake	1.500	95%	$183,000,000
2004 Athens	3.800	72%	$228,000,000

Source: Adapted from IOC, *2006 Marketing Fact File*, 59. NB: 95 percent of ticketing revenue stays with the local OCOG; 5 percent goes to the IOC.

host city. Also, since the Games are often spread over more than two weeks, these visitors may spend a significant amount of time in the host area, generating substantial spending in the lodging, and food and beverage sectors.

The Olympic Games require large spending on constructing and updating venues. These include facilities for the actual competition, accommodations for the participants, and visitors, and facilities for the army of media covering the Games. Many of these venues are specific structures like a velodrome for bicycle racing or a bobsled/skeleton/luge run, which involve costly construction due to their specialized nature. In addition, Olympic venues typically have huge seating capacities. The stadiums that have hosted the opening and closing ceremonies for the Summer Olympic Games often seat 100,000 spectators.

In addition to venue construction, hosting the Olympic Games often requires expansive infrastructure to move the participants, officials, and fans to and from the venues. A majority of past transportation infrastructure construction has been on roads. But host cities and regions have also spent considerable sums on airport construction as well as on the renovation and construction of public transportation systems.[21] In less-developed cities, the building of a modern telecommunications capacity also represents a substantial investment. The construction of this infrastructure generates appreciable economic activity in the host community. Large numbers of construction workers must be hired and large quantities of construction materials must be purchased and transported.

Beyond the construction period, Olympics-generated infrastructure can provide the host metropolitan area or region with a continuing stream of economic benefits. The venues built for Olympic events can be used for years or decades after the Games are over. The existence of these venues can generate some ongoing economic benefits. But more important, upgrades to the transportation infrastructure can provide significant benefits to the local and regional economy if local businesses are able to make use of the improved transportation infrastructure. These benefits take the form of reduced production costs and prices charged by local businesses.[22]

The economic benefits to local securities markets are typically associated with the announcement of the awarding of the Olympic Games, and not with the hosting itself of the Games. If the awarding of the Games generates significant expected future profits in the host economy, this could lead to a current increase in stock returns in the host country. A permanent increase in wealth, generated by increases in returns to stock shares, could lead to increases in current consumption and investment. However, the magnitude of these wealth effects are likely to be small, and a temporary increase in stock returns associated with the Olympic selection decision may indicate, at best, a small increase in future profits by firms in specific industries or, alternatively, spurious correlation.

The indirect economic benefits generated by the Olympic Games are potentially more important than the direct benefits and also more difficult to quantify. One possible indirect benefit is the advertising effect of the Olympic Games. Many Olympic host metropolitan areas and regions view the Olympics as a way to raise their profile on the world stage. Cities and regions compete intensely for a share of international tourism spending, and the Olympic Games are possibly one way to make the host stand out in this crowded marketplace. In this sense, the intense media coverage before and during the Olympic Games is a form of advertising. If hosting the Olympic Games is an effective form of advertising in that it leads tourists who would not have otherwise considered this to be a destination to visit the host city or region, then this advertising effect can generate significant economic benefits over a long period of time. These potential economic benefits take the form of increased tourist spending, just like the direct benefits discussed above. The difference is that these potential benefits may be long lasting, and may be spread more diffusely over the host city or region, and not concentrated in and around the Olympic venues like the direct benefits associated with hosting the Games.

TYPES OF EVIDENCE

Hosting the Olympic Games may produce a variety of benefits in the host economy. However, just because hosting the Games can produce economic benefits, this does not imply that hosting the Games actually generates economic benefits. A thorough assessment of the economic benefits generated by hosting the Olympic Games should include evidence about the size of the economic impact of the Games. A considerable body of evidence on past economic impacts, as well as some prospective evidence about the potential impact of future Olympic Games in Beijing, Vancouver, and London, exists. Before reviewing this evidence, it is useful to discuss the types of evidence that are available.

The evidence on the economic impact of the Olympic Games falls into four categories: retrospective evidence based on econometric analysis; case studies of individual Olympic Games; evidence derived from computable general equilibrium (CGE) models; and, "multiplier-based" estimates of future economic impact. Note the important temporal element associated with each of these types of evidence. The "multiplier-based" estimates are prospective; these studies are basically forecasts of economic benefits that will take place at some time in the future. Because this type of evidence is a forecast, it should be judged by the same criteria as any other economic forecast. The other three types of evidence are retrospective. They are based on an examination of what actually happened in the past when a metropolitan area or region hosted the Olympic Games. This fundamental difference between "multiplier-based" estimates and other types of evidence is sometimes not clearly delineated in the popular press, or among careless analysts of economic impact, but it is critically important for understanding the differences in estimates of the economic impact of the Olympic Games.

Econometric-based evidence on the economic impact of sporting events uses historic data on the performance of the local economy before, during, and after the event takes place. This approach uses statistical methods to determine how much of the past local economic activity could be attributed to the sporting event, and how much would have taken place without the sporting event occurring. The most commonly used statistical methods are reduced form or structural regression models.

Case studies of the economic impact use a similar approach to the econometric method. This approach examines past indicators of economic activity, but does not use sophisticated regression techniques. Case studies often examine a broader set of economic indicators than econometric studies, and use unconditional statistical tests like tests of differences in means, cross-tabs, or chi-square tests of statistical independence.

CGE models are complex representations of the entire economy, including sectors that are not related to sporting events. These models explicitly account for the interconnected nature of the economy. Because the Olympic Games are large-scale events involving significant numbers of participants, officials, staff, and spectators, the effects of the Games may spread beyond the immediate area and affect a number of distinct sectors of the economy in different ways. CGE models can account for complex economic effects like, for example, the effect of the additional borrowing needed to finance venue and infrastructure construction on the availability (or price) of funds to finance other construction projects in the economy. CGE models can also explicitly account for long-run economic effects.

The use of multipliers to estimate the economic impact of sporting events is discussed in detail in several other chapters in these volumes, so we will not belabor the details here. The basic idea behind multipliers is straightforward, and emerges from input-output models of the economy. When a consumer purchases a one-dollar pack of gum at a local store, the economic effects of that transaction extend well beyond the consumer handing a dollar to the cashier, who places that dollar in the till. Some of that one dollar in spending finds its way into the pocket of the cashier, in the form of wages, some finds its way into the pocket of the store owner, some into the pocket of the driver who delivered the gum, and so on. If the clerk, store owner, and delivery person live in the local community, then this money is further distributed in the local economy as these individuals pay rent, buy groceries, and so on. A multiplier is an analytical device used to estimate the broad economic impact of each dollar spent in the local economy in terms of the total amount of additional revenues earned by firms, the total amount of personal income, and the number of jobs generated in the local economy.

Estimating the economic impact of a sporting event using the multiplier approach is relatively simple in theory. First, estimate the number of people who attend the sporting event; second, estimate the amount of spending by these attendees; third, apply a multiplier to this spending to estimate the broad, overall impact of this spending on the economy. However, upon closer examination, this process requires a significant amount of discretionary input on the part of the researcher, and coming up with accurate estimates of several of these components is not a straightforward process.

THE PROBLEM WITH MULTIPLIERS

Multiplier-based estimates of the economic impact are subject to a number of potentially damaging criticisms.[23] Although these criticisms are widely known in academic circles, the continued use of multiplier-based estimates of the economic impact of sporting events suggests that these limitations are not understood in other settings.

One important problem with multiplier-based estimates stems from the estimate of the number of attendees. New economic impact can only be generated by the spending of spectators, participants, and officials from out-side the host area. Spending by local residents does not represent new eco-nomic impact, it represents spending that would have taken place in the host area even if the Olympic Games were held elsewhere; this spending needs to be removed from the estimate.[24] However, estimating the total number of attendees is much easier than estimating the number of attendees from outside the host area. From Table 5.3, 8.3 million tickets were sold to events at the 1996 Atlanta Summer Olympic Games. Some of these tickets were clearly sold to residents of Atlanta. But how many of these 8.3 million tickets were purchased by Atlantans? This number is difficult to estimate accurately.

Further complicating the process are "time-switchers" and "casuals." "Time-switchers" are attendees who would have visited the host area at some other time, for some other reason, but instead choose to visit the host area during the sporting event. "Casuals" are attendees who visit the host area at the same time as the sporting event for some other reason and decide to attend the event out of convenience. The spending by both types of attendees needs to be removed from the economic impact estimate, as it cannot be directly attributable to the sporting event. This spending would have taken place whether or not the sporting event was in the area. Failure to remove this spending leads to over estimates of the economic impact gen-erated by the event.

A second important problem with multiplier-based economic impact esti-mates is their failure to account for crowding out. In many cases, the host area for the Olympic Games is a tourist destination in its own right; tourists would visit this area even if the Olympic Games were held elsewhere; Lon-don, for example, is a major tourist destination. Crowding out takes place when outside visitors attending the Olympic Games buy hotel rooms, meals, and other travel-related goods and services that would have been purchased by other visitors absent the Olympic Games. Crowding out implies that each dollar of new economic impact estimated by multiplier-based methods needs to be offset by some corresponding lost economic impact that was crowded out, or else the net economic impact will be overstated.

It is extremely difficult to determine how much crowding out actually takes place when an area hosts the Olympic Games. However, one study found that gate arrivals at the Atlanta airport during the 1996 Summer Games was identical to gate arrivals in the same months in 1995 and 1997, implying that quite a few tourists to Atlanta were crowded out by the 1996 Games.[25] In late 2004 Athens tourism officials were estimating about a 10 percent drop in summer tourism in 2004 due to the Olympics. The Utah Skier Survey found that nearly 50 percent of nonresidents would stay away from Utah in 2002 due to the expectation of more crowds and higher prices. Even though the size of crowding out is difficult to determine, it exists, and multiplier-based estimates of economic impact typically ignore it, and, consequently, overestimate the actual economic impact.

A third problem with multiplier-based estimates is the displacement phenomenon. Some local residents may choose to leave town to avoid the congestion during the Games. The displaced people spend money outside the local area that they would have spent locally absent the Games. For instance, a survey in Barcelona indicated that fully one-sixth of the city's residents planned to travel outside the city during the 1996 Olympics.

A fourth important problem with multiplier-based estimates of the economic impact of sporting events is the selection of the multiplier. Economic theory does not provide exact guidance on the size of the multiplier to use in any particular application. The size of the multiplier used is at the discretion of the analyst. More important, the larger the multiplier used, the larger the estimate of the economic impact. This creates an incentive for researchers to systematically choose large multipliers in order to generate large estimates of the economic impact of sporting events.

Despite all these problems, the majority of published estimates of the economic impact of the Olympic Games come from multiplier-based estimates. Multiplier-based estimates are widely used because, relative to the other approaches discussed above, this approach requires little data, little technical expertise, and very little in the way of computing power. Multiplier-based estimates are relatively cheap to produce and easy to manipulate.

EVIDENCE ON THE ECONOMIC IMPACT OF THE OLYMPICS

Considering the size and prominence of the event, relatively little objective evidence on the economic impact of the Olympic Games exists. Much of the existing evidence has been developed by the host cities or regions, which have a vested interest in justifying the large expenditures on the games that were documented above. These "promotional" studies suffer from a number of the flaws discussed in the previous section, and must be taken with a very large grain of salt. Given these caveats, Table 5.4 shows some estimates of the economic impact of past Olympic Games, as well as some published estimates of the number of outside visitors who attended the Games. In all cases, the estimated dollar values of the economic impacts have been converted to 2006 U.S. dollars using contemporaneous exchange rates.

Column 4 in Table 5.4 contains the published estimated economic impact generated in eight past Olympic Games. In all cases, these impacts were generated using multiplier-based economic impact estimates. In all but

TABLE 5.4
Estimated Economic Impacts and Visitors from Promotional Studies

Host	Year	Period	Total Estimated Impact Real 2006 U.S. Dollars	Visitors	Notes
Tokyo	1964	1964		70,000	Actual
Munich	1972	1972		1,800,000	Estimated
Montreal	1976	1976		1,500,000	Estimated
Moscow	1980	1980		30,000	Actual
Los Angeles	1984	1984	$4,488,522,780	600,000	Multiplier
Calgary	1988	1988		1,339,000	Unknown
Seoul	1988	1982–88	$4,598,146,717	279,332	Multiplier
Albertville	1992	1992		942,000	Estimated
Barcelona	1992	1987–92	$42,834,973	400,000	Multiplier
Lillehammer	1994	1994		1,208,000	Estimated
Atlanta	1996	1991–97	$6,526,821,761	1,100,000	Multiplier
Sydney	2000	1994–2006	$1,565,371,660	700,000	Multiplier
Salt Lake	2002	1996–2003	$1,696,475,533	850,000	Multiplier
Athens	2004	1998–2011	$16,983,139,800	5,900,000	Multiplier
Turin	2006	2006	$2,000,000,000	1,500,000	Multiplier

Source: Compiled from various media sources, author's calculations.

one of these Games, the estimated economic impact was significant, ranging from $1.5 billion to nearly $17 billion U.S. dollars. The time frame for these economic impacts varies significantly, from a single year to a thirteen-year period. Because the actual underlying economic impact is not constant across time, it does not make sense to express these figures on an annual basis. The extremely large estimated impact from the Athens Games, for instance, is in part due to the exceptionally long period of analysis used.

Because these estimates of economic impact are all based in part on spending by tourists who attend the Games, the information on estimated tourist attendance shown in column 5 of Table 5.4 is also interesting. Like the economic impact estimates, the visitor estimates show a wide amount of variation, ranging from a low of 30,000 for the 1980 Moscow Olympic Games to a high of nearly 6 million, over a thirteen-year period, for the 2004 Athens Games. Again, the host cities or regions have an incentive to overstate these estimates to justify their large expenditures on the Games.

The figures for both the 1964 Tokyo Games and the 1980 Moscow Games are interesting, in that these are actual visitor totals based on the number of tourist visas issued by these two countries. The Moscow Games are clearly an outlier, both because of the boycott of those games by the United States and some other countries over the ongoing war in

Afghanistan, and the difficulties of travel behind the Iron Curtain at that time. The Tokyo Games took place far from both Europe and North America, which meant considerable travel costs in the early 1960s.[26] But still, the modest size of these two actual visitor counts, even given these caveats, makes some of the larger estimates in the table questionable.

Estimates of the economic impact of the Olympic Games derived from academic research published in peer-reviewed journals is a more reliable type of evidence than the figures from promotional studies shown in Table 5.4, because the researchers who develop these estimates have no vested interest in the economic success of the Games and also because the peer review process provides an important check on the methods and assumptions used to generate these estimates.

Only a few such studies exist. One study focused on the effect of the 1996 Atlanta Olympic Games on the economy in Georgia.[27] The paper concludes that hosting the games increased employment in Georgia by 17 percent, or approximately 293,000 new jobs in the counties that contained Olympic venues or were contiguous to counties with Olympic venues in the four-year period 1996–2000, but had no effect on real wages. This result implies new employment, but no benefit for the existing workers in these counties in Georgia.

This paper used a novel, high-frequency panel data set for counties in Georgia over the period 1985–2000. The results, based on estimates of reduced form econometric models of the determination of county-level employment and real wages, are strong because of the length and breadth of this panel data set and the careful econometric analysis. This paper contains the strongest evidence of economic benefits flowing from the Olympic Games. However, the reduced form nature of the analysis does not identify a particular mechanism through which hosting the Olympic Games raises employment in the counties in and near the Olympic venues.

A second paper examined the effects of hosting the Olympic Games on migration into North American regions.[28] This paper examined population and employment in the regions surrounding Lake Placid, New York (1980), Los Angeles, California (1984), Calgary, Alberta (1988), and Atlanta, Georgia (1996). The results indicate a 1 percent increase in employment in these regions in a variable period following the Olympic Games, along with a decline in per capita income in this period, after controlling for other factors that affect employment and income.

The evidence in this paper is based on estimated reduced form econometric models of migration into these four regions using pooled data. While the econometric approach is appropriate, the study uses relatively little data from before the Lake Placid and Los Angeles Games and after the Atlanta Games. This data limitation reduces the strength of the results.

These two papers find evidence that hosting the Olympic Games increases employment in the host region, but do not contain any evidence that hosting the Olympics increases compensation in the host region. The lack of an effect on compensation implies that the distributional effects of the overall impact of hosting the Olympic Games may be different than the employment effects, if local prices and the local cost of living rose as a result of hosting the games. This could be the case even in Atlanta, where local wages were deflated by a national price measure, the Consumer Price Index for all Urban Employees (CPI-U). If prices and the cost of living in Atlanta increased more than national average prices reflected in the CPI-U, then real wages in the Atlanta region could have declined as a result of hosting the 1996 Games.

A third paper examined the effects of the 2000 Sydney Olympic Games in the context of a multiregional computable general equilibrium (CGE) model. CGE models consider the broad impact of the Olympic Games across many different sectors of the economy, including both labor and capital markets, as well as across different regions of a country. This study concluded that the Sydney games increased real gross domestic product (GDP) in Australia by $6.5 billion 1996 Australian dollars, or about 0.12 percent, each year over a twelve-year period. The study also concluded that the Sydney Games increased employment in Australia by 7,500 jobs per year over this twelve-year period. However, these results depended critically on the assumptions made about the Australian labor market. In particular, if wages actually rose in response to this increase in employment (rather than a constant wage), then the net impact of the Games in Australia was zero, with a negative effect in states outside New South Wales (the host region) being offset by a positive effect in the host state. This effect is due to the equilibrium labor market response to a change in employment. If the effect of the new jobs created by the Games is to raise wages in all sectors of the economy, some of the jobs created by the Games will be offset by other jobs destroyed because of higher prevailing wages.

A retrospective study of the long-term economic impact of the 1994 Winter Olympic Games in Lillehammer, Norway, found little long-term benefit.[29] Despite extremely optimistic predictions from local and national authorities about the impact of the Lillehammer Games on local tourism, within a few years 40 percent of the hotels built in and around Lillehammer for the Games had gone bankrupt and two large alpine skiing facilities built for the Games had been sold for less than one dollar to prevent bankruptcy. In general, the long-term effects on tourism in the Lillehammer area were a fraction of the impact forecasted by planners. Even the Games themselves were something of a disappointment in Lillehammer: "February 1994 became a major disappointment for many hotels in the host region."[30]

The results in these studies present a consistent picture of the economic impact of hosting the Olympic Games on regions. Some jobs will be created as a result of hosting the Games. However, there appears to be no detectable effect on income, suggesting that existing workers do not benefit from the Games. Moreover, as the CGE results highlight, the overall economic impact of hosting the Games depends on the overall labor market response to the new jobs created by the Games. When taking into account the overall labor market situation, the net impact of the Games on a region may not be positive. The negative impact on regional income found by the study that examined four North American regions is consistent with a negative overall labor market response to hosting the Games. Furthermore, the long-run impacts on tourism in the host region may be overstated, based on evidence from Lillehammer.

Clearly, the results from academic research on the economic impact of hosting the Olympic Games call into question the reported economic impact from the promotional studies shown in Table 5.4. Economic impacts on the order of $5 to $10 billion should be easily detectable in retrospective economic data from a geographic region. The fact that no peer-reviewed research published in a scholarly journal has found any evidence of billions of dollars of new income in any Olympic host regions suggests that the promotional studies vastly overstate the economic impact of hosting the Olympic Games.

The Lillehammer Games are not the only one to experience a disappointing post-Olympic surge in tourism. Recall that one of the economic benefits allegedly generated by the Olympic Games is an increase in the worldwide profile of the host city or region, leading to a long-run increase in tourism. One study examined the awareness of former Olympic host sites in both Europe and North America.[31] Based on several thousand telephone interviews carried out over the period 1986–89, fewer than 10 percent of the North American residents surveyed, and less than 30 percent of the Europeans, could correctly recall where the 1976 Winter Olympic Games were held (Innsbruck, Austria). Only 28 percent of the North Americans and 24 percent of the Europeans surveyed could recall that the 1980 Winter Games took place in Lake Placid, New York. These low recall numbers are not consistent with a large, long-lasting "advertising effect" generated by hosting the Olympic Games. Further, to the extent that the Games are accompanied by bad weather, pollution, unsavory politics, or terrorist acts, the Games may actually damage a city's or an area's reputation.

Economists have looked beyond income and employment measures for evidence that hosting the Olympic Games has an economic impact on the host economy. One area examined is stock markets.[32] The relationship between hosting the Olympic Games and stock markets is straightforward. To the extent that hosting the Olympic Games generates any benefits, including tangible economic benefits associated with increased tourism, or intangible benefits like national pride, sporting benefits, or increased visibility, stock markets should be efficient mechanisms for valuing these benefits far into the future and discounting them back to the present. Positive benefits, if present, may be capitalized into stock prices at the time that the Games are awarded. Research on the effect of hosting the Olympic Games on stock markets exploits the nature of the process through which the Games are awarded. A large number of potential applicants are winnowed down to a small number of candidate hosts, and an announcement of the winner is made. Until this announcement is made, there is considerable uncertainty about who will be awarded the games, and the contest is winner-take-all. The announcement about the winner of the Games takes place at a specific time (seven years prior to the Games) and represents a natural experiment in stock prices.

The existing evidence is mixed. The announcement that Sydney would host the 2000 Summer Olympic Games produced modest increases in stock returns in a limited number of industries: building materials, developers and contracts, and engineering. The announcement that Athens would host the 2004 Summer Olympic Games produced a short-term, significant increase in overall stock returns on the Athens Stock Exchange, but had no impact on the Milan Stock Exchange. Milan was one of the cities in the running for the 2004 Summer Games. Stock returns in construction-related industries on the Athens Stock Exchange increased more than other sectors following the announcement, suggesting that much of the economic benefit accrues to this sector.

This evidence is limited to only two Olympic Games, and the increases in stock returns reported in the studies are modest, short-term, and primarily limited to the construction industry and related sectors of the economy. The empirical model used to analyze stock returns on the Athens Stock Exchange explains only 6 percent of the observed variation in returns. Overall, the evidence from this literature suggests that stock markets do not forecast large positive economic impacts flowing from the Olympic Games. While the idea that hosting the Olympic Games affects stock returns may appear important to the general public, a careful reading of this literature reveals that the underlying effects are small, transitory, and limited to a few sectors of the economy. This evidence does not support net economic impact on the order of those reported in Table 5.4 accruing to the host city or region.

CAN THE OLYMPIC GAMES BE AN ECONOMIC SUCCESS?

Our review of the existing peer-reviewed evidence on the economic impact of the Olympic Games reveals relatively little evidence that hosting the Games produces significant economic benefits for the host city or region. If the economic gains are modest, or perhaps nonexistent, what can host cities and regions do to leverage hosting the Olympic Games? A careful examination of past experiences suggests two important avenues for leveraging the Olympic Games: host cities or regions need to make careful land-use decisions and maximize the post–Olympic Games use of new and renovated facilities and infrastructure.

Land is an increasingly scarce resource in both large urban areas that typically host the Summer Games and in the mountainous areas that host the Winter Games. Hosting the Olympic Games requires a significant amount of land for facilities, the Olympic Village, housing for the media and staff, accommodations for spectators, and parking. Unsuccessful Games leave behind legacies of seldom- or never-used structures taking up valuable land. For example, one recent study concluded that the primary legacy of the Nagano Games are a rarely used bobsled track and a huge speed-skating venue that has generated significant operating losses since the Games. Likewise, the long-term impact of the Calgary Games is viewed as less important than the annual rodeo, the Calgary Stampede, and the signature venue in Calgary, the SaddleDome, is viewed as obsolete and in need of replacing less than twenty years after the end of the Games.[33] Although it was used for years following the 1976 Montreal Games, the Olympic Stadium was widely viewed as one of the worst facilities in Major League Baseball, and many "features" like the retractable roof never worked. Many of the venues used in the 2004 Athens Games are either vacant or seldom used, and occupy valuable land in a crowded urban center.

Successful Games, like the 1984 Los Angeles Summer Games, utilize existing facilities as much as possible, consuming as little scarce urban land as possible. The stadium used for the opening and closing ceremonies in the 1996 Atlanta Games was reconfigured to a baseball stadium immediately following the conclusion of the Games. The bullet train built for the Nagano Games greatly reduced the travel time between that city and Tokyo.

Tying up scarce land for seldom-used Olympic venues in both urban areas and alpine recreation areas cannot be an optimal use of this valuable resource. Olympic planners need to design facilities that will be useful for a long time after the Games are over, and are constructively integrated into the host city or region.

Clearly, the impact of the Olympic Games will vary according to the differing levels of development in the host city and country. Properly planned, hosting the Games can catalyze the construction of a modern transportation, communications, and sport infrastructure. Such a potential benefit is bound to be greater for less-developed areas. But even in such areas, hosting the

Games will require a significant outlay of public funds to finance the infrastructural improvements. These improvements can also be made without hosting the Games. Thus, it is relevant to ask whether the planning for the Olympics produces an optimal use of scarce public monies. It is also relevant to consider that in many circumstances the public policy process is so gridlocked that needed infrastructural investments may be delayed for years, if not decades, without the Olympic catalyst and that the Games do provide at least some capital to facilitate the completion of desirable projects.

Conversely, in more developed regions, where land is even more scarce during the initial bid planning (and destined to become scarcer still over the ten-year period of Olympic selection and preparation) and labor and resource markets are tight, hosting the Games can occasion a gross misuse of land as well as provoke wage and resource price pressure, leading to higher inflation.

Finally, it is important to recognize that hosting the Olympic Games generates significant nonpecuniary benefits to the host city or region. The residents of the host city or region are likely to derive significant pride and sense of community from hosting the Games. Their homes are the focus of the world's attention for a brief, but intense period. The planning and work required to host the Games take considerable time and effort, and much of the hard work is done by volunteers. Pulling off such a huge endeavor is a source of considerable local and national pride. These factors are both important and valuable, even though researchers find it difficult to place a dollar value on them.

Some recent research has attempted to quantify the value of the nonpecuniary benefits generated by the Olympic Games.[34] Economists have used the Contingent Valuation Method (CVM) to place a dollar value on such diverse intangible benefits as cleaning up oil spills in pristine wilderness areas and preserving green space in urban areas. The basic approach in CVM is to elicit people's willingness to pay for some intangible through hypothetical questions involving referendum voting or changes in taxes. A recent estimate of the total willingness to pay for the intangible benefits generated in the United Kingdom from hosting the 2012 Summer Games was in excess of two billion pounds sterling.

In the end, the economic and noneconomic value to hosting the Olympic Games is a complex matter, likely to vary from one situation to another. Simple conclusions are impossible to draw. Prospective hosts of future Games would do well to steer clear of the inevitable Olympic hype and to take a long, hard, and sober look at the long-run development goals of their region.

NOTES

1. Montreal city officials initially projected that the Games would only cost $124 million. Rick Burton, "Olympic Games Host City Marketing: An Exploration of Expectations and Outcomes," *Sport Marketing Quarterly* 12 (2003): 38.

2. According to one report, the Soviet government spent $9 billion on facilities for the 1981 games. Ibid., 38.

3. Holger Preuss, *The Economics of Staging the Olympic Games* (Northampton, Mass.: Edward Elgar, 2003), 194.

4. Quoted in Burton, "Olympic Games Host City Marketing," 35.

5. For instance, in the recent Games hosted in the United States, the federal government provided $1.3 billion in Salt Lake City in 2002, $609 million in Atlanta in 1996, and $75 million in Los Angeles in 1984 (all reckoned in 1999 prices). Bernard L. Ungar, *Olympic Games: Federal Government Provides Significant Funding and Support* (Collingwood, Pa.: Diane Publishing Co., 2000), 5. For the 2010 Winter Games in Vancouver, in addition to the provincial government of British Columbia and the federal government of Canada putting up $9.1 million each to help finance the bidding process, the provincial government is putting up an additional $1.25 billion to finance the Games (and providing a guarantee to cover cost overruns) and the federal government is contributing another $330 million. The city of Vancouver is putting up $170.3 million. www.mapleleafweb.com, accessed August 22, 2007.

6. Preuss, *Economics of Staging the Olympic Games,* 195.

7. International Olympic Committee (hereafter IOC), "2006 Olympic Marketing Fact File," http://www.olympic.org/uk/organisation/facts/revenue/index_uk.asp. 23 (accessed October 28, 2007).

8. Preuss, *Economics of Staging the Olympic Games,* 110.

9. IOC, "2006 Marketing Fact File," 51-54.

10. Ibid., 82–83. From the Salt Lake Games revenues, the IOC also provided $305 million to the NOCs.

11. In addition to providing for facilities, infrastructure and security, and devoting large tracts of land on which to build the facilities, the eventual host city, along with its bidding competitors, typically spend $30 to $50 million to conduct their bid. The bidding process involves a roughly ten-year commitment for the eventual host city. Further, and as discussed elsewhere in this paper, host cities must maintain most Olympic facilities for decades into the foreseeable future.

12. Preuss, *Economics of Staging the Olympic Games,* 195.

13. Of course, not all OCOGs manage to break even; the Albertville OCOG lost $57 million. Burton, "Olympic Games Host City Marketing," 39.

14. Herein lies another conundrum. The lower figure appears to include only operating costs or the budget of the Beijing OCOG. This is the figure that is generally publicized. The higher range also includes facility and infrastructure costs. The latter includes the expansion of the Beijing subway system and, hence, will likely serve the city productively well after the Games are over. Before and after comparisons are often plagued by this apples and oranges confusion.

15. Brendan Carlin, "Olympic Budget Trebles to £9.3bn," *London Telegraph*, March 15, 2007. Also see Bernard Simon, "Cost of Canadian 2010 Winter Olympics Escalates," *Financial Times*, February 6, 2006.

16. To be sure, the Winter Games involve fewer participants, fewer venues, and less construction; hence, the cost of these Games is lower than for the summer Games.

17. Not surprisingly, the PR hype does not always match this reality. For instance, the director of planning and budgeting of the Atlanta Games told Holger Preuss (author of *The Economics of Staging the Olympics*): "We can only give you the analyses which carry a positive image. Other analyses remain unpublished so as not to make the population insecure."

18. The Sydney bid cost $46.2 million and its Games cost $3.24 billion. Preuss, *Economics of Staging the Olympics,* 233. The Sydney Games were originally projected to earn the Australian Treasury a surplus of $100 million. Burton, "Olympic Games Host City Marketing," 39. One of the goals of the Sydney Games was to generate increased tourism, yet Graham Mathews, a former forecaster for the Australian Federal Treasury stated: "While having the Olympics may have made us feel warm and fuzzy and wonderful, in cold hard terms it's actually hard in international experience to determine if there has been a positive, lasting impact on tourism from having that brief burst of exposure." Burton, "Olympic Games Host City Marketing," 40.

19. Similarly, maintenance costs on the Athens Olympics facilities in 2005 reportedly will come in around $124 million and there appears to be little to no local interest being expressed for the two Olympic soccer stadiums. "Cost of 2004 Athens Games Continues to Escalate," *Washington Post*, August 10, 2005, http://www.washingtonpost.com. Torino had several white elephants, including its bobsled-run venue which cost $108 million to construct. Deputy President of Torino Games Evelina Christillin commented to a *Wall Street Journal* reporter: "I can't tell you a lie. Obviously, the bobsled run is not going to be used for anything else. That's pure cost." The speed-skating arena in Nagano (1998) is sometimes used for flea markets. Gabriel Kahn and Roger Thurow, "Quest for Gold—Torino 2006," *Wall Street Journal*, February 10, 2006, A1.

20. The total reported cost of the Barcelona Games was $9.3 billion, of which private sources covered $3.2 billion and public sources covered $6.1 billion. See Burton, "Olympic Games Host City Marketing," 39. For a related account of large public expenditures on infrastructure for the Salt Lake City Olympics, see D. L. Bartlett and J. B. Steele, "Snow Job," *Sports Illustrated*, December 21, 2001, 79–98. Bartlett and Steele report that the U.S. government spent $1.5 billion of taxpayer money on the purchase of land, road construction, sewers, parking lots, housing, buses, fencing, a light-rail system, airport improvements, and security equipment, *inter alia*. Some have argued that a part of these expenditures would have occurred even if Salt Lake City did not host the Olympics.

21. Stephen Essex and Brian Chalkley, "Mega-sporting Events in Urban and Regional Policy: A History of the Winter Olympics," *Planning Perspectives* 19, no. 1 (2004): 205.

22. Terance Rephann and Andrew Isserman, "New Highways as Economic Development Tools: An Evaluation Using Quasi-Experimental Matching Methods," *Regional Science and Urban Economics* 24, no. 6 (1994): 728.

23. John Crompton, "Economic Impact Analysis of Sports Facilities and Events: Eleven Sources of Misapplication," *Journal of Sport Management* 9 (1995): 15

24. This statement assumes that residents have a fixed budget for leisure spending. To the extent that they may expand their leisure spending or that they substitute local

leisure spending for leisure spending outside the local area, then this claim must be modified.

25. Philip Porter, "Mega-Sports Events as Municipal Investments: A Critique of Impact Analysis," in *Sports Economics: Current Research*, ed. J. Fizel, E. Gustafson, and L. Hadley (Westport, Conn.: Praeger, 1999)

26. Of course, the city of Tokyo may have benefited from Japanese tourists coming from other parts of the country. Any such benefit would have been at the expense of other places in Japan and would not have constituted a benefit to the whole country.

27. Julie L. Hotchkiss, Robert E. Moore, and Stephanie M. Zobay, "Impact of the 1996 Summer Olympic Games on Employment and Wages in Georgia," *Southern Economic Journal* 69 (2003): 691–704.

28. Travis J. Lybbert and Dawn D. Hilmany, "Migration Effects of Olympic Siting: A Pooled Time Series Cross-sectional Analysis of Host Regions," *Annals of Regional Science* 34 (2000): 405-420.

29. Jon Tiegland, "Mega-events and Impacts on Tourism; the Predictions and Realities of the Lillehammer Olympics," *Impact Assessment and Project Appraisal* 17 (1999): 305–317.

30. Ibid., 309.

31. J. R. Brent Ritchie and Brian H. Smith, "The Impact of a Mega-Event on Host Region Awareness: A Longitudinal Study," *Journal of Travel Research* 30 (1991): 3–10.

32. Gabrielle Berman, Robert Brooks, and Sinclair Davidson, "The Sydney Olympic Games Announcement and Australian Stock Market Reaction," *Applied Economics Letters* 7 (2000): 781–784; Nikolas Veraros, Evangelia Kasimati, and Peter Dawson, "The 2004 Olympic Games Announcement and its Effect on the Athens and Milan Stock Exchanges," *Applied Economics Letters* 11 (2004): 749–753.

33. David Whitson and John Horne, "Understated Costs and Overstated Benefits? Comparing the Outcomes of Sports Mega-events in Canada and Japan," *Sociological Review* 54 (2006): 75.

34. Giles Atkinson, Susana Mourato, and Stefan Szymanski, "Quantifying the 'Unquantifiable': Valuing the Intangible Benefits of Hosting the Summer Olympic Games," *Urban Studies* (2008), in press.

Six

New Revenue Streams in Professional Sports

Daniel S. Mason and Dennis R. Howard

The unprecedented prosperity of the 1990s was a boon for professional sports teams in North America as both consumers and corporations spent increasing amounts on the 123 franchises comprising the four "major league" sports leagues. From 1992 to 2000, total revenues generated by professional sports franchises more than doubled, growing from $4.9 billion to $11 billion.[1] In 2006 *Forbes* estimated that gross revenues topped $17.1 billion for sports teams in the United States and Canada.[2] The explosive growth of revenues has transformed the overall value of sports teams. In 1992 *Financial World* estimated the cumulative market worth of sports teams to be around $10 billion.[3] By 2007 that figure had almost tripled to $29.1 billion.[4]

Over the last fifteen years, leagues and teams have taken full advantage of professional sports' growing popularity to maximize revenue production. Owners and operators have done this in two ways. First, they have grown traditional revenue sources like gate receipts and media sales to unprecedented levels. Second, they have created new, abundant sources of income in the form of premium-seating options and corporate partnerships. Teams and leagues have also taken advantage of the promise of developing technologies, such as the Internet and virtual signage, to create promising new streams of revenue. This chapter will examine the many traditional and innovative sources of revenue that have had a transformational impact on the economic well-being of professional sports.

The following provides an overview of the types of gate and media revenues that teams and league generate. The chapter then discusses new media advancements and how leagues receive revenue from merchandising and sponsorships. It concludes with a discussion of how owning franchises can also lead to additional revenue opportunities.

GATE REVENUES

The most staple source of revenue for professional sport franchises since their inception has been the sale of admission tickets. Ticket sales or gate receipts remain the most important single source of income for all sports leagues except the National Football League. According to *Forbes.com*, Major League Baseball (MLB) leads the four major leagues in the United States and Canada with total gate revenues in 2006 of $1.831 billion, followed by the National Football League (NFL) at $1.4 billion (for 2005), the National Basketball Association (NBA) at $1.111 billion for the 2006 season, and the National Hockey League (NHL) with $947 million in total gate receipts for the 2005/06 season. While the National Hockey League's total gate receipts are the smallest among the four major leagues, NHL teams rely most heavily on ticket sales with on average about 41 percent of their total annual income derived from box office revenues. Major League Baseball and the NBA depend on over a third of their gross revenues from ticket sales, at 36 and 31 percent, respectively. Interestingly, the most prosperous of all the major leagues, the NFL, is the least dependent on ticket sales, which account for only 23 percent of the total revenues generated by NFL teams. The relatively small contribution of gate receipts in the NFL is a result of the league's enormous popularity on television. National television rights fees claimed by the NFL have grown to almost $3 billion a year, more than doubling the $1.4 billion NFL teams realized from ticket sales in 2005.

Premium Seating

The introduction of "premium seating" options in the early 1990s has allowed professional sport franchises to grow gate receipts dramatically over the past fifteen years. Perhaps, no single development in the last several decades has had a more transformational effect on team sports than premium seating. "Luxury" suites, loge boxes, and various forms of club seats have become an almost universal feature of stadium and arena construction. The introduction of this type of high-yield seating is a fairly recent phenomenon. A few years ago, the executive director of the Association of Luxury Suite Directors commented, "Ten years ago, only about 3% of the seating in stadiums and arenas was designated as premium and club seating. Now that figure is approaching 20%."[5] The average NBA arena now contains eighty-eight luxury suites and 1,974 club seats.[6]

TABLE 6.1
Cost of Premium Seating, 2005/06

Price	MLB	NBA	NFL	NHL
Average regular ticket	$22.41	$45.92	$58.95	$41.19
Average premium ticket	NA	$156.97	$176.26	$87.49

Source: Adapted from Team Marketing Report (2007).

The primary reason that premium seating has become so popular is that the sale of this inventory yields such abundant revenues. In both the NBA and NFL, club seats are sold on average for more than three times the price of a regular (nonpremium) game ticket and for more than double the price or a regular ticket in the NHL (see Table 6.1). Given that the average premium customer spends considerably more on food and beverage during a game, the average "per cap" yield for someone purchasing a club or loge seat in the NBA or NFL exceeds $200 a game. With teams generating three to four times as much on a per-capita or per-seat basis from premium customers, it is not surprising that sports facilities built over the past ten to fifteen years have emphasized the inclusion of this high-priced seating inventory.

As shown in Table 6.2, the venues in which teams in the four major leagues play contain over 12,000 luxury suites and close to 500,000 club seats. The current prominence of premium-seating inventory is amazing in that in that prior to 1990 only a handful of stadiums and arenas contained any kind of luxury seating. The development of two privately financed facilities in 1989 ignited the premium-seating boom. The Palace at Auburn Hills (home of the NBA Detroit Pistons) and Joe Robbie Stadium (now called Dolphin Stadium, home of the NFL Miami Dolphins) were the first two venues to incorporate what was at the time an unprecedented number of luxury suites and club seats. The Palace included 180 suites and over 2,000

TABLE 6.2
Number of Suites and Club Seats in Major League Venues

League	Number of Suites (average)	Number of Club Seats (average)
MLB	2,310 (77)	119,990 (3,988)
NBA	2,640 (88)	58,220 (1,974)
NFL	4,564 (143)	246,816 (7,713)
NHL	2,820 (94)	62,820 (2,094)
Total	12,334	488,346

Source: 2006 Revenues Adapted from Sports Venues: Pro Edition (Milwaukee, Wis.: Mediaventures, 2006).

club seats and the new Dolphins stadium contained 216 luxury suites. In Detroit the Pistons presold their premium inventory, which allowed them to finance the construction of their new state-of-the-art arena. The team generated over $18 million annually from the sale of suites and club seats. The Dolphins realized gross revenues of close to $20 million from leasing the 216 suites the first year in their new stadium. These two facilities had a transformational effect on sport-venue development. Every new arena or stadium built since the early 1990s has been fully loaded with premium seating inventory. The income-generating potential of this new generation of sports venues was most fully exploited with the opening of the Staples Center in Los Angeles in late 1999. This $400-million arena, home to the NBA Lakers and Clippers and the NHL Kings, generates an estimated $70 million per year from the sale of 160 suites (ranging in price from $307,000 to $188,278) and 2,476 club seats (selling at an average of $14,000).[7]

The spectacular revenue production of the Staples Center will be surpassed by the next generation of sports venues, which are currently under construction. In 2009 two new stadiums and two new ballparks are scheduled to open. The NFL Dallas Cowboys and the New York Giants and Jets (the teams will share a new stadium at the Meadowlands) are building new state-of-the-art facilities, whose construction costs are projected to run $1.1 billion and $1.6 billion, respectively. A new ballpark for the New York Yankees is projected to cost $1.2 billion. Finally, the New York Mets are currently building a new venue in which projected construction costs may also exceed $1 billion. These construction costs are noteworthy because they represent the most expensive sports venues ever built in North America, and by a significant margin. The most expensive sport facility built to date in the United States was Safeco Field in Seattle. This publicly financed ballpark was built for $520 million in 1999. From 2000 through 2007 twenty-nine new major sports facilities were built in the United States and Canada. Significantly, the price tag for not one of these modern venues exceeded $600 million. While part of the extraordinarily higher cost of building the new facilities may be a function of inflation, particularly related to construction materials like steel and concrete, and the generally higher cost of building in the New York City market area, a primary factor in the heightened cost is that the design of all of these new facilities maximizes the inclusion of expensive premium-seating options. The new Cowboys stadium will include 300 luxury suites and 15,000 club seats. Club seat patrons will have access to four lavishly appointed club rooms inside the stadium; two of these hospitality areas will be 60,000 square feet. While the stadium will be expensive to build, the return on investment will be abundant for the Cowboys, with gross revenues from the sale of this premium inventory projected to yield more than $75 million a year.

Luxury suites have been particularly attractive to corporations who have found sports venues to be a unique and highly effective place to entertain key clients. Although the physical features of suites may vary from one venue to another, they are likely to include amenities such as carpeting, wet bars, lavish furnishings, and seating accommodations for twelve to fourteen patrons. Private restrooms used to be built into luxury suites, but many new facilities have provided easily accessible restrooms outside of the suites. These generally upscale restrooms are available exclusively to suiteholders and their guests. Because of the numerous exclusive benefits afforded suiteholders, luxury or private suites are commonly the most expensive seating options available in stadiums or arenas. Suite prices vary according to location, size, and number of amenities. Table 6.3 provides the average annual lease prices for luxury suites across the four major leagues. The gross annual income produced by the more than 12,000 luxury suites in major league venues exceeded $600 million in 2005.[8]

Many professional teams offer suites on an extended contract basis. Rather than selling the entire inventory on an annual basis, prospects are offered the opportunity to lease or rent a suite on three-, five-, seven-, up to a ten-year arrangement. Often payment terms are designed to encourage clients to select extended lease agreements. Suite holders who elect a seven-year lease would pay less on an annual basis than those choosing a three-year term. Staggering the length of the contracts over several intervals also ensures that the school or team would not have to renew or replace all current suiteholders every year.

Due to the considerable investment required of those purchasing private suites, the prospect pool is often limited to large corporations. Companies find suites an ideal place to entertain key clients and/or reward high-performing employees. In addition, corporations can mitigate the higher cost of leasing suites by writing off a considerable portion of the investment. Direct payments for game tickets, food, parking, and other goods may be written off as a business expense if used to entertain clients. In addition, companies and individual taxpayers can deduct most of the lease fee from their taxable income.

TABLE 6.3
Annual Luxury Suite Prices by League

League	Average Low Price	Average High Price
MLB	$89,987	$177,661
NBA	$128,017	$231,203
NFL	$59,600	$183,850
NHL	$111,501	$216,333

Source: 2006 Revenues Adapted from Sports Venues: Pro Edition (Milwaukee, Wis.: Mediaventures, 2006).

Over the past ten to fifteen years, club seats have become a very popular premium-seating option. Club seats have become the preferred option for growing numbers of individual fans who are willing to pay a premium for the special benefits provided by this seating arrangement. Not only are club seats located close to the action, they also provide fans with superior comfort. Typically fans sit in chair-back, wide-bottom, cushioned seats. In addition, individuals purchasing club seats receive access to a variety of specialty services and amenities. These special services may range from in-seat wait service during games to offering club seatholders exclusive access to a club lounge for pre- and post-game food and beverage. Figures 6.1–6.3 show a number of premium seating options in a new sports facility.

While most often club seats are sold on an annual basis, several professional sports teams sell them on an extended-lease basis, ranging from three to ten years. Under this arrangement, the purchaser prepays the entire amount upfront or contracts to make several payments over a stipulated period of time, typically two to five years, depending on the length of the agreement.

Currently, the most popular premium-seating innovation, according to the Association of Luxury Suite Directors, is the emergence of loge box or terrace table seating.[9] This recent seating alternative takes the traditional box seat concept to a completely different level. It combines the special vantage point benefit of traditional box seats with the ultimate VIP experience. In fact, in the Charlotte Bobcat arena, these premium seats are referred to as "Royal Boxes." Typically, these seats are the closest to the action of all the premium-seating options. This loge seating is provided in private, opera-styled, open-air boxes with accommodations for four to six people. Further

FIGURE 6.1
Loge Box

Source: Author's photograph.

FIGURE 6.2
Loge Box Seating

Source: Author's photograph.

differentiating the experience are several unique benefits, including a flat-screen television monitor in each box with access to live-game and instant replays, bench tables, comfortable seating, in-box wait service, and immediate access to semiprivate bathrooms. In addition, loge-box patrons also have access to an exclusive hospitality area before, during, and after games where they can enjoy upscale food and beverage.

Ticket sales remain the most important source of annual operating revenues for professional sport franchises. The key driver in sustaining the prominence of gate receipts has been the increased emphasis on selling premium-seating opportunities. Ever since the Palace at Auburn Hills demonstrated the abundant yield from the provision of premium-seating options,

FIGURE 6.3
Terrace Table Seating

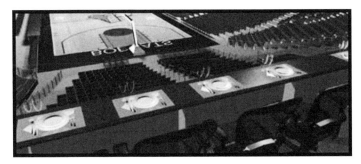

Source: Author's photograph.

teams have clamored to build new facilities loaded with luxury suites, club seats, and, most recently, loge boxes. Suites have proven to be highly attractive to corporations interested in finding unique and impactful opportunities to entertain important clients. Club seats offer more affluent fans the opportunity to be treated to a special game experience. The result has meant that teams can realize substantially greater revenues from the sale of their seating inventory, with premium options often yielding three to four times as much income on a per-capita or per-seat basis. Given the magnitude of revenue return, the creation and sale of premium-seating options will continue to be a priority for professional teams into the foreseeable future.

Personal Seat Licenses

A new and innovative driver of gate revenues has been the advent of personal seat licenses (PSLs). Like premium seating, selling seat licenses became a widespread practice during the 1990s. The concept requires an individual to make an advance payment to purchase the right to secure a particular seat in the venue. Often that particular seat may include a club seat. Buyers make a one-time payment which allows them to purchase the season ticket to that designated seat for a specified period of time. The seat license provides the buyer with an exclusive claim to that seat as long as the seat licenseholder continues to purchase season tickets.

Seat licenses are often referred to as PSLs, but there is no common agreement to what the "P" means in the term PSL. Over the last fifteen years, PSL programs have been alternatively called personal, private, and/or permanent seat licenses. The most recent PSL sales programs have tended to prefer the term *permanent* because the teams selling the licenses wanted to convey that the advance payment gave the fan lifetime control over the seat(s) being purchased. This approach was in contrast to early programs in which *personal* or *private* seat licenses were sold for a fixed period of time. Examples include the Oakland Raiders' disastrous seat license program, which limited seat guarantees to a ten-year period, at which time seat license owners were expected to pay an extravagant renewal price. The Raiders abandoned their seat license program before the renewal period because of their fans' angry reaction to the prospect of paying another high premium for the privilege of buying season tickets to seats they had occupied for an extended period of time.

Seat license programs have been a very effective way for teams to raise development capital to help construct new facilities. As the cost of modern sports venues has increased dramatically over the past fifteen to twenty years, team owners have had to pay an ever-increasing share of the construction costs. For example, the original estimate for building the Dallas Cowboys' new football stadium was $650 million. In 2004 the voters of the city of Arlington passed a referendum that obligated the city to pay half of the anticipated construction cost or $325 million. Jerry Jones, the Cowboys' owner, agreed to pay the other half of the stadium development expenses. That original, preconstruction estimate, however, eighteen months into actual development rose to a revised cost projection of over $1 billion. Fortunately for Jones, it is conceivable that the Cowboys will be able to presell as many as 50,000 seat licenses in their new 80,000-seat domed stadium and raise as much as $150 million, all of which could be applied to offset the increased cost of building the new stadium. While the seat license revenues will not cover entirely the inflationary expenses related to stadium construction, Mr. Jones will also be able to sell the naming rights to the new venue. Analysts believe that the naming rights to the new Cowboys stadium be worth as much as $300 to $400 million. Clearly, these two revenue streams alone will adequately cover the additional cost of construction. Most important, Mr. Jones will not have to spend an additional dollar from his own personal resources.

In 1993 the NFL Carolina Panthers became the first team to successfully implement a PSL program. The then-expansion team pledged the monies raised from the sale of seat license toward building a planned downtown stadium. The first day PSLs went on sale, the Panthers sold 41,632 licenses. Eventually, the new NFL franchise sold 62,000 seat licenses, ranging from $600 to $5,000, providing the team with $125 million in revenues in *advance* of stadium construction.[10] This phenomenal success spurred other teams to employ the seat license concept. To date, over thirty professional sports teams have initiated seat license programs. The scope and magnitude of some of the most successful PSL programs is illustrated in Table 6.4.

TABLE 6.4
Size, Price, and Economic Magnitude of Current (PSL) Programs

Team (League)	Total (Venue # of PSLs/Capacity)	Price Range	Total Revenue
Philadelphia Eagles (NFL)	29,000/66,000	$1,760–$3,617	$50–$60 mm
Seattle Seahawks (NFL)	8,300/67,000	$2,000–$3,000	$16–$17 mm
Pittsburgh Steelers (NFL)	48,000/65,000	$250–$2,700	$35–$40 mm
San Francisco Giants (MLB)	15,000/40,930	$1,500–$7,500	$40–$45 mm
Cincinnati Bengals (NFL)	50,000/65,600	$300–$1,500	$35–$40 mm
Baltimore Ravens (NFL)	59,000 /69,000	$250–$3,000	$65–$70 mm
Houston Texans (NFL)	50,000/69,500	$600–$3,900	$74 mm
Tennessee Titans (NFL)	57,000/67,000	$450–$4,500	$60 mm
Houston Astros (MLB)	2,300/40,950	$2,000–$20,000	$15–$20 mm

Source: Compiled from various media sources.

Demand is the key ingredient to achieving success with seat license programs. Thus, PSL sales have been most successful in those markets with pent-up demand for professional sports, such as when the NFL rewarded Charlotte with an expansion franchise, or in existing markets with particularly fervent fan bases such as in many NFL cities. For example, the Cleveland Browns and Pittsburgh Steelers, two franchises with storied histories, both sold more seat licenses than they had originally placed on the market. The Browns sold 64,000 licenses, raising more than $74 million. In the case of the Steelers, the original plan to sell 35,000 seat licenses had to be quickly adjusted up to 48,000 to more fully accommodate local interest.[11]

Of the sixteen NFL teams moving into new venues between 1993 and 2006, twelve sold seat licenses.[12] Other leagues have approached PSLs more conservatively, because each has a much greater inventory of games to sell. For example, MLB teams have eighty-one games to sell each season (versus the NFL's ten home dates). Fans, therefore, have many more opportunities to buy tickets and the necessity of paying a premium to *guarantee* the right to purchase a ticket is not nearly as compelling. Consequently, the small number of MLB teams that have implemented seat license programs have offered only a limited inventory. The San Francisco Giants offered 13,700 seat licenses (approximately one-third of the total seating capacity in their new ballpark) priced from $1,500 for an upper box seat location to $7,500 for a premium field seat. The one-time, upfront payment provided purchasers with a "lifetime guarantee" to buy season tickets to the charter seats they purchased. The Giants' entire seat license allocation sold out in less than six months. The club attributed the program's success to its ability to convince the public that all revenues raised would be used to finance the construction of the new ballpark and, according to a team representative, "not line the pockets of team owners."[13]

A dimension of seat license programs that has made them very attractive to consumer is that most programs allow the rights holder to transfer the PSL by gift or bequest and/or to sell the seat license to any interested party. The transfer feature allows seat holders to pass their seats on to family members. In addition to establishing a family legacy, PSLs have also proven to be reasonable investments. In Charlotte, for example, the Carolina Panthers' fully transferable PSLs, which originally sold for $600 to $5,400, were recently being sold for as much as $975 to $12,000, respectively, in what is called the PSL aftermarket. After seeing the success of the Panthers, most teams have established the rights transfer benefit as a prominent feature of their PSL programs.

NAMING RIGHTS

Over three-fourths, 94 of 122 major-league sports teams, currently play in corporate-named venues. The growth in the number of stadium and arena naming rights deals has been spectacular over the past decade. In 1997 only 36 percent of major-league teams played in venues that bear the name of corporate sponsors. The cumulative value of all of the naming rights partnerships currently in place comes close to $6 billion. As shown in Table 6.5, in 2006 alone the seven companies that entered into naming right deals with major professional sport franchises committed close to a billion dollars. While 1998 and 1999 were the most active years for naming rights agreements, with several major deals including Reliant Stadium ($300 million) and FedEx Field ($205 million), the two largest naming rights agreements to date were consummated in early 2007. Citigroup, Inc., an international financial services firm headquartered New York City, agreed to pay $400 million ($20 million per year over twenty years) for the naming rights to the new ballpark being built for the MLB New York Mets. The Citi Field contract is the most expensive sports-stadium naming rights deal ever, superseding the previous record agreement, Reliant Stadium by a substantial margin. Shortly after the Citi Field announcement, Barclays Bank announced that it would become the naming rights partner with the NBA New Jersey Nets and pay between $300 and $400 over twenty years for the naming rights to a proposed arena to be called the Barclays Center.[14]

Why are companies willing to pay so much for the naming rights to sports facilities? There are three fundamental reasons corporations enter into naming agreements with sports franchises. Initially, the principal reason companies found naming rights so attractive was the unique exposure

TABLE 6.5
Trends in Sports Naming Right Deals: Average Price of Naming Rights from 1996–2006

Year	No. of Venues Corp. Named	Total Amount Committed	Average Total Price	Average Length	Average Annual Price
2006	7	$956 m	$137 m	18.6 yrs	$5.45 m
2005	2	$147 m	$73 m	15 yrs	$4.9 m
2004	3	$295–$335 m	$98–$112 m	20–21.7 yrs	$4.93–$5.3 m
2003	5	$359 m	$71.8 m	21 yrs	$3.87 m
2002	5	$441 m	$88.2 m	20.6 yrs	$4.28 m
2001	3	$265 m	$88.5 m	21 yrs	$4.01 m
2000	8	$793 m	$92.9 m	20 yrs	$4.26 m
1999	10	$1,020 m	$102.0 m	20.2 yrs	$4.80 m
1998	9	$468 m	$52.0 m	18.1 yrs	$2.75 m
1997	8	$418 m	$52.3 m	24.3 yrs	$2.24 m
1996	2	$62 m	$31.2 m	17.5 yrs	$17.5 m

Source: Compiled from various media sources, author's calculations.

opportunities provided by taking the name of a conspicuous public attraction. From an exposure perspective, naming rights agreement offer companies several significant advantages over traditional advertising alternatives:

> You can't bypass a name on a stadium the way you zap through a commer-
> cial—it's tougher to ignore. While each sponsorship needs to be measured for
> its effectiveness, a lot of marketers are looking for a less cluttered, high impact
> way to get a brand in front of the public eye. Associating with marquee prop-
> erties is one great way to accomplish this.[15]

The unique "24/7" exposure afforded by naming rights deals is an appealing benefit, particularly for companies with little or no brand recognition.
Swedish telecommunications giant Ericsson, Inc., was virtually unknown in
the United States before it paid $20 million in 1995 for the naming rights
to the NFL Carolina Panthers' new stadium in Charlotte, North Carolina.
The exposure received by the company over the first three years had a remarkable impact on Ericsson's brand awareness. Market research conducted
in 1998 found that in less than three years the Ericsson brand grew from
almost no public presence to being recognized by 50 percent of the adults in
the Carolinas and by 44 percent nationally.

While enhancing a company's awareness is an important benefit of naming rights agreements, the most important reason companies are willing to
pay so much for the association with sport venues is the company's desire to
use the facility as a platform for increasing sales. In fact, the amount of the
rights fee is often based largely on the company's estimate of the amount of
incremental sales that will be realized from the partnership. The incremental
sales benefits are most apparent in naming rights transactions that convey
exclusive selling rights to the entitled company. For example, the Pepsi Center in Denver, Colorado, home to the NBA Nuggets and NHL Avalanche,
provides Pepsi USA with exclusive pouring rights in the building, allowing
the company to recapture a significant portion of the $3.4 million they pay
in rights fees annually. Philips Electronics paid $185 million for the naming
rights to Atlanta's 20,000-seat arena, home to the NBA Hawks and NHL
Thrashers. The twenty-year agreement provides Philips with a 10,000-
square-foot consumer products display area, The Philips Experience, where
the company can showcase its latest consumer entertainment products. In
addition, the agreement required the $213-million venue to be fitted exclu-
sively with Philips equipment and products from the state-of-the-art turn-
stiles to the hundreds of big screen monitors located throughout the
arena.[16] Companies also use their affiliation with a popular sports team to
create traffic-driving promotions, such as player appearances at retail outlets,
to derive tangible benefits from their naming rights agreements.

The final benefit, closely related to increasing sales, is the unique entertainment opportunities provided to companies through naming rights partnerships. An almost universal element of every naming rights contract is that the corporate partner receives access to at least one luxury suite in the sports venue. This allows the company to create indirect selling opportunities with key customers by hosting them in premium surroundings at games or concerts. The goodwill engendered through these kinds of hospitality efforts is intended to strengthen business relationships that translate into increased or renewed sales opportunities.

Many teams and venue operators have been able to exploit the abundant revenue-generating potential of modern sports facilities. The relatively recent development of three sources of income—premiums seating, seat licenses, and the sale of naming rights—have had a dramatic impact on the financial growth and viability of professional sport franchises. Even through troubling economic times such as 2002 and late 2007, both individual fan and corporate investment in these three important revenue sources has remained stable. Premium seating options, seat licenses, and long-term naming rights agreements will all continue to be prominent elements of the professional sports landscape into the foreseeable future.

MEDIA REVENUES

Media rights fees continue to comprise a growing share of overall league revenues. Initially, leagues feared that broadcasting games on radio and/or television would hurt attendance at games, and were reluctant to enter into agreements with providers. During the 1940s and 1950s, many baseball teams were unable to sell the rights to broadcast their games in opposing cities; to circumvent this stations would "recreate" games in studio with announcers improvising play-by-play using telegraph reports in order to air away games.[17] In addition, limitations to early technologies did not provide a very good representation of the games on television, thus limiting their appeal. Despite these early issues, television rose to prominence in the 1950s and 1960s, and sporting events became a viewing staple. A key development was the advent of communications satellites, which allowed sporting events to be aired live across the world. In 1962 Telstar was launched, and the 1964 Tokyo Olympics were seen live in thirty-nine countries.[18]

The rights to air sports contests are valuable to broadcasters for a number of reasons. High interest in games generates advertising and sponsorship revenues, where advertisers seek to engage the desirable male, eighteen to thirty-four age demographic. As a result, sports audiences can allow advertisers to target a specific consumer group and are viewed in the industry as a way to break through the "clutter" of other channels and advertising. In addition, associating with a league can improve a broadcaster's overall brand by giving it legitimacy and driving subscription penetration.[19] This differentiates sports programming from many other kinds of programming, as "its value is directly tied to a program suppliers' market reputation and legitimacy."[20] This creates high demand for sports programming that may exceed other programming with similar ratings.

A key determinant of revenues for broadcasters is the ratings that the programming generates. A *rating* represents the percentage of television households that are tuned into the program. Another indicator is the *share* that the program has, which represents the percentage of households with sets in use that are tuned into the program.[21] Thus, broadcasters judge the success of programming content on the basis of the total number of households watching and also on how the programming fares against other programming options available at the same time.

To maximize revenues from media sources, sports leagues encourage a bidding process between providers:[22]

> There is currently monopoly control of each of the four pro team sports of baseball, football, basketball, and hockey, as there has been over most of the histories of the sports. Through exclusive territorial franchises, leagues provide each member team with a local monopoly in the sport, giving it special bargaining power in its dealings with local radio and TV stations, with the municipally owned stadium or arena in its city, and even with the ticket-buying public. The league is a monopolist in its negotiations with competing network and cable TV systems, in contracting for national TV coverage of its sport.[23]

Different types of media revenue sources are discussed below.

Broadcast

Broadcast agreements with sports leagues typically come in three forms. The first are the direct sale of rights, where a fee is paid by the broadcaster. The second involves in-house production, where the team and/or league owns and controls the production. A third form involves a cooperative production between the sport and provider that usually involves revenue sharing between the parties.[24] However, leagues and teams will try to avoid the latter scenario, as it involves an assumption of risk.

In some cases, broadcasters are willing to assume significant financial risks in order to contract with certain leagues. For example, Fox Television made inroads into becoming the fourth major U.S. television network after acquiring the rights to NFL football games in 1994. Fox ended up losing over $350 million on this agreement; however, the rest of the network showed an increase in profitability, which was attributed in part to the increasing legitimacy of the network due to its association with the NFL brand.[25]

Rights fees for the four major professional sports leagues continue to climb, with the exception of the NHL. The NFL currently has six-year agreements with three U.S. networks, which expire in 2011. Fox is paying $4.27 billion, CBS $3.73 billion, and NBC $3.6 billion. The NBA has a $2.4-billion, six-year agreement with ABC/ESPN that expires at the end of 2007/08. Major League Baseball just completed a six-year, $2.5-billion contract with Fox.[26] The NHL has an agreement with NBA to share revenues generated by telecasts, and the most recent contract in Canada is with CBC through 2008.

Cable

In addition to network television agreements, sports leagues and teams televise programming on cable. In contrast to network television, which is aired for free, cable channels must be paid for by the fan/subscriber. Where network television once dominated, cable channels are becoming more and more competitive for ratings. By the early 2000s basic cable services cost in excess of $154/year, with ESPN receiving $24 of that amount.[27] ESPN, an all-sports channel, was launched in September of 1979 and moved to a twenty-four-hour hour broadcast the following year. The channel was not widely regarded and few felt that it would survive. However, by May of 1981, ESPN was shown in over 10 million homes, and by January of 1989, over 50 million.[28] Today ESPN reaches over 100 million U.S. households.

Cable rights fees generate substantial revenues. The NFL currently has an eight-year, $8.8-billion agreement with ESPN to show Monday Night Football through 2013. ESPN is also paying MLB $2.37 billion over eight years, with Turner Broadcasting (TBS) also holding some rights. The NBA has a $2.2-billion contract with TBS through 2007/08. Finally, the NHL has a two-year, $135-million agreement with Versus; in Canada the NHL has an agreement with TSN through 2008.

Local

In some leagues teams can sell the rights to local providers to televise games. These are typically aired on regional sports networks. Traditionally, teams have taken one of three approaches to the production of local programming. One is to sell rights to a local provider, who in turn hires announcers, provides technical support, and then sells commercial time to sponsors. The second involves the team packaging its own games, then selling it to sponsors and providers. The final option involves selling directly to a sponsor, who in turn resells a portion of the rights to other noncompeting products and services, and contracts with the broadcasters.[29]

Local contracts can be very lucrative, depending on the size of the market the team is playing in. In leagues where local revenues are not shared, this can create a significant financial disparity among clubs. It also provides an opportunity for team owners to find synergies with their other business interests, if they also have a stake in the media property.

NEW MEDIA

Another emerging interest to sports leagues is the development of what is called "new media." New media can be considered new ways in which viewers can consume sports programming, and typically includes the Internet, digital television, and mobile telephones.[30] These new platforms change the ways in which fans consume games, and make sports programming more accessible.[31] A term for this is *convergence,* where there is an increasing integration of mass communication, telecommunication, data transference, and the delivery of media content. This will become increasingly important as technology improves the quality of these alternative means of viewing or listening to games:[32]

These new forms of delivery relates involve more interactivity with the consumer:

> A key to the new media environment is interactivity. Where traditional mass media were about the one-way flow of information, new media incorporate the ability to interact with the medium in a two-way or multilateral communication without the control of intermediaries (producers, editors, schedulers and so on).[33]

An example of an emerging power in new media has been Major League Baseball Advanced Media (MLBAM). The subsidiary of MLB was created in 2000 and today has revenues of $300 million. It is estimated that if MLBAM was to be offered publicly, it would be valued at over $2 billion.[34] While MLB.com is not as popular a website as other sports offerings, like ESPN.com, MLBAM has aggressively pursued a number of different growth areas, including ticketing, merchandise sales, and fantasy gaming. In addition, MLBAM has created a diversified portfolio, handling e-commerce for the city of New York, providing online video for the U.S. Figure Skating

Association, and working with CBS's March Madness on Demand programming.[35]

MLBAM serves as baseball's interactive provider, distributing over 18,000 hours of live video of games per year and over 30,000 of live game audio. In addition, MLBAM bought tickets.com for $66.5 million, and the interactive rights from the MLB Players' Association. The former resulted in the sale of over 24 million of MLB's 76.04 million tickets sold in 2005; the latter allowed MLBAM to reconfigure its fantasy baseball platform. As explained by John Brody, MLB senior vice president of corporate sales and marketing, "There's a much more unified effort going on now to tie everything together, whether it's marketing, sponsorship, merchandise, what have you."[36]

Following in the footsteps of MLBAM, the NBA has recently announced that it will launch its own video download store. Close to 4 million hours worth of video was watched on NBA.com during the 2006/07 NBA regular season, twice the previous year's totals. The league will also make video available on YouTube, Yahoo!, MySpace, Facebook, and through wireless devices.

> Located on NBA.com, the store venture essentially replaces a deal struck with Apple last year for the 2006 playoffs to get video content on iTunes. Somewhat similar to the pricing structure on iTunes, individual, full-length games will cost $2.99 each, full playoff series will cost $12.99 and the entire postseason will be available for $79.99.[37]

Out-of-market television packages have also emerged as a revenue source for leagues. This has created some intense competition among providers, who often seek to improve their market position by entering into exclusive contracts with leagues for content. For example, recent discussions between DirecTV and MLB for exclusive access to MLB's Extra Innings package were considered potentially a "huge blow to the cable industry and one that will certainly grab attention on Capitol Hill."[38] DirecTV began offering the package in 1996, with cable operators starting in 2001 and rival Dish Network in 2004. Over 750,000 subscribers pay $179 per season to access games. In contrast, the NFL's Sunday Ticket package (offered by DirecTV exclusively), has over 2 million subscribers. DirecTV pays the NFL $700 million per year for these rights.[39]

The advent of satellite radio has also created a new revenue stream for leagues and teams. For example, as of July 1, 2007, XM became the exclusive satellite radio home for the NHL, broadcasting over 1,100 games per season across the United States and Canada. It also features the only twenty-four-hour hockey radio channel. Other leagues have lucrative agreements: the

NFL has a seven-year, $220-million agreement with Sirius lasting through 2010, and MLB receives $650 million over eleven years through 2015. When XM became partners with MLB in 2004, it had 2.5 million subscribers. Since then subscriptions have tripled and research by XM has shown that 23 percent of new subscriptions were driven by the baseball package.[40]

MERCHANDISING AND SPONSORSHIPS

Another growing source of revenues for major-league sports teams is through licensing its names and logos to other companies, who produce official products on behalf of the league. Although licensed league properties can be big-ticket items, most revenues come from sales of low-priced, "impulse" products.[41] On average, licensing fees are 8 percent of gross sales.[42] Thus, sales figures of total sales of items such as player jerseys can be misleading, as leagues and their respective teams only receive a small portion of this amount. However, some franchises generate significant revenues; for example, Manchester United, which has a worldwide following, had more revenues from merchandising as it did from ticket sales in 1998.[43]

All four major professional sports leagues have developed their own central licensing office, and royalties are then split among league clubs:[44]

> Each sports team has a logo, consisting of a name, design, and color scheme that represents the team and is easily identifiable by the sports viewing public. The logo is a trademark and can be registered with the Patent and Trademark Office on the Principal Register as a mark for entertainment services in the form of professional sports games. Team logos are placed on merchandise to indicate sponsorship and authorization by the team represented by the logo. Each team owns the trademark rights in the logo, including the right to license the logo.[45]

The first league to organize centrally was the NFL, who created NFL Properties in 1981. At the time, twenty-six of the twenty-eight franchises entered into a trust agreement, transferring the exclusive rights to their marks to the NFL Trust. A licensing agreement was then created between the NFL Trust and NFL Properties, with the latter then able to enter into negotiations with other firms, such as Nike, or Coca-Cola.[46]

Three years later, Major League Baseball formed MLB Properties, a subsidiary of MLB Enterprises. MLB Properties owns and controls the licensing of all teams and all events associated with MLB, along with the marks of both the American League (AL) and National League (NL).[47] MLB Properties distributes income equally among league teams, despite the fact that some specific teams may generate much more income due to their popularity. In return for providing this service to teams, MLB Properties takes a 30 percent commission for revenues under $50 million and 15 percent for income greater than $50 million.[48] In 2006 MLB Enterprises generated revenues of $300 million, up from $195 million in 2003. Players' associations also generate substantial revenues from licensing; for example, EA Sports (a video-game firm) pays a licensing fee of $3 million to the Major League Baseball Players' Association; the NFLPA was paid $33 million by the same company. The NFL currently has a five-year, $300-million agreement with EA through 2009. In professional basketball, the National Basketball Players' Association (NBPA) assigns its licensing rights to the NBA; it received $33.5 million from the NBA in 2006.

Sales of licensed merchandise remains strong. In 2006 U.S. and Canada sales of licensed merchandise for the NHL was $750 million. The NFL had $3.3 billion in retail sales, MLB $3.2 billion, and the NBA $2.2 billion.[49] Overall licensing revenues can be threatened by the behavior of individual team owners and declines in interest for team products. Teams may "cheat" by entering into independent agreements with licensees; an example would be a team signing an agreement with a footwear manufacturer that is a competitor of a company that has paid to be the "official" footwear of the league as a whole. In most cases, leagues are content to assign licensing rights to their partners, as they are reluctant to assume any financial risks in licensing ventures.[50] As a result, licensees can lose significantly should leagues enter work stoppages due to strikes or lockouts.

Similar to licensing, sponsorships involve a company paying in order to associate with a league or team. Sports sponsorships date back nearly 150 years, when a catering firm sponsored a cricket tour. However, the widespread use of sponsorships did not emerge in the four major North American sports leagues until the 1960s.[51] Currently, MLB has eighteen official sponsors in seventeen categories; the NBA sixteen in sixteen categories; the NFL twenty-one in eighteen, and the NHL nineteen in sixteen categories. Examples include official airline, automobile, battery, beer, hotel, and soft drink. The number of sponsors for the four major leagues ranges from sixteen to nineteen, and categories from sixteen to twenty-one. This is in contrast with NASCAR, which has much more aggressively pursued sponsorships. NASCAR has forty-four official sponsors in thirty-six different categories.

TEAM OWNERSHIP

Another source of significant revenues for teams and leagues is through expansion fees, which are typically divided equally among existing franchises. However, the amount that individual teams profit in the long run is dependent upon the amount of revenue sharing among league clubs. For example, where revenues are widely shared, existing teams will be foregoing future shares of revenues as there will be more teams to divide revenues among. Where teams share little revenues, receiving expansion fees are ideal as long as the new team does not reduce the existing team's revenue. In addition, teams have an incentive to expand where fees are not included in designated revenue pools that are used to determine salary caps in some leagues; in other words, teams will receive revenues without having to increase payrolls where they are set at a fixed percentage of league revenues. However, although leagues have an incentive to expand to gain expansion fees, the addition of too many new teams can dilute the quality of play in a league and increase the number of teams that pooled revenues are shared with. Thus, from a fan's perspective, it may be desirable to have restrictions on the total number of teams in a given league.

Expansion fees have grown dramatically in recent years, with the NFL's most recent expansion franchise, Houston, paying $700 million to enter the league. It is anticipated that the next expansion team to enter the NFL will have to pay $1 billion. By way of comparison, the most recent NBA expansion team, in Charlotte, North Carolina, paid $300 million in 2004/05, and the wave of expansion in the NHL in the 1990s topped out at $80 million. Perhaps a good way of tracking growth in expansion fee revenues is to examine MLB over the past few decades.[52] When the AL expanded by two teams in 1961, no expansion fee was required; however, each new team was required to purchase players from existing team rosters, resulting in over $2.1 million per expansion team being paid to other clubs. In addition, the new Los Angeles franchise, the Angels, had to pay a $550,000 indemnification fee to the Los Angeles Dodgers for playing in their market. In the NL similar rules were adopted for the two new franchises added the following year, except each expansion franchise ended up paying over $1.8 million each.

In 1969 in the AL, Kansas City and Seattle each paid a $100,000 franchise fee and acquired three players from each existing team for a total of thirty, at a total cost of $5.25 million per team. The two new teams were also unable to share in national television revenues for the next three years, which cost each team $2,062,500. The same year in the NL, Montreal and San Diego joined, paying a $4-million franchise fee. The two teams drafted 30 players each at a cost of $6 million. As a result, it cost teams $10 million to join the NL, although the new franchises could share in television revenue.

In 1977 Seattle and Toronto joined the AL, with Toronto paying $7 million and Seattle $6.5 million. This fee included the cost of drafting thirty players each from existing teams. In 1993 Colorado and Florida paid $95 million to join the NL. These clubs were not initially able to share in television revenues, costing each an additional $14 million. In addition, $42 million of the total $190 million was shared with AL clubs; in return, the AL clubs had to make players available for the expansion draft. In 1998 the Arizona Diamondbacks and Tampa Bay Devil Rays entered the NL and AL, respectively. Each paid a $130-million expansion fee and had to forego future $5 million annual payments from MLB's central fund, for a total cost of $155 million per franchise.

As the discussion above suggests, franchise fees have been climbing steadily in recent years, and fees are often tied to specific conditions related to expansion, such as the sharing of pooled revenues and the availability of players from other existing teams. Although it seems as though all four leagues have saturated the available markets in their respective sports, the lure of expansion fees should result in more new teams in the coming years.

A frequent headline in the sports pages concerns team owners who continue to complain about how their teams are losing millions of dollars a year. Notwithstanding the fact that some team owners are not motivated purely to make money, and that creative accounting practices and related party transactions (to be discussed below) can make losses seem even more pronounced, team owners and professional sports can generally bank on the appreciation of their franchise's value over time.[53] An example would be a recent offer by Jim Balsillie to purchase the Nashville Predators of the NHL. The team paid an expansion fee of $80 million to join the league in 1997; the city of Nashville actually chipped in $25 million of that amount, so the initial investment was $55 million. According to team owner Craig Leipold, the team has lost in excess of $70 million over the course of its history. However, the recent offer of $238 million for the franchise clearly suggests that owning the team has been a wise investment for Leipold.[54]

Due to their unique characteristics, sports franchises seem to be unaffected by economic conditions that might influence the vale of other businesses in other industries. A study by sports industry consultants Moag and Company reviewed the U.S. economy in recent decades, and found that the Standard and Poor's 500 grew at a compound annual rate of 8.4 percent. Over that span, they identified five bear market periods, but acknowledged that businesses in the sports industry experienced either no decline or less of a decline than the broader market average. They concluded that sports-focused businesses thrive regardless of economic conditions: "In both robust and declining economies, people turn to sports out of loyalty, passion, and a need for an entertaining distraction from the regularities of life. Accordingly, the sports industry represents an attractive investment opportunity."[55]

Other research has supported this claim. For example, during the 1990s the average annual rate of franchise appreciation was 11.3 percent in MLB, 17.7 percent for NBA franchises, 10.7 percent in the NHL, and 12.7 percent in the NFL.[56]

Another way team owners can profit from team ownership is by selling stock in their franchises. Some leagues allow this on the condition that voting control is maintained by a dominant shareholder.[57] Wayne Huizenga, then owner of the Florida Panthers of the NHL, conducted an Initial Public Offering (IPO) of a portion of his franchise in 1996. The Panthers had entered the NHL as an expansion franchise in 1993 and Huizenga had paid an expansion fee of $50 million. Three years later, he netted $71.4 million based on the sale of 7.3 million shares of Panthers stock, representing approximately half the franchise. A rationale provided for Huizenga to undertake the IPO was to generate money to build a new arena for the team. However, after it was decided that the arena would be publicly funded, Huizenga then used a portion of the money he received from the IPO to invest in hotel resort properties.[58]

In addition, franchise owners may benefit where they also own related properties in the entertainment industries, which allow them to leverage their sports teams. In 1998 Disney—who at the time owned both the Mighty Ducks of the NHL and Angels of MLB—entered into a ten-year, $120-million cable contract with Fox Sports Net West II to show games of both teams. While the contract amount was deemed under market value, economist Andrew Zimbalist noted that Disney likely received additional benefits from Fox, such as carriage on Fox's parent company, News Corporation's worldwide satellite distribution systems.[59]

Some owners have bought franchises and used the team as media content for their other businesses. When media mogul Ted Turner bought the Atlanta Braves in 1976, the Braves provided much-needed programming for his new cable station, which would eventually become TBS. The rise of TBS and the Braves as a popular team in the United States coincided with the ability of Braves games to reach many parts of the country, especially those with no local major league team.[60] It is this demand that may also drive up the value of franchises, as owning teams may be more valuable to some ownership interests than others.[61]

A recent trend has been for teams to develop their own regional sports networks. They can generate significant revenues for teams and also help franchises control media coverage of their teams. Table 6.6 lists some of the regional sports networks that are owned or jointly owned by professional sports franchises.

In owning both the team and the network, franchise owners can engage in what are called related party transactions. The owner has control of both

TABLE 6.6
Team-owned Regional Sports Networks

Network	Franchise
Comcast SportsNet Chicago (2004)	Ownership groups of the Chicago White Sox, Bulls and Blackhawks; Comcast Corp.
Mid-Atlantic Sports Network (2005)	Baltimore Orioles, Major League Baseball (Washington Nationals)
New England Sports Network (1984)	Boston Red Sox, Boston Bruins
Rogers Sportsnet (1998)	Rogers Communications Inc. (Toronto Blue Jays)
SportsNet New York (2006)	Sterling Entertainment (New York Mets), Time Warner, Comcast
SportsTime Ohio (2006)	Cleveland Indians
YES Network (2002)	Yankee Global Enterprises LLC (New York Yankees), Goldman Sachs Capital Partners, Providence Equity Partners
Altitude Sports & Entertainment (2004)	Kroenke Sports Enterprises, parent company of the Denver Nuggets, Colorado Avalanche, MLS Colorado Rapids, NLL Colorado Mammoth and the Pepsi Center

Source: Compiled from various media reports.

parties that are entering into a transaction—for example, a team and a sports network—so regardless of what price is charged, the money all goes into the pockets of the same group or individual. This can reduce franchise revenues, where the profits are channeled through the other business entity. This occurs frequently where the franchise owner also owns the venue that the team plays in. A notable case occurred in 1997 when the owner of the Florida Marlins of MLB, who had just won the World Series, claimed to have lost $30 million during that year:

> However, revenues from luxury suites, premium seats, naming rights, parking, signage, merchandising and concessions were all attributed to the stadium that he also owned, not to the team. The estimated revenues from these sources were $36 million. In addition, the value of the media outlet increased by $40 million in that year as a result of the team's success.[62]

An excellent example of how a franchise owner has been able to leverage the team occurred with New York Yankees team owner George Steinbrenner and Yankees Entertainment & Sports (YES) Network. Steinbrenner purchased the Yankees in 1973 for $10 million. Through the 1980s, the Yankees had a local cable television contract with MSG Network for $50 million. At the conclusion of that contract, Steinbrenner signed a multiyear cable rights agreement for an unprecedented $493 million. This taught him the value of the Yankees as programming content, and the Yankees decided to develop their own network to take advantage of their property. In 2002 YES was launched, co-owned by Yankee Global Enterprises LLC (New York Yankees), Goldman Sachs Capital Partners, and Providence Equity Partners. The Yankees reportedly own 35 percent of YES.

> The 2002 plan was to carry all but thirty-two Yankees games on the YES network (twenty going to CBS-TV and twelve to exclusive national coverage as part of MLB's package deal with Fox and ESPN), and to insist that cable distributors in the New York market offer the YES network in their expanded basic package. YES would charge each cable distributor approximately $2 per subscriber per month to carry its programming.[63]

It is estimated that subscriber revenues total $188.5 million per year, and advertising sales generate $38 million per year, for a total of $227 million. Today, although the Yankees continue to report losses for their baseball operations, *Forbes* magazine values the Yankees at $1.2 billion, up from $636 million in 2001.

CONCLUSION

This chapter has reviewed the ways in which professional sports leagues have found new and increasing revenue streams. While gate revenues remain a staple, it is the luxury component of seating that is the most lucrative and has been a focus of teams in recent years. In addition, the last several years have seen a dramatic increase in the fees companies have been willing to pay for the naming rights to sports venues. PSL programs provide teams with the ability to raise an abundant amount of development capital for new facility construction. With the exception of the NHL, television revenues continue to grow, and all leagues have actively cultivated new revenues through new media. In the coming years, it will be interesting to see what new technologies will emerge that will change the consumption experience for fans, while at the same time increasing the revenues of teams and leagues in the multibillion dollar professional sport industry.

NOTES

1. The revenue figures were compiled from data furnished by *Forbes* in their annual valuation of professional sports leagues.
2. M. Ozanian and S. Taub, "Big Leagues, Bad Business," *Financial World*, July 7, 1992, 34–42.

3. D. Howard and J. Crompton, *Financing Sport* (Morgantown, W.V.: Fitness Information Technology, Inc., 1995), 10.

4. The valuation figures were compiled for data furnished by *Forbes* in their annual valuation of professional sports teams.

5. B. Dorsey, "Premium Seating: The Next Ten Years," *SEAT Magazine* (Summer 2001), http://www.alsd.com/publications.

6. *2006 Revenues from Sport Venues* (Milwaukee, Wis.: Mediaventures, 2006).

7. T. J. Simers and D. Wharton, "How the Game Was Played," *Los Angeles Times Magazine*, October 10, 1999, 28–31, 128–131.

8. *2006 Revenues from Sport Venues.*

9. "Why the Big Deal about Premium Seating?" *SEAT Magazine* (Winter 2007): 13.

10. R. Noll and A. Zimbalist, "Build the Stadium—Create the Jobs!," in *Sports, Jobs, and Taxes,* ed. R. Noll and A. Zimbalist (Washington, D.C.: Brookings Institution Press, 1997).

11. Dennis R. Howard and J. L. Crompton, *Financing Sport,* 2nd ed. (Morgantown, W.V.: Fitness Information Technology, 2004), 289.

12. *2006 Revenues from Sport Venues.*

13. A. Feurerstein, "Giants Take the Early Lead in Seat Sales," *San Francisco Business Times* (1996): 12.

14. T. Dworetzky, "Barclays, Nets Team Up on Atlantic Yards Naming Rights," *Commercial Property News,* January 18, 2007, http://www.commercialpressnews.com/cpn/article_display.ysp.

15. J. Zoghley, "Ericsson Makes Name with N.C. Stadium," *Sports Business Journal,* November 1–7, 1999, 14.

16. Howard and Crompton, *Financing Sport,* 281.

17. Robert Bellamy Jr., "The Evolving Television Sports Marketplace," in *MediaSport,* ed. L. A. Wenner (London: Routledge, 2000), 73; T. Ashwell and M. A. Hums, "Sale of Broadcasting Rights," in Howard and Crompton, *Financing Sport,* 390.

18. T. Hoehn and D. Lancefield, "Broadcasting and Sport," *Oxford Review of Economic Policy 19* (2003): 554.

19. Bellamy, "Evolving Television Sports Marketplace," 76.

20. Ashwell and Hums, "Sale of Broadcasting Rights," 388–389.

21. Rodney D. Fort, *Sports Economics* (Upper Saddle River, N.J.: Prentice-Hall, 2003), 51.

22. James Quirk and Rodney Fort, *Pay Dirt: The Business of Professional Team Sports* (Princeton, N.J.: Princeton University Press, 1992), 16.

23. Ashwell and Hums, "Sale of Broadcasting Rights," 397.

24. Fort, *Sports Economics,* 50.

25. This agreement includes the transfer of some cable rights to ESPN.

26. Hoehn and Lancefield, "Broadcasting and Sport," 557.

27. See M. Freeman, *ESPN: The Uncensored History* (Dallas: Taylor Publishing Company, 2000).

28. Ira Horowitz, "Sports Broadcasting," in *Government and the Sports Business*, ed. R. G. Noll (Washington, D.C.: Brookings Institution, 1974), 277–278.

29. R. Boyle and R. Haynes, *Power Play: Sport, the Media, and Popular Culture* (London: Pearson Education Ltd., 2003), 95–96.

30. M. Lewis, "Franchise Relocation and Fan Allegiance," *Journal of Sport Social Issues* 25 (2001): 8.

31. Boyle and Haynes, *Power Play,* 96–97.

32. Ibid., 98.

33. "Score Another for MLBAM: Under Bob Bowman's Leadership, Baseball's Digital Arm Stays Agile in an Ever-Changing Marketplace," *Sports Business Journal,* February 19, 2007, 15.

34. Ibid., 15.

35. Eric Fisher, "Special Report: MLB Season Preview," *Sports Business Journal*, April 3, 2006, 1.

36. Ibid.

37. Eric Fisher, "Opening Up Their Books," *Sports Business Journal,* May 7, 2007, 4.

38. John Ourand and Eric Fisher, "DirecTV-Only MLB Package? Possible Exclusive Extra Innings Deal Could Draw Congress's Eye," *Sports Business Journal*, December 25, 2006, 1.

39. Ibid.

40. "XM to Become Exclusive Satellite Radio Carrier of NHL," Newswire.ca, http://www.newswire.ca/en/releases/archive/June2007/28/c9748.html (accessed June 29, 2007).

41. "Thank You, Technology, for Allowing Us to Go Home Again," *Sports Business Journal,* May 7, 2007, 29.

42. J. A. Garcia, "The Future of Sports Merchandise Licensing," *Hastings Commercial and Entertainment Law Journal* 18 (1995): 221.

43. B. L. Grusd, "The Antitrust Implications of Professional Sports' League-Wide Licensing and Merchandising Arrangements," *Virginia Journal of Sports and the Law* 1 (1999): 5.

44. W. Andreff and P. D. Staudohar, "European and U.S. Sports Business Models," in *Transatlantic Sport: The Comparative Economics of North American and European Sports,* ed. C. P. Barros, M. Ibrahimo, and S. Szymanski (Cheltenham: Edward Algar, 2002), 32.

45. Garcia, "Future of Sports Merchandise Licensing," 220.

46. Ibid., 221.

47. Grusd, "Antitrust Implications," 10–11.

48. Ibid., 8–9. MLB Properties set up MLB Properties Canada to work with the two Canadian clubs.

49. Ibid., 9.

50. Jenn Abelson, "NHL Suits Up Like Never Before: Hopes Look Will Lure Fans," *Boston Globe,* June 21, 2007, http://www.boston.com/business/articles/2007/06/21/nhl_suits_up_like_never_before (accessed June 22, 2007).

51. G. D. Way, "Sudden Death: League Labor Disputes, Sports Licensing, and Force Majeure Neglect," *Marquette Sports Law Journal* 7 (1997): 430.

52. Gerald W. Scully, *The Market Structure of Sports* (Chicago: University of Chicago Press, 1995), 23.

53. The following discussion has been gleaned from http://www.roadsidephotos.com/baseball/expansion.htm (accessed May 23, 2007).

54. Tim Wharnsby, "Nashville Consortium Throws Hat into Ring to Buy Franchise," *Globe and Mail,* http://www.theglobeandmail.com/servlet/story/LAC.20070704.PREDATORS04/TPStory/Sports. (accessed July 5, 2007).

55. Moag and Company, *Analysis and Reporting on Emerging Financial Trends and Developments in the Sports Industry* (Baltimore: Author, 2002), 1.

56. Andrew Zimbalist, "Sport as Business," *Oxford Review of Economic Policy* 19 (2003): 508.

57. R. Bacon, "Initial Public Offerings and Professional Sports Teams: The Regulations Work, But Are Owners and Investors Listening?" *Seton Hall Journal of Sport Law* 10 (2000): 145.

58. Zimbalist, "Sport as Business," 509.

59. Fort, *Sports Economics,* 62.

60. Ibid., 64–65.

61. Zimbalist, "Sport as Business," 508.

62. Howard and Crompton, *Financing Sport,* 33.

63. Andrew Zimbalist, *May the Best Team Win: Baseball Economics and Public Policy* (Washington, D.C.: Brookings Institution Press, 2003), 12–13.

Seven

The European Perspective on Team Ownership, Competitive Balance, and Event Impacts

Arne Feddersen and Wolfgang Maennig

In the literature of sports economics, several studies have identified significant differences between the American and the European sports model.[1] Since the European perspective on sports economics or sports business is a broad subject, the following remarks concentrate on the central aspects of team ownership, competitive balance, and event impacts, while considering the most recent experiences and developments, especially in European soccer.

OWNERSHIP IN EUROPEAN SOCCER: NONPROFIT ASSOCIATIONS, MAGNATES, AND PUBLIC LIMITED COMPANIES

Owner Objectives: Profit versus Utility Maximization

Why is it important to identify owner objectives? The answer is that, due to the local monopoly position held by most sport clubs, their discretion over pricing and output is much greater than that of competitive firms.[2] As the owner objective has direct implications for the firm's behavior, regarding both factor and product markets, it must be taken into account in decisions affecting regulations in the team sports market.

In the literature on American sports, it is widely accepted that owners maximize profits.[3] This assumption is derived from the theory of the firms. However, some authors have discussed alternative objectives of a firm, such as sales revenue maximization, growth maximization, and utility maximization.[4] With few exceptions, the objective of utility maximization is favored in the sports economics literature on European sports. Regarding European team sports, some economists have argued that profit maximization is not descriptive of leagues whereas the utility obtained from winning per se can be an important decision-making factor.[5] Nevertheless, as the commercialization of European soccer progresses, tendencies toward profit maximization can be found.

Constraints on Profit Maximization in European Soccer

League Design

The most striking difference between the American and the European sports system is league design. While the American major leagues are closed leagues, European leagues are open leagues. Moreover, European soccer leagues provide greater incentives for good table rankings than U.S. major leagues: (1) The first position is equivalent to winning the championship, (2) positions 2–6 qualify for participation in one of the supranational competitions of the Union of European Football Associations (UEFA), and (3) the bottom positions are consistent with relegation to the second tier.

It is important to note that the gap in revenue from one of the groups (1) to (3) to another is significant. Winning the championship guarantees a team's participation in the UEFA Champions League (UCL), with additional revenues of about $20 million per team.[6] Also, teams in positions 2–6 participate in a European supercompetition, which means additional revenues of several million U.S. dollars. Nonetheless, the gap between the first and second tiers in European soccer is very large.[7] Thus, a club is hurt tremendously if it does not reach one of the positions that guarantee participation in a supranational competition or if it is relegated at the end of a season.

Accordingly, there is enormous incentive for clubs to be competitive and for teams at the bottom of the league to perform well, even at the end of a season. One strategy of those clubs is to hire new players during the winter break or to hire a new coach for the remainder of the season. However, these strategies are associated with unforeseen expenses. As most of the other teams may use the same strategy, an arms race may ensue.[8] Furthermore, due to this overinvestment strategy, almost no profits are made in Europe's open leagues.

Nonrestricted Player Markets

Regulations used by sports associations differ between Europe and the United States. Generally, all sport associations believe in the necessity of regulating interventions to adjust competitive balance, but the methods used differ across the Atlantic Ocean. While American leagues prefer to regulate the input (player) market, European leagues have opted to regulate the output market.[9] The few regulations of the player market that had been established in European soccer (transfer fee even after a contract ends, restriction of foreign players on the roster) were abolished by the European Union with the Bosman verdict of December 1995.[10] Since there are no restrictions for players to switch teams, the situation is comparable to that of unrestricted free agents in the United States. Also, important limitations concerning a team's roster no longer exist.

As there is no salary cap, only weak pressure through the licensing system, and unrestricted free agency, the European player market can be called unrestricted.[11] The result is that the position of the players is more powerful in Europe than in the United States. In combination with more or less altruistic motives on the part of the clubs, it is clear that most of the revenues will be used to improve the talent stock of a club and thus its league position. As a consequence, clubs overbid for talented players without increasing league revenues due to these activities.

Immobility of Clubs

In Europe, the only way to become a first-division soccer club is promotion. The European sports associations do not permit a club to move to another city.[12] As the clubs cannot threaten their home city with an exit option, they lack a powerful position to obtain subsidies from it. Consequently, public funding in Europe is less than in the United States. Due to promotion and relegation, the number of teams located within a single city may vary between seasons. In particular, it is possible that two or more of a city's clubs play in the top division.[13] Another constraint in profit maximization results from the fact that, due again to promotion and relegation, some teams with a very small market can be members of the first tier, which is never the case in the American major leagues.[14]

The situation in the United States is indeed completely different. Since the leagues allow franchises (teams) to relocate, teams are located in markets with high revenue potential. Moreover, the league association will normally avoid more than one major-league franchise within one city.[15] However, besides this effect of market size, there is the possibility to relocate, which may translate into higher revenues and profits. Clubs can force cities to pay high subsidies, especially regarding stadium infrastructure.[16]

Legal Form of the Clubs

The sports systems in the United States and Europe also differ in terms of the legal forms of the clubs and thus the organization of the teams. While

TABLE 7.1

Ownership Rules in the Big Five European Soccer Leagues

	England	France	Germany	Italy	Spain
Ownership	Freedom of choice	Restricted; 50% must remain with the registered membership association	Restricted; 50% must remain with the registered membership association	Freedom of choice	Freedom of choice
Legal form	Public company	Special form of a public company	Registered membership association/public or limited company	Public company	Special form of public company
Conversion	Entire club	Only the professional department	Only the professional department	Entire club	Entire club

Sources: Thomas Hoehn and Stefan Szymanski, "The Americanization of European Football," *Economic Policy* 28 (1999); Ingo Kipker, *Die Ökonomische Strukturierung Von Teamsportwettbewerben* [*The Economic Design of Team Sports Competitions*] (Aachen: Shaker, 2002).

teams in the United States are organized as franchises, European teams are generally controlled as not-for-profit membership associations (see Table 7.1).

The structure of ownership has implications on profit maximization. In particular, open membership associations have no incentive for profit maximization. Due to their not-for-profit nature, dividends cannot be paid out. Thus, individual incentives to be a member of the club are restricted to intangible effects. Since the executive officers are, in general, elected by the general assembly of the association, they are motivated by re-election, and the best way to be re-elected might be to maximize the club's reputation (e.g., by maximizing wins). Even some publicly traded clubs lack any incentive to maximize profits because their shareholders are barred from receiving dividend payments.[17]

New Model of Ownership in European Soccer: Publicly Traded Clubs

For nearly one hundred years, soccer clubs were organized as not-for-profit organizations. Most clubs were publicly owned or established as open-membership associations. However, since the beginning of the 1980s, European soccer clubs have been converted into (public) limited companies (see Table 7.2).

Individual countries differ with respect to which part of a sports club can or must assume the structure of a corporation. In Germany and

TABLE 7.2
Publicly Traded European Soccer Clubs

	Country	Currency	Date of IPO	Minimum	Maximum
Aalborg BK	DK	DKK	Sep 1998	26.10	201.38
AFC Ajax	NL	EUR	May 1998	3.25	13.75
Århus GF	DK	DKK	Sep 1987	1.15	50.19
Arsenal FC	ENG	GBP	–	120,000.00	715,000.20
AS Roma	ITA	EUR	May 2000	0.47	4.96
Aston Villa	ENG	GBP	May 1997	102.50	1,100.00
Besiktas JK	TUR	TRY	–	0.83	14.40
Birmingham City	ENG	GBP	Mar 1997	10.00	58.00
Borussia Dortmund	GER	EUR	Oct 2000	1.64	10.40
Brøndby IF	DK	DKK	Jan 1987	3.20	210.00
Celtic FC	SCO	GBP	Sep 1995	22.50	472.09
Charlton Athletic	ENG	GBP	Mar 1997	14.00	80.00
Fenerbahçe SK	TUR	TRY	–	10.40	26.50
Futebol Clube do Porto	POR	EUR	Nov 1997	2.12	7.98
Galatasaray SK	TUR	TRY	–	29.00	160.00
Heart of Midlothian	SCO	GBP	May 1997	14.50	141.50
Juventus FC	ITA	EUR	Dec 2001	1.11	3.70
Lazio Società Sportiva	ITA	EUR	May 1998	0.25	57.50
Manchester City FC	ENG	GBP	Sep 1998	13.50	51.50
Manchester United	ENG	GBP	Jun 1991	13.05	412.50
Millwall FC	ENG	GBP	Oct 1989	0.03	12.53
Newcastle United	ENG	GBP	Apr 1997	19.50	140.00
F.C. København	DK	DKK	Nov 1997	143.00	1,990.00
Preston North End	ENG	GBP	Sep 1995	102.50	600.00
Rangers FC	SCO	GBP	Jun 1996	0.63	715.00
Akademisk BK	DK	DKK	Dec 1998	2.65	115.00
Sheffield United	ENG	GBP	Jan 1997	4.03	1,151.78
Silkeborg IF	DK	DKK	Apr 1989	8.00	290.00
Southampton FC	ENG	GBP	Jan 1997	23.50	151.50
Sporting Clube de Portugal	POR	EUR	Oct 1997	2.32	8.15
Tottenham Hotspur	ENG	GBP	Oct 1983	9.92	138.00
Trabzonspor AS	TUR	TRY	May 2005	4.12	6.10
Watford FC	ENG	GBP	Aug 2001	20.50	755.40

Sources: Deutsche Bank, *Datastream: Data on Stock Prices of European Soccer Clubs* (email from May 29, 2007); STOXX Limited, "Dow Jones Stoxx Football," review of Reviewed Item (2007), http://www.stoxx.com/indices/download.html?symbol=FCTP; WGZ-Bank and Deloitte et Touche, *Fc €Uro Ag* (Duesseldorf: Planet Macro GmbH, 2001).

France, only the professional football department can be incorporated whereas the core of the sports club remains a not-for-profit organization. In England, Italy, and Spain, by contrast, the entire club becomes a corporation.

FIGURE 7.1

Stock-Price Development of Selected Clubs, January 1, 1985, to May 23, 2007

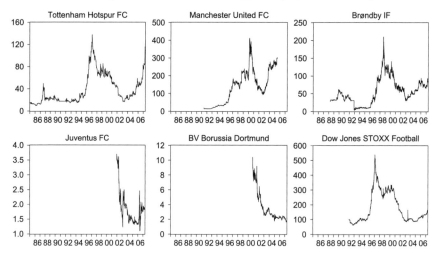

Coincident with the increasing professionalization of European soccer, the attraction of new financial resources has gained in importance. The opportunity to receive equity capital by going public is one possible strategy. In 1983 the English club Tottenham Hotspur was the first club to be listed on the stock exchange. During the next twenty-five years, other clubs followed this example; presently over thirty clubs are listed. Most of the publicly traded clubs are located in England, followed by Denmark, whereas only one German team has risked going public. Some clubs, such as Arsenal FC and Manchester City FC, are off-market traded.

After a slow start, the market strengthened during the mid-1990s. However, by the end of the decade, the soccer clubs' share prices followed the general developments of the international stock markets. Figure 7.1 plots the sequences of selected European soccer clubs and the Dow Jones STOXX Football Index.

Peculiarities of Soccer-Club Shares

The primary interest of a shareholder is generally directed toward a return on his or her financial commitment. Return potential results from issue yield, dividend payments, and share-price development. Since the issue yield can be gained only once, repeating returns takes center stage. In most cases, listed soccer clubs have paid only small or no dividends and the prospects for future payments are bleak.[18] Thus, the only remaining significant potential for future returns resides in the development of the share price.[19]

Important peculiarities of soccer-club shares have to be considered. As is the case for shares of "normal" business enterprises, the share prices of soccer clubs depend on future returns. It is in the nature of a professional sports team that future short-term returns are highly correlated with success in that sport.[20] From a shareholder's point of view, future sporting success cannot be predicted precisely.

Long-term returns on investments are subject to certain boundaries due to the special structures of (European) sports leagues.[21] First, football enterprises are limited in their rights of disposal in important marketing areas—particularly with regard to television rights—as these rights are often collectively sold by the leagues association and not by the club itself. Accordingly, the opportunities for profit-making are reduced, as are the yield prospects for those clubs that would benefit from decentralized marketing. This dependency and the tie to the league organization not only limit the rights of the enterprise but also the rights of the individual shareholders. Compared with enterprises in other markets, the requirements for a high degree of coordination in the field of marketing and other areas (e.g., game schedules, championship regulations) are particularly exacting, which means that football enterprises and their activities can only partially be explained by the model of maximizing individual business. It therefore seems more appropriate to undertake an analysis of the activities of football enterprises within the context of a cartel or joint venture.[22]

In addition, one of the driving factors of stock-price changes is takeover fantasies. This is also true for soccer-club shares, as shown by the example of the interdicted takeover of Manchester United by BSkyB in 1998/99.[23] Besides the rules of the national and European competition authorities, additional restrictions on majority participations exist. Table 7.1 shows that majority participation by an investor is not possible in France or Germany, since at least 50 percent of the club's shares must remain with the registered membership association. There are no national restrictions for clubs in Italy or Spain. In England, shares of one club cannot be bought if the potential investor already holds more than 10 percent of the shares of another club. Moreover, since the 1998/99 season, UEFA has established its own rules regarding multiple participations by one investor in European soccer clubs. Two clubs with the same owner are not allowed to participate in the same UEFA supranational competition.[24] These regulations are necessary to avoid distortion of sports competition.

It can be concluded that short-term price changes caused through sporting success/failure are dominating the share price of a club. If the shares of several soccer clubs are pooled into a stock market index (like the DJ STOXX Football or the Bloomberg KICK-Index), the short-term sporting success of an individual club outweighs that of all the others due to the zero-sum character of league competition, so that developments in the stock market index are mostly affected by long-term determinants of returns (marketing strategy, takeover ambitions, and so on).

The Gold Rush in the English Premier League: Takeovers by Foreign Billionaires

After almost one hundred years of publicly owned teams or teams controlled by not-for-profit membership associations, a new era was recently initiated in the English Premier League. Starting with the takeover of Fulham FC by the Egyptian Mohamed Al Fayed in 1997, an increasing number of English soccer clubs have been sold to foreign investors (see Tables 7.3 and 7.4). The best-known foreign billionaire engaged in the English Premier League is the Russian Roman Abramovich, of Chelsea FC. Since 2005 the number of takeovers has increased. Currently, U.S. investors are discovering the English top tier as an investment target (starting with the takeover of Manchester United by Malcolm Glazer in May 2005).

These owners can be divided into two groups: (1) those (mostly from the United States) with a clear focus on financial returns and (2) those who use

TABLE 7.3
Foreign Owners in English Soccer

Team	New Owner	Country	Date	Cost
Manchester United	Malcolm Glazer	USA	May 2005	£790.0m
Aston Villa	Randy Lerner	USA	Sep 2006	£62.6m
FC Chelsea	Roman Abramovich	Russia	Jun 2003	£120.0m
West Ham United	Bjorgolfur Gudmundsson	Iceland	Nov 2006	£107.5m[a]
Queens Park Rangers	Gianni Paladini	Italy	Sep 2005	£1.0m[b]
FC Fulham	Mohamed Al Fayed	Egypt	May 1997	£7.5m
FC Portsmouth	Alexandre Gaydamak	Russia/France	July 2006	£36.9m
FC Liverpool	George Gillett and Tom Hicks	USA	Feb 2007	£174.1m

[a]95 percent share.
[b]30 percent share.

Sources: BBC Sport, "US Pair Agree Liverpool Takeover," Review of Reviewed Item (2007), http://news.bbc.co.uk/go/pr/fr/-/sport1/hi/football/teams/l/liverpool/6323037.stm; Sam Wallace, "Football's Foreign Invasion: A Global Cause for Concern for the Most 21st-Century Fan," Review of Reviewed Item, *The Independent* (2006), http://sport.independent.co.uk/football/premiership/article2055525.ece.

TABLE 7.4
Foreign Owners in English Soccer

Name	Net Worth (in billion US$)	Teams	Source of Income
Malcolm Glazer	$2.0	Manchester United (ENG)	Investments
Randy Lerner	$1.6	Aston Villa (ENG) Cleveland Browns (NFL)	Finance
Roman Abramovich	$18.7	FC Chelsea (ENG)	Oil/gas
Bjorgolfur Gudmundsson	$1.2	West Ham United (ENG)	Finance
Mohamed Al Fayed	$0.7	FC Fulham (ENG)	Real estate
Silvio Berlusconi	$11.8	AC Milan (ITA)	Media
Massimo Moratti	n/a	Internationale FC (ITA)	Oil
Agnelli Family	$2.7	Juventus FC (ITA)	Manufacturing
Robert Louis-Dreyfus	$3.4	Olympique Marseille (FRA)	Oil/gas
Dermot Desmond	$1.8	Celtic FC (SCO)	Finance
Paul Allen	$18.0	Seattle Seahawks (NFL) Portland Trail Blazers (NBA)	Software
Phillip Anschutz	$7.9	Los Angeles Kings (NHL)	Investment
Mickey Arison	$5.8	Miami Heat (NBA)	Service
Preston Tisch	$2.1	New York Giants (NFL)	Investment
William Davidson	$4.1	Detroit Pistons (NBA)	Manufacturing
Carl Pohad	$2.6	Minnesota Twins (MLB)	Banking
H. Wayne Huizenga	$2.1	Miami Dolphins (NFL)	Service
Glen Taylor	$2.3	Minnesota Timberwolves (NBA)	Printing
Richard DeVos	$3.5	Orlando Magic (NBA)	Service
Arthur Blank	$1.4	Atlanta Falcons (NFL)	Retailing
Mark Cuban	$2.3	Dallas Mavericks (NBA)	Technology
Stanley Kroenke	$2.1	Colorado Avalanche (NHL)	Retailing
Robert McLane Jr.	$1.3	Houston Astros (MLB)	Retailing
Alexander Spanos	$1.1	San Diego Chargers (NFL)	Real estate
Jerral Jones	$1.3	Dallas Cowboys (NFL)	Oil/gas

Sources: "The World's Billionaires," *Forbes,* Review of Reviewed Item., no. (2007), http://www.forbes.com/lists/2007/10/07billionaires_The-Worlds-Billionaires_Rank.html; Michael Leeds and Peter von Allmen, *The Economics of Sports,* 2nd ed. (Boston: Pearson Addison Wesley, 2005).

their investment as both a financial asset and entertainment. The implications for the European soccer system are immense. Since teams with magnates as owners seem to have no budget constraints, the competitive balance can change dramatically.[25] Hence, the attempts by other teams to remain competitive can lead to an arms race. Rich owners or magnates can be found in other European leagues as well. Especially in Italy, such magnates have a long tradition of team ownership (e.g., the Agnelli family and Juventus FC, or Silvio Berlusconi and AC Milan).

COMPETITIVE BALANCE IN EUROPE'S TOP SOCCER LEAGUES

Measuring Competitive Balance

A central aspect in the literature of sports economics is the uncertainty of outcome hypothesis. Many studies have treated the concept of competitive balance, either theoretically or empirically.[26]

A widespread and frequently used measure of (within-season) competitive balance is a concept based upon the work of Noll, Scully, and Quirk and Fort.[27] This measure represents a normalized standard deviation that normalizes the actual standard deviation of the winning percentage using an idealized standard deviation. In this context, a league is regarded as absolutely balanced (ideal) when all teams have equal playing strengths and hence have a winning percentage of 0.500. With n matches in a season, this results in an idealized standard deviation of $0.500/\sqrt{n}$. This measure assumes a value of 1 when the actual and the idealized standard deviation are identical. The larger the ratio of standard deviation of actual winning percentage to standard deviation of winning percentage in an ideal league (RSD), the greater the resulting imbalance and the lower the competitive balance.

It should be mentioned that other measures of competitive balance have been described in the literature, such as the Gini coefficient and the Herfindahl-Hirschman Index (HHI). Some authors have tried to measure the dynamic component of competitive balance in order to consider not only the static one-season measure of win dispersion but also changes in the win percentage distribution from one season to another. Examples of such studies are Szymanski and Smith, Eckard, Humphreys, Hadley, Ciecka and Krautmann, and Feddersen.[28]

Competitive Balance in the Big Five European Soccer Leagues

The average RSD calculation of competitiveness for the period 1949/50 to 2006/07 as well as for decade-long subperiods, shown in Table 7.5, refers to the final league tables of the Big Five European soccer leagues.[29] These are distinguished on the basis of overall league revenue and consist of the English Premier League, the French Ligue 1, the German Bundesliga, the Italian Serie A, and the Spanish Primera División.

Since a higher RSD value indicates a lower competitive balance, Italy has the most imbalanced league, closely followed by the English league. The most competitive league among the Big Five is the French league, with the German and Spanish leagues in-between. A glance at the subperiods discloses no clear trend over time. The highest RSD values (lowest competitive

TABLE 7.5
Average Competitive Balance (RSD) of the Big Five

	England	France	Germany	Italy	Spain
1949/50 to 2006/07	1.386	1.251	1.336	1.421	1.316
1949/50 to 1958/59	1.165	1.145	—[a]	1.221	1.302
1959/50 to 1968/69	1.336	1.209	1.130	1.459	1.290
1969/70 to 1978/79	1.415	1.265	1.315	1.403	1.127
1979/80 to 1988/89	1.396	1.350	1.457	1.324	1.409
1989/90 to 1998/99	1.392	1.341	1.291	1.543	1.457
1999/2000 to 2006/07	1.669	1.181	1.422	1.614	1.309

[a]The German Bundesliga was not founded until 1963/64.

balance) have occurred during the last decade for the Premier League and for Serie A.

Figure 7.2 shows an exemplary representation of the standard deviation of the winning percentage. It can be seen that the within-season competitive balance is not necessarily maintained; in other words, a low-imbalance season can follow one marked by high imbalance. Additionally, this visual representation fails to confirm a secular trend toward a reduced balance of competition, as repeatedly assumed by associations and competition organizers—particularly in Europe—and which is often a source of demand for greater intervention in sports policy.

To empirically test trends in competitive balance, ordinary least-squares regressions using a constant were carried out.[30] The significance of the

FIGURE 7.2
RSD of the Big Five European Soccer Leagues, 1949/50 to 2006/07

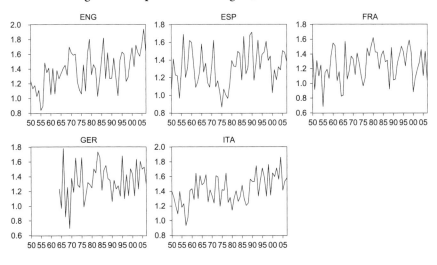

individual trends was determined on the basis of the usual critical values for the t-statistics. To take into account potential developments in the recent past, the calculations were performed for the entire observation period 1949/50 to 2006/07 and for the subperiods.

In the overall period of 1949/50–2006/07, a trend toward competitive balance was significant only for the English and Italian top soccer leagues (see Table 7.6). These trends were significant at the 1 percent level even though the value was small compared to the RSD values for England (1.386) and Italy (1.421). A trend toward competitive balance was also determined for the remaining leagues (France, Germany, and Spain). Different results were obtained for the individual subperiods. The German Bundesliga was the only league that did not display a significant trend during anytime in their history. The significant trend in the overall sample for the Italian Serie A did not hold for the subsamples. The English Premier League and the French Ligue 1 showed a significant trend at the 5 percent level only for one subperiod. By contrast, increasing competitive balance was determined in the Spanish Primera División during the period 1969/70 to 1978/79.[31]

In summary, there is little evidence for an increase in seasonal imbalance over time for the Big Five European soccer leagues.[32] For some of those leagues, especially those of England and Italy, there might be a significant, albeit small trend in the long run. For shorter periods, there is no evidence of a decrease in competitive balance. This result also persists in the presence of a large exogenous shock. Specifically, even the changes in the labor markets of European team sports that occurred after the Bosman verdict did not lead to a decrease in competitive balance in the Big Five, contrary to what has been claimed by many league officials and fans.

As the RSD only covers the within-season competitive balance (uncertainty of seasonal outcome), there might be other aspects influencing the

TABLE 7.6
Trends in Competitive Balance

	England	France	Germany	Italy	Spain
1949/50 to 2006/07	0.008	0.002	0.004	0.006	0.003
1949/50 to 1958/59	0.025	−0.001	−[a]	−0.017	0.035
1959/50 to 1968/69	0.044	−0.016	−0.079	0.000	−0.024
1969/70 to 1978/79	−0.001	0.018	−0.018	−0.002	−0.044
1979/80 to 1988/89	0.016	−0.030	−0.004	0.016	0.013
1989/90 to 1998/99	0.012	0.045	0.021	−0.007	0.001
1999/2000 to 2006/07	0.026	0.035	0.003	−0.017	0.028

[a]The German Bundesliga was not founded until 1963/64.

TABLE 7.7
Championship Concentration in the Big Five European Soccer Leagues, 1949/ 50 to 2006/07

	HHI	CR(1)	CR(2)	CR(5)
England	0.140	0.241	0.466	0.707
France	0.111	0.172	0.310	0.655
Germany	0.227	0.432	0.545	0.773
Italy	0.221	0.351	0.596	0.842
Spain	0.313	0.466	0.741	0.948
UCL	0.083	0.173	0.308	0.558

uncertainty of league outcome. To assess the dominance of one or a few teams, the persistence in winning championships is analyzed below. Again, while there are many different measures of team dominance, we have restricted our analysis to: (a) the HHI and (b) the concentration ratio (CR).[33] The period analyzed is the same as that in the analysis of the within-season competitive balance (1949/50 to 2006/07).

The results in Table 7.7 reveal strong differences in the championship concentration among the Big Five European soccer leagues. The English and the French leagues are the most competitive, while the Spanish Primera División is the most imbalanced. Nearly three-quarters of the championships since 1949/50 (43 out of 58) have been won by the top two clubs, Real Madrid (27) and FC Barcelona (16). Only three of the fifty-eight championships were not won by one of the top five clubs. The long-term competitive balance in Germany and Italy is somewhere between those extremes. Also, the absolute number of clubs that have won a championship differs. The minimum number of different champions can be observed in Spain, where only seven teams were able to win a championship. By contrast, the English Premier League had sixteen different champions during the same period. A broader distribution of champions than in Spain is found in France (13), Germany (11), and Italy (13).

In addition to the championship distribution of the Big Five, the four measures of long-term dominance were also calculated for the championship distribution of the UCL. This supranational club competition is more comparable to postseason play in the U.S. major leagues and is therefore included in Table 7.7. The championship concentration for the UCL is clearly lower than in the Big Five. This may be due to the fact that the best European clubs from each league compete against each other. Since parts of this competition are played as knock-out rounds (similar to the playoffs in the American sport system), chance and luck become important.

Competitive Balance in Small European Soccer Leagues

Although the Big Five is the focus of the larger part of the literature on European sports, the UEFA consists of other member associations as well. However, only a very few studies have devoted their attention to the competitive balance in small European soccer leagues.[34] In the following, nine of the smaller European leagues are examined.

To compare these values it should be noted that the RSDs of the Big Five vary from 1.251 (France) to 1.421 (Italy). Three leagues (Norway, Poland, and Sweden) have clearly lower values and thus a higher competitive balance (see Table 7.8). The values of three other leagues (Austria, Belgium, and Turkey) are slightly higher than those of the Big Five but close to the level of competitive balance of the Italian Serie A. The RSDs for the Netherlands, Portugal, and Scotland are higher than those of the Big Five. Since there are groups of leagues that are more, evenly, or less balanced than the Big Five, no general hypothesis describing differences in the competitive balance of small leagues can be formulated.

This contradicts (anecdotal) evidence of a lower competitive balance in these smaller leagues than in the Big Five. The most frequently used example is the Scottish Premier League. Celtic Glasgow and the Glasgow Rangers together have accounted for forty-seven of the fifty-eight championships since 1949/50, with a total of eight different champions. Other heavily dominated championships are found in Portugal and Turkey (see Table 7.9). In both of those leagues, only four different teams have won the championship since 1949/50. Similar findings are obtained for Greece (five champions). The remaining leagues have had between ten and fifteen different champions, which corresponds to the level of the Big Five (with the exception of Spain). Regarding the HHI, the leagues in Belgium, Greece, Portugal, Scotland, and Turkey can be designated as very imbalanced. Only the Danish Superligaen nearly reaches the low level of imbalance of the UCL.

European Big Five versus U.S. Major Leagues: A Comparison

More similar to the economic background of the Big Five European soccer leagues are the major leagues in the United States. Major League Baseball (MLB), the National Basketball Association (NBA), the National Football League (NFL), and the National Hockey League have been chosen here as the basis for comparison. Analogous to the previous procedure, the RSD for the period 1949/50 to 2006/07 was calculated (see Table 7.10).

The within-season competitive balance in the U.S. major leagues is lower than that of European soccer. It should be kept in mind that a value of one implies a perfectly balanced league and that the average of the Big Five

TABLE 7.8
Average Competitive Balance (RSD) of Small European Soccer Leagues, 1949/50 to 2006/07

	Austria	Belgium	Netherlands	Norway	Poland	Portugal	Scotland	Sweden	Turkey
1949/50 to 2006/07	1.584	1.505	1.701	1.260	1.268	1.709	1.812	1.274	1.426
1949/50 to 1958/59	1.875	1.283	1.418	–	1.250	1.580	1.526	1.374	–
1959/50 to 1968/69	1.593	1.324	1.510	1.226	1.212	1.857	1.844	1.349	1.223
1969/70 to 1978/79	1.369	1.490	1.879	1.358	1.024	1.787	1.707	1.230	1.154
1979/80 to 1988/89	1.513	1.617	1.688	1.123	1.132	1.721	2.075	1.241	1.347
1989/90 to 1998/99	1.665	1.652	1.723	1.347	1.543	1.680	1.721	1.172	1.749
1999/2000 to 2006/07	1.468	1.705	1.883	1.232	1.510	1.611	2.045	1.283	1.610

TABLE 7.9

Championship Concentration in Small European Soccer Leagues, 1949/50 to 2006/07

	HHI	CR(1)	CR(2)	CR(5)
Austria	0.222	0.345	0.603	0.862
Belgium	0.284	0.466	0.672	0.879
Denmark	0.090	0.172	0.276	0.534
Greece	0.355	0.483	0.793	1.000
Ireland	0.100	0.155	0.293	0.638
Netherlands	0.255	0.362	0.672	0.879
Norway	0.175	0.345	0.483	0.776
Poland	0.133	0.241	0.379	0.741
Portugal	0.344	0.431	0.759	1.000
Scotland	0.338	0.379	0.810	0.914
Sweden	0.149	0.259	0.466	0.759
Switzerland	0.147	0.241	0.431	0.793
Turkey	0.279	0.333	0.647	1.000

(all considered European soccer leagues) is 1.342 (1.446). The average of the U.S. major leagues is 1.947 (see Figure 7.3). Only the NFL, with an RSD of 1.523, reaches the low level of European soccer.

This pattern changes completely if the long-term competitive balance instead of the seasonal imbalance is analyzed. The championship concentration in the U.S. major leagues is very low for the MLB and NFL (see Table 7.11). An HHI value of 0.10 and less is only reached by the UCL, the Danish Superligaen, and the Irish Premier Division. Of the Big Five, only the RSD value of the French league is nearly as low as those of the two aforementioned U.S. leagues. The NBA and NHL both have values of about 1.50, comparable to that of the English league. As the remaining leagues of the Big Five have RSDs above 1.20, they must be considered as dominated leagues. With the

TABLE 7.10

Average Competitive Balance (RSD) of the U.S. Major Leagues

	NBA	NFL	NHL	MLB (AL)	MLB (NL)
1949/50 to 2006/07	2.547	1.523	1.982	1.903	1.779
1949/50 to 1958/59	2.022	1.482	1.863	2.346	1.935
1959/50 to 1968/69	2.737	1.614	1.841	1.900	2.067
1969/70 to 1978/79	2.323	1.626	2.557	1.852	1.767
1979/80 to 1988/89	2.666	1.431	1.974	1.669	1.560
1989/90 to 1998/99	2.960	1.475	1.795	1.631	1.630
1999/2000 to 2006/07	2.580	1.505	1.815	2.075	1.685

FIGURE 7.3
RSD of the U.S. Major Leagues, 1949/50 to 2006/07

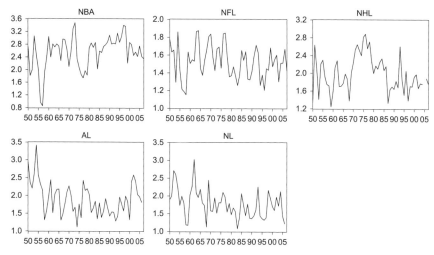

exception of the NBA, the cumulative championship share of the five most successful clubs in all of the other U.S. major leagues is 55 percent and below. This is an expression of a balanced league characterized by the absence of long-term domination. None of the European soccer leagues considered herein is as balanced as these three leagues. Only the UCL, with a CR(5) of 0.558 has a comparable low level of long-term competitive balance.

Why Competitive Balance Differs: Structural Disparity and Different Forms of Regulations

Two important empirical facts can be derived from the above findings: (1) The within-season competitive balance in the European soccer leagues is higher than that in the U.S. major leagues and (2) the Big Five European soccer leagues are dominated to a much greater extent by one or a few teams than is the case in the U.S. major leagues. If there are such strong

TABLE 7.11
Championship Concentration in the U.S. Major Leagues, 1949/50 to 2006/07

	HHI	CR(1)	CR(2)	CR(5)
MLB	0.103	0.250	0.357	0.554
NBA	0.153	0.276	0.500	0.707
NFL	0.086	0.128	0.256	0.538
NHL	0.145	0.316	0.439	0.526

(opposing) patterns in the within-season and long-term competitive balance, then it is necessary to consider the reasons.

One of the main reasons for the difference in the within-season competitive balance might be the existence of relegation in European soccer.[35] Weaker clubs have the incentive to perform well even if they have no chance to win the championship after a given point in the season. This pressure of relegation is missing in the U.S. major leagues, such that weaker teams can reduce their efforts at the end of a season.[36] This leads to a wide dispersion among the clubs and hence to a lower within-season competitive balance in a closed league.

In the literature of sports economics, the effects of specific regulations on the sports leagues have been widely discussed. League associations use different instruments to increase competitive balance, such as salary caps, the draft, and reserve clauses. The effect of free agency on competitive balance was analyzed by Maxcy, and Maxcy and Mondello. Larsen, Fenn, and Spenner examined the impact of salary caps on competitive balance in the NFL, and the effects of the draft were analyzed by Grier and Tollison.[37]

Regarding long-term dominance, the method of electing the champion, which differs between U.S. and European leagues, must be examined. The U.S. major leagues use a playoff system, while in the European leagues the team placing first in the regular season wins the championship. Thus, chance is a more influential factor in the U.S. major leagues. As randomness rises, the competitive balance increases, too. This argument is supported by the example of the UCL. This European supercompetition is played in a playoff format with knockout rounds (two games, home and away) in its late phase. Thus, the degree of randomness is higher than in league competition and, consequently, the long-term balance is as high as in the NFL or MLB.

STRUCTURAL DIFFERENCES BETWEEN U.S. AND EUROPEAN LEAGUES AND THEIR REGIONAL ECONOMIC IMPACTS ON SPORTS

Analyzing the Economic Impact of Professional Sports: A Lack of Positive Empirical Evidence

The abovementioned differences in the structure and ownership of soccer clubs and the nature of the leagues themselves, together with differences between European relegation and the U.S. franchise system, may lead to differences in the choice of stadium locations within or outside a city, These, in turn, can affect the role that the presence of the stadium or sporting events plays in the regional economy, employment, and the generation of tax income.

Concerning the regional economic effect of U.S. major league sports, most of the econometric studies have come to the conclusion that sporting events or sports stadia have no significant impact on regional income and/or employment.[38] A number of analyses, particularly those of Baade, Baade and Dye, Baade and Matheson, Coates and Humphreys, even found significant negative effects.[39]

Only a few studies have reported significant positive effects. For example, Baim noted positive employment effects of major-league baseball and football for fifteen cities in the United States. Carlino and Coulson recorded positive effects of NFL teams on the rent prices of housing, but no significant increase in wages; they nonetheless interpreted this finding as a positive effect of NFL sports. Tu found significant positive effects of the FedEx Field (Washington) on the prices of neighboring real estate as did Ahlfeldt and Maennig for the values of land near the "Olympic Arenas" in Berlin.[40]

Nelson argued that studies concluding insignificant or even negative effects on the home cities of stadia are misleading, since the data are based on stadia built in the 1960s–1980s.[41] These were frequently located either in suburban or far-removed locations. On closer examination of the economic impact, it is evident that stadia built in Central Business Districts (CBD) or downtown sites have a positive effect while for suburban stadia the effects on regional economic development are insignificant or even negative.[42]

Whereas in the United States, in many metropolitan regions, downtown areas were long-neglected, beginning in the 1990s it was discovered "for the first time in 30 years, that downtown has much to offer." Indeed, since the early 1990s, with few exceptions, all new U.S. stadia have been built in urban settings.[43] The earlier trend toward suburban locations has been reversed, leading to stadia built at the most accessible sites decision-makers could afford. Empirically, the 1965–1985 period of stadium building, with its decentralizing trend, was significantly different from that in the 1985–1997 period, with its trend to construction in cities, albeit not necessarily downtown.[44]

Downtown versus Suburban Locations of Stadia

What might be the reasons that the U.S. suburban stadia of the 1960s, 1970s, and 1980s have not generated positive economic effects? First of all, earlier stadia were not intended to be economic development tools;[45] rather, by isolating the stadia from the economy of the city, fan consumption is isolated as well and instead easily internalized by the stadia, owned by the clubs, thus adding to their profits. Moreover, a suburban location implicitly means less team visibility and less importance for the status of the city.[46]

Why have the more central stadia of the 1990s positively affected urban economies, effects larger than those that can be ascribed to a "shift of economic activity to an area that needs redevelopment"?[47] Here it is worth asking why cities or urban communities usually have a higher per-capita income than more rural areas. One explanation lies in the innovative milieus that are a feature of the former. Camagni defines innovative milieus as

> the set, or the complex network of mainly informal social relationships on a limited geographical area, often determining a specific external "image" and a specific internal "representation" and sense of belonging, which enhance the local innovative capability through synergetic and collective learning processes.[48]

These milieus facilitate personal contact such that milieu-specific aspects such as the transfer of knowledge and the learning process are also simplified.

A second reason is that cities offer a large number of social contacts and networking opportunities, such that there is homogenization and coordination within and between different occupations and interest groups as well as recognition of common rules of behavior, moral values, and conventions. The resulting synergy, in the form of a local identity and an external image, equips the cities with a special form of capital.[49]

A third explanation is based on the urban income and productivity advantages offered by agglomeration economies through the reduced transaction costs associated with the acquisition of inputs and resources (personnel, capital, knowledge), not only in the production process but also with respect to marketing and sales as well as consumption. A high reduction of the transaction costs assumes that the entire spectrum of capital outlay, resources, and consumer possibilities thereby benefit. The agglomeration advantages of cities thus differ not only regarding traditional "hard" and "soft" factors but also with respect to a city's unique features as well as to synergistic factors consisting of elements such as interaction, cooperation and other, similar processes.[50] The agglomeration advantages that have the most to do with the synergistic process are essentially elements of the above-described milieu.

Centrally located stadia have access to all three mechanisms for increasing their income. With respect to the concept of innovative milieus, stadia and sports events have positive effects on local urban identity, the quality of life that residents experience, and the city's external image. Regarding the second, relationship-building capital aspect, stadia offer a location for interactions and potential personal as well as professional contacts (especially in the case of the seats purchased by firms or the loges).

In light of the explanation concerning agglomeration economies, stadia can be viewed as "hard" location factor. As for similar facilities (recreational and those that offer social and cultural meeting places), they might be without significance when considered individually. Like the pieces in a mosaic, the full effect is achieved only when all the other pieces are arranged in a certain way. Likewise, a stadium is an indivisible part of a city.

At the same time, it must be emphasized that it is not the existence of a stadium that exerts a positive effect, rather its successful integration in the social fabric and structure of the city. While this holds true for the infrastructure (access to public transportation, adequate parking spaces) it also applies to intangible aspects of city life. Stadia (and thus the sports and cultural/entertainment events they host) must be part of the city's culture and of the identity of its citizens, appreciated historically and politically. A centrally located stadium positively contributes to a city's development, especially when it is in the vicinity of related businesses and cultural opportunities.[51]

Nonetheless, mistakes can be committed even for stadia located in within cities, such that positive effects on urban development are hindered; for example, a stadium that is isolated from the rest of the downtown area by a moat of surface parking or through several wide streets that cannot be crossed by pedestrians.[52] Additionally, it must be recognized that stadia and sporting events (like other economic activities) exert positive effects (e.g., enhanced image, "feel-good" benefits, employment opportunities) as well as negative ones (noise, pollution, increased traffic, lack of sufficient parking). Only when the advantages outweigh the disadvantages can an overall benefit for the city be expected. Or, as Chema stated: "It is not the sport activity, but the context which is key."[53]

Due to the amount of freedom conferred by the U.S. major leagues on (private) franchise owners, clubs can optimize their stadia on a macro scale according to determinants such as population distribution, area buying power, size of the television market, and location relative to other franchises. The size of the influence of these determinants explains the increased likelihood of interurban moves by clubs. Intraurban moves can be explained by microlevel determinants. At the micro scale, factors such as accessibility, ingress and egress, environmental impact, land availability, and costs are most important.[54] These are joined by the determinant of income, and during the suburbanization of stadia in the 1960s to 1980s income generated by fan consumption predominated. Such profits are higher for stadia outside of cities, as long as they are able to internalize consumption (e.g., by preventing the establishment of competing restaurants, shops, and facilities in the surrounding area).

The tendency since the 1990s to situate new stadia in or near city centers was the result of increases in corporate support and sponsorship, especially when the stadium investor owned at least some of the land targeted for the stadium. The land values in that area of the city would be expected to increase by relocation of the stadium there because of the added investment and the increased scarcity of nearby real estate.[55] Tu estimated that the construction of FedEx Field near Washington, D.C., raised the land values in a one-mile radius by 5–9 percent, while Ahlfeldt and Maennig found that, for the three arenas being built in Berlin, the prices of properties as far as 1.5 kilometers away have risen by 4–8 percent.[56]

Without a similar threat of leaving their home cities, European clubs lack a convincing bargaining tool, which substantially lowers their bargaining power to demand subsidies. Together with "new" income sources, such as VIP and business seats, as well as naming rights, this has led to a tendency of reduced subsidies for European stadia over the last several decades. For example, whereas subsidies for the stadia of the 1974 Soccer World Cup in Germany were 100 percent, they were less than 40 percent for the stadia of the 2006 World Cup (see Table 7.12). The share of direct public financing is even less, some 20 percent, if Berlin and Leipzig are excluded.[57]

Interestingly, in the United States, where the private sector usually takes a larger role than in a European economy, the pendulum has started to

TABLE 7.12
Costs of the 2006 FIFA World Cup Stadia in Germany

Location	Costs					
	Total	Federal	State	City	Operator	External
Berlin	242.0	196.0	0.0	0.0	0.0	46.0
Dortmund	36.0	0.0	0.0	0.0	36.0	0.0
Frankfurt	126.0	0.0	20.5	64.0	0.0	41.5
Gelsenkirchen	192.0	0.0	0.0	0.0	33.8	158.2
Hamburg	97.0	0.0	0.0	11.0	16.0	70.0
Hannover	64.0	0.0	0.0	24.0	0.0	40.0
Kaiserslautern	48.3	0.0	21.7	7.7	18.9	0.0
Cologne	117.5	0.0	0.0	25.5	0.0	84.5
Leipzig	90.6	51.0	0.0	12.2	27.4	0.0
Munich	280.0	0.0	0.0	0.0	280.0	0.0
Nuremberg	56.0	0.0	28.0	28.0	0.0	0.0
Stuttgart	51.6	0.0	15.3	36.3	0.0	0.0
Sum	1401.0	247.0	85.5	208.7	412.1	440.2

Source: FIFA, Auf Nach Deutschland Stadien, 2006, http://fifaworldcup.yahoo.com/06/de/d/stadium/index.html (accessed March 12, 2006).

swing the other way, that is, towards greater public subsidies. While from 1990 to 1999 around 57 percent of the costs for new major-league sports facilities were publicly financed, this figure rose in the period 2000–2005 to 67 percent.[58]

Concerning the intraurban location of the stadia and clubs, it is apparent that, with few exceptions, the situation in Europe has not changed. For example, of the Bundesliga clubs that play in the 2006 World Cup stadia, in the last thirty years in Germany only Bayern Munich moved from its former location (Olympic Stadium from 1972; see Table 7.13). In this case, the move was from a central urban location to a suburban one. A similar argument applies to France, the only other European nation that organized a Soccer World Cup in the last fifteen years. For the 1998 World Cup in France, only one new stadium was built at a new location—in an inner-city region that had been targeted for economic recovery (see Table 7.14). However, no top-tier club plays regularly in this new stadium, implying that the rate of intra-urban moves of French clubs is very low as well.

The reasons for the lack of European intraurban immobility are linked to the lack of opportunities in Europe for interurban moves, which as discussed

TABLE 7.13
Distances between Stadia and City Centers of the 2006 FIFA World Cup in Germany

Location	Distance from previous venue	Location changed since 1974	Distance from town hall (miles)	Travel time/ private (min)[a]	Travel time/ public (min)[b]
Berlin	0.000	No	7.9	24	20
Dortmund	0.000	No	2.1	6	4
Frankfurt	0.000	No	3.98	9	26
Gelsenkirchen	0.720	No[c]	2.7	6	16
Hamburg	0.000	No	5.8	18	37
Hannover	0.000	No	0.8	2	19
Kaiserslautern	0.000	No	2.0	6	4
Cologne	0.000	No	5.0	15	28
Leipzig	0.000	No	1.8	6	8
Munich	9.250	Yes	7.1	17	21
Nuremberg	0.000	No	3.9	12	8
Stuttgart	0.000	No	3.4	10	7
Average	—	—	3.9	10.92	16.50

[a]The time needed for, e.g., searching for a parking place and walks from parking place to stadium are not included.
[b]Durations for, e.g., line changes and walks are included.
[c]Location changed by some 700 meters.

TABLE 7.14

Distances between Stadia and City Centers of the 1998 FIFA World Cup in France

Location	Name of Stadium	Distance from town hall (km)	Location changed since 1974	Opening
Saint-Denis	Stade de France	7.6	–[a]	1998
Marseille	Stade Vélodrome	13.0	No	1937
Paris	Parc des Princes	11.2	No	1897
Lens	Stade Félix Bollaert	3.0	No	1932
Lyon	Stade Gerland	6.5	No	1926
Nantes	Stade de la Beaujoire	5.8	Yes[b]	1984
Toulouse	Stadium de Toulouse (Municipal)	8.5	No	1937
Saint-Étienne	Stade Geoffroy-Guichard	2.9	No	1931
Bordeaux[c]	Stade Chaban-Delmas	2.2	No	1924
Montpellier	Stade de la Mosson	6.3	No	1972
Average		6.7		

[a]No previous venue before 1998.
[b]Previous venue was the Stadium Marcel-Saupin (from 1963 until 1984).
[c]Former Parc Lescure.

above, provides U.S. teams with the opportunity to bargain for new locations. Second, European cities are subject to restrictive and hardly changeable zoning laws. This makes it difficult to find alternative sports locations and to sell the old sites, generally allocated to sports uses, to investors seeking profitable inner-city locations. With the lower bargaining power of clubs toward urban decision-makers, the goal of internalizing fan consumption to the stadium (a target also of clubs' U.S. counterparts) cannot be achieved.

As a consequence, almost all European stadia and clubs have always had urban locations. On average, the twelve German Soccer World Cup stadia are located 3.9 miles away from the town halls of their respective cities, with an average commuting time by private transportation, assuming normal congestion, of some 11 minutes.[59] Since the number of parking places is restricted at the stadia, most spectators use public transportation, which is well developed in most large European cities.[60] In Germany, the average traveling time with public transportation from the main stations of cities to the stadia is 16.5 minutes. The large number of users of public transportation, especially among nonlocal fans, more or less leads fans to interact with local urban economies, even in CBD (where Europe's main stations are located). This provides opportunities to patronize local shops and merchants without large transactions costs. In support of central urban locations for stadia is also the fact that for certain international sporting events, the centrality of the local sports facilities can be a deciding criterion that improves the likelihood of attracting these events.[61]

Urban Locations for Stadia: Scant Empirical Evidence for Better Regional Economic Effects

There is thus a basis for systematic differences between stadia and sports events impacts in the European Premier Leagues, with their traditionally centrally located stadia, and the U.S. major leagues. Up to now, there has been scant empirical evidence. In Germany the 1972 Olympic Games, its sport facilities, and the activities in these facilities led to significant income for the host regions, but not significant employment.[62] The 1974 Soccer World Cup, its stadia, and the activities in them since 1974 have not been able to induce significant short- or long-term employment effects in the host cities.[63] The 2006 Soccer World Cup was well able to improve Germany's international reputation and to generate a substantial feel-good effect, but there were few measurable positive effects on merchant sales, tourism income, and so on.[64] In addition, there were no significant short-term effects on unemployment in the host cities.[65] Thus, for urban stadia and sporting events in Europe the impact on income and employment can hardly be seen as more positive compared to the situation in the United States.

A way to increase the urban economic efficiency of stadia in the future—in the United States and in Europe—is: to improve the architectural quality of stadia, which thus far in both continents "give the impression more of a fort."[66] A more attractive, spectacular, or even "iconic" stadium architecture could create a strong urban impulse in the respective city.[67] There is no standard definition of "iconic buildings," but there are plenty of examples among existing structures: the Sydney Opera House is inseparable from the worldwide image of that city, and the Guggenheim Museum in Bilbao has converted that Spanish city, which hitherto went largely unnoticed internationally, into one of the five most visited cities of Spain.

The effect of "iconic" architecture is valued worldwide, and it is often one of the most important parts of a city's development strategy. Thus far, the concept of "iconic" buildings has been limited to opera houses, museums, and other cultural buildings. Nevertheless, Gehry's Atlantic Yards Arena in Barclays Center, the future home of the Brooklyn Nets basketball team, the Bejing Olympic Stadium, and the Durban (South Africa) stadium for the 2010 Soccer World Cup are three recent examples of explicit attempts to copy the "Bilbao-effect" for other cities through architecturally innovative sports facilities.[68]

Event Impacts: A Summary

Due to the differences between the United States and Europe with respect to club and league ownership, decisions regarding inter- and intraurban location have differed as well. U.S. clubs have undertaken a substantial number of interurban moves, in contrast to the situation in Europe. As for intraurban moves, the trend of the 1965–1985 period toward suburban locations for new U.S. stadia was eventually reversed, such that subsequent stadia have been built at highly accessible urban sites. In Europe, stadia have more or less invariantly remained in central urban locations. Although there are arguments that more centrally located stadia should have more beneficial economic effects on urban development, there is hardly any empirical evidence that European stadia and the sport events therein have had a significant impact on their host cities.

NOTES

1. Wladimir Andreff and Paul D. Staudohar, "The Evolving European Model of Professional Sports Finance," *Journal of Sports Economics* 1, no. 3 (2000); Rodney Fort, "European and North American Sports Differences(?)," *Scottish Journal of Political Economy* 47, no. 4 (2000); Thomas Hoehn and Stefan Szymanski, "The Americanization of European Football," *Economic Policy* 28 (1999); Didier Primault and Arnaud Rouger, "How Relevant Is North American Experience for Professional Team Sports in Europe," in *Competition Policy in Professional Sports: Europe after the Bosman Case,* ed. C. Jeanrenaud and S. Késenne (Antwerp: Standaard Editions, 1999), 181–193; Stefan Szymanski, "Is There a European Model of Sports?" in *International Sports Economics Comparisons,* ed. Rodney Fort and John Fizel (Westport, Conn.: Praeger, 2004).

2. Robert Sandy, Peter J. Sloane, and Mark S. Rosentraub, *The Economics of Sport: An International Perspective* (New York: Palgrave Macmillan, 2004), 11.

3. Fort, "European and North American Sports Differences(?)"; Rodney Fort and James Quirk, "Cross-Subsidization, Incentives, and Outcomes in Professional Team Sports Leagues," *Journal of Economic Literature* 33, no. 3 (1995); Andrew Zimbalist, *Baseball and Billions: A Probing Look Inside the Business of Our National Pastime* (New York: Basic Books, 1992).

4. William J. Baumol, *Business Behavior, Value and Growth* (New York: Macmillan, 1959); Oliver E. Williamson, "Managerial Discretion and Business Behavior," *American Economic Review* 53, no. 5 (1963).

5. John A. Cairns, Nicholas Jennett, and Peter J. Sloane, "The Economics of Professional Team Sports: A Survey of Theory and Evidence," *Journal of Economic Studies* 13, no. 1 (1986); George Daly and William J. Moore, "Externalities, Property Rights and the Allocation of Resources in Major League Baseball," *Economic Inquiry* 19, no. 1 (1981); Walter C. Neale, "The Peculiar Economics of Professional Sports," *Quarterly Journal of Economics* 78, no. 1 (1964); Peter J. Sloane, "The Economics of Professional Football: The Football Club as a Utility Maximizer," *Scottish Journal of Political*

Economy 17, no. 2 (1971); Fort and Quirk, "Cross-Subsidization, Incentives, and Out-comes in Professional Team Sports Leagues." For an overview of profit versus utility maximization see, e.g., Paul Downward and Alistair Dawson, *The Economics of Profes-sional Team Sports* (New York: Routledge, 2000); Sandy, Sloane, and Rosentraub, *Eco-nomics of Sport.*

6. Arne Feddersen, "Economic Consequences of the UEFA Champions League for National Championships—the Case of Germany," *Hamburg Contemporary Economic Discussions* (2006): 15.

7. The first tier in Germany ("Bundesliga") created revenues of $1.723 billion while the second tier ("2. Bundesliga") only generated $0.314 billion or 15.5% of the overall revenues. DFL, *Bundesliga Report* (Frankfurt: Deutsche Fußball Liga GmbH, 2007), 46.

8. See, e.g., George Akerlof, "The Economics of Caste and of the Rat Race and Other Woeful Tales," *Quarterly Journal of Economics* 90, no. 4 (1976).

9. Most regulations in the four U.S. major leagues (MLB, NBA, NFL, and NHL) tend to restrict the market power of players and to enhance the position of the owners. This applies especially to salary caps (luxury tax) and the draft. The most commonly used method of European soccer leagues is the redistribution of collective sold broadcast-ing rights and, with less importance, gate sharing.

10. For further information about the Bosman case and its consequences, see, e.g., Stefan Késenne, "The Bosman Case and European Football," in *Handbook on the Eco-nomics of Sport*, ed. Wladimir Andreff and Stefan Szymanski (Cheltenham: Edward Elgar, 2006); Eberhard Feess, "Transfer Fee Regulations in European Football," *Euro-pean Economic Review* 47, no. 4 (2003); Eberhard Feess and Gerd Muehlheusser, "The Impact of Transfer Fees on Professional Sports: An Analysis of the New Transfer Sys-tem for European Football," *Scandinavian Journal of Economics* 105, no. 1 (2003); Thomas Ericson, "The Bosman Case: Effects of the Abolition of the Transfer Fee," *Journal of Sports Economics* 1, no. 3 (2000); Stefan Szymanski, "The Market for Soccer Players in England after Bosman: Winners and Losers," in *Competition Policy in Profes-sional Sports: Europe after the Bosman Case*, ed. Stefan Késenne and Claude Jeanrenaud (Antwerp: Standaard Ed., 1999).

11. Some European soccer leagues (especially the German "Bundesliga") and the UEFA for their supranational competitions use a licensing system. A team is not allowed to participate in a competition if liquidity is not proven for the next season, but as the long-term balance sheet is not considered teams can use short-term debt to improve their sporting performance.

12. There are only a few exceptions: In the first German hockey league (DEL), the Munich Barons relocated in 2002 to Hamburg as the Freezers. The German first-division handball club VfL Bad Schwartau was moved to Hamburg, also in 2002, and was renamed HSV Hamburg.

13. As of the 2007/08 season, five clubs of the English "Premier League" are located in London or the greater London area: Arsenal FC, Chelsea FC, Fulham FC, Totten-ham Hotspur FC, and West Ham United FC. Four teams are from Manchester or the greater Manchester area: Manchester City FC, Manchester United FC, Wigan Athletic FC, and Bolton Wonderers FC. The metropolitan area of Madrid hosts three teams of the Spanish "Primera División" (2007/08): Club Atlético de Madrid, Getafe CF, and Real Madrid CF.

14. Examples of very small market teams are Energie Cottbus (GER/102,265), Blackburn Rovers FC (ENG/105,085), Villarreal CF (ESP/48,055), AC Siena (ITA/54,498), Udinese Calcio (ITA/96,750), Empoli FC (ITA/46,017), AJ Auxerre (FRA/37,790), and RC Lens (FRA/36,823). For a theoretical analysis on the relationship between revenue potential and the size of the market of a team, see, e.g., John Vrooman, "A General Theory of Professional Sports Leagues," *Southern Economic Journal* 61, no. 4 (1995), or Fort and Quirk, "Cross-Subsidization, Incentives, and Outcomes."

15. Only very big cities or broader metropolitan areas, such as New York, have more than one major league franchise, e.g., New York Giants and New York Jets (NFL), New York Rangers and New York Islanders (NHL), New York Yankees and New York Mets (MLB), New York Knicks and New Jersey Nets (NBA).

16. Sandy, Sloane, and Rosentraub, *Economics of Sport*, 23.

17. For the example of Borussia Dortmund, see Arne Feddersen and Wolfgang Maennig, "Sporting Success and Capital Market Performance—An Event Study of Borussia Dortmund," *Journal of Applied Social Science Studies* 124, no. 2 (2003): 287. A similar situation can be found for the Green Bay Packers.

18. Erik Lehmann and Jürgen Weigand, "Wieviel Phantasie Braucht Die Fußballaktie? [How much fantasy does a football share need?]," *Zeitschrift für Betriebswirtschaft Ergänzungsheft* Special Issue 2 (1998): 107, 108.

19. Feddersen and Maennig, "Sporting Success and Capital Market Performance," 286.

20. For empirical analysis of the relationship between sporting success and stock-price reactions, see, e.g., Georg Stadtmann, "Frequent News and Pure Signals: The Case of a Publicly Traded Football Club," *Scottish Journal of Political Economy* 53, no. 4 (2006); Feddersen and Maennig, "Sporting Success and Capital Market Performance"; and John K. Ashton, Bill Gerrard, and Robert S. Hudson, "Economic Impact of National Sporting Success: Evidence from the London Stock Exchange," *Applied Economics Letters* 10, no. 12 (2003).

21. Mirko Dahlke and Armin Rott, "Fußballaktionäre in Der Abseitsfalle? Erste Erfahrungen Mit Dem Bvb-Papier [Football club stockholders in the offside trap? First experience with the Bvb share]," in *Dortmunder Diskussionsbeiträge Zur Wirtschaftspolitik* [Dortmund Discussion Paper in Economic Policy], ed. Hartmut Berg and Ulrich Teichmann (N.p., 2000), 6.

22. Michael A. Flynn and Richard J. Gilbert, "The Analysis of Professional Sports Leagues as Joint Ventures," *The Economic Journal* 111, no. 469 (2001).

23. In 1998 the television network BSkyB, owned by Rupert Murdoch, bid for a takeover of the soccer club Manchester United. This merger was rejected by the UK Monopolies and Mergers Commission. Simon Lee, "The Bskyb Bid for Manchester United Plc—All the Passion of a Banknote," in *A Game of Two Halves? The Business of Football*, ed. Sean Hamil, Jonathan Michie, and Christine Oughton (Edinburgh: Mainstream Publishing, 1999); Andrew McKenzie, "Football Takeover Trends," review of Reviewed Item, *BBC Sport*, no. 1 (2007), http://news.bbc.co.uk/sport2/hi/football/eng_prem/6179569.stm. During the bidding phase, the stock price of Manchester United Plc increased by 30%. WGZ-Bank and Deloitte et Touche, *Fc €Uro Ag* (Duesseldorf: Planet Macro GmbH, 2001), 108.

24. WGZ-Bank and Deloitte et Touche, *Fc €Uro Ag*, 108, 109.

25. Roman Abramovich invested round about £440 million between June 2003 and January 2007, especially into new players. See Matt Williams, "Abramovich Second in UK Rich List," review of Reviewed Item (2006), http://www.sportinglife.com/football/premiership/chelsea/news.

26. Theoretically: Stefan Késenne, "Revenue Sharing and Competitive Balance on Professional Team Sports," *Journal of Sports Economics* 1, no. 1 (2000); Stefan Szymanski and Stefan Késenne, "Competitive Balance and Gate Revenue Sharing in Team Sports," *Journal of Industrial Economics* 52, no. 1 (2004); Vrooman, "A General Theory of Professional Sports Leagues." Empirically: Bill Gerrard, "Still Up for Grabs? Maintaining the Sporting and Financial Viability of European Club Soccer," in *International Sports Economics Comparisons*, ed. Fort and Fizel; Jonathan Michie and Christine Oughton, "Competitive Balance in Football: Trends and Effects," Football Governance Research Centre, Research Paper no. 2, 2004; James Quirk and Rodney D. Fort, *Pay Dirt: The Business of Professional Team Sports* (Princeton, N.J.: Princeton University Press, 1992); Martin B. Schmidt and David J. Berri, "Competitive Balance and Attendance: The Case of Major League Baseball," *Journal of Sports Economics* 2, no. 2 (2001).

27. Roger G. Noll, "Professional Baseball," *Stanford University Studies in Industrial Economics,* no. 144 (1988); Gerald W. Scully, *The Business of Major League Baseball* (Chicago: University of Chicago Press, 1989); Quirk and Fort, *Pay Dirt.*

28. Stefan Szymanski and Ron Smith, "Equality of Opportunity and Equality of Outcome: Static and Dynamic Competitive Balance in European and North American Sports Leagues," in *Transatlantic Sport: The Comparative Economics of North American and European Sports*, ed. Carlos Pestana Barros, Muradali Ibrahimo, and Stefan Szymanski (Northampton, Mass.: Edward Elgar, 2002). E. Woodrow Eckard, "Baseball's Blue Ribbon Economic Report: Solutions in Search of a Problem," *Journal of Sports Economics* 2, no. 3 (2001); Eckard, "Free Agency, Competitive Balance, and Diminishing Returns to Pennant Contention," *Economic Inquiry* 39, no. 3 (2001); Eckard, "The NCAA Cartel and Competitive Balance in College Football," *Review of Industrial Organization* 13, no. 3 (1998); Brad R. Humphreys, "Alternative Measures of Competitive Balance in Sports Leagues," *Journal of Sports Economics* 3, no. 2 (2002); Lawrence Hadley, James Ciecka, and Anthony C. Krautmann, "Competitive Balance in the Aftermath of the 1994 Players' Strike," *Journal of Sports Economics* 6, no. 4 (2005); Arne Feddersen, "On the Use of Markov-Chains as a Measure of Competitive Balance in European Soccer," *Hamburg Contemporary Economic Discussions* (February 2006).

29. Since the basis of the RSD is the winning percentage of each club, the change from the two-point-system (two points for a win, one point for a draw, no points for a loss) to the three-point-system (three points for a win, one point for a draw, no points for a loss) in European soccer, at least at the beginning of the 1995/96 season, is not considered. In their analysis of the correlation between the sporting outcome (points and league positions) under a given point regime (winning percentage, two-point-system, three-point-system) and a hypothetical outcome under an alternative regime, Feddersen and Maennig showed that no bias is conditioned by the point regime. Thus, the RSD can be chosen even if the actual ranking system is not based upon winning percentages. Arne Feddersen and Wolfgang Maennig, "Trends in Competitive Balance: Is There Evidence for Growing Imbalance in Professional Sport Leagues?" *Hamburg Contemporary Economic Discussion* (January 2005).

30. Rainer Schlittgen and Bernd H. Streitberg, *Zeitreihenanalyse* (Time Series Analysis), vol. 4 (Munich: R. Oldenburg Verlag, 1991).

31. It should be mentioned that this trend is only significant at the 10% level.

32. These findings are consistent with previous studies. See, e.g., Jean-Francois Bourg, "Professional Team Sports in Europe: Which Economic Model?" in *International Sports Economics Comparisons*, ed. Fort and Fizel; Luigi Buzzacchi, Stefan Szymanski, and Tommaso M. Valletti, "Equality of Opportunity and Equality of Outcome: Open Leagues, Closed Leagues and Competitive Balance," *Journal of Industry, Competition and Trade* 3, no. 3 (2003); Feddersen and Maennig, "Trends in Competitive Balance"; Stefan Szymanski, "Income Inequality, Competitive Balance and the Attractiveness of Team Sports," *Economic Journal* 111 (2001).

33. The HHI is a summation of all quadratic firm market shares in an industry. Higher values of this index indicate a higher concentration. For use of the HHI as a measure of long-term competitive balance, see, e.g., Bill Gerrard, "Analysing the Win-Wage Relationship in Pro Sports Leagues: Evidence from the Fa Premier League, 1997/98–2001/02," in *Sports Economics after Fifty Years: Essays in Honour of Simon Rottenberg*, ed. Plácido Rodríguez, Stefan Késenne, and Jaume García (Oviedo: Servico de Publicaciones de la Universidad de Oviedo, 2006). The CR(n) displays the cumulative market share of the top n teams. In the following, n is chosen to be one, two, or five. These numbers reflect the dominance of a few teams.

34. See, e.g., Ruud H. Koning, "Balance in Competition in Dutch Soccer," *Journal of the Royal Statistical Society: Series D (The Statistician)* 49, no. 3 (2000), for Dutch soccer, or Kelly Goossens, "Competitive Balance in European Football: Comparison by Adapting Measures: National Measure of Seasonal Imbalance and Top 3," Working Paper 2005034, University of Antwerp, Faculty of Applied Economics, 2005, for six small leagues (Belgium, Denmark, Greece, Netherlands, Portugal, Sweden).

35. The number of games played by each team in a league and thus the degree of chance in the league outcome is certainly a main factor for competitive balance, but the RSD is constructed to consider these effects in light of the number of games. See Gerald W. Scully, *The Market Structure of Sports* (Chicago: University of Chicago Press, 1995), 67.

36. As a consequence of a closed league in combination with a draft system, it is possible that weaker teams "compete" for the worst possible league table ranking in order to improve their draft position.

37. Joel G. Maxcy, "Rethinking Restrictions on Player Mobility in Major League Baseball," *Contemporary Economic Policy* 20, no. 2 (2002); Joel G. Maxcy and Michael J. Mondello, "The Impact of Free Agency on Competitive Balance in North American Professional Team Sports Leagues," *Journal of Sport Management* 20, no. 3 (2006); Andrew Larsen, Aju J. Fenn, and Erin Leanne Spenner, "The Impact of Free Agency and the Salary Cap on Competitive Balance in the National Football League," *Journal of Sports Economics* 7, no. 4 (2006); Kevin B. Grier and Robert D. Tollison, "The Rookie Draft and Competitive Balance: The Case of Professional Football," *Journal of Economic Behavior and Organization* 25, no. 2 (1994).

38. Robert A. Baade, "Professional Sports as Catalysts for Metropolitan Economic Development," *Journal of Urban Affairs* 18, no. 1 (1996); Baade, "Stadiums, Professional Sports, and Economic Development: Assessing the Reality," *The Heartland Institute Policy Study* (1994); Baade and Victor Matheson, "An Assessment of the Economic Impact

of the American Football Championship, the Super Bowl, on Host Communities," *Reflets et Perspectives* 39, nos. 2–3 (2000); Baade and Allen R. Sanderson, "The Employment Effect of Teams and Sports Facilities," in *Sports, Jobs, and Taxes: The Economic Impact of Sports Teams and Stadiums*, ed. Roger G. Noll and Andrew Zimbalist (Washington, D.C.: Brookings Institution Press, 1997); Dennis Coates and Brad R. Humphreys, "The Economic Consequences of Professional Sports, Strikes and Lockouts," *Southern Economic Journal* 67, no. 3 (2000).

39. Robert A. Baade, "Is There an Economic Rationale for Subsidizing Sports Stadiums?" *Heartland Policy Study* 13 (1987); Baade and Richard F. Dye, "The Impact of Stadiums and Professional Sports on Metropolitan Area Development," *Growth and Change* 21, no. 2 (1990); Baade and Victor Matheson, "Bidding for the Olympics: Fool's Gold?" in *Transatlantic Sport: The Comparative Economics of North American and European Sports*, ed. Carlos Pestana Barros, Muradali Ibrahimo, and Stefan Szymanski (Northampton, Mass.: Edward Elgar, 2002); Dennis Coates and Brad R. Humphreys, "The Growth Effects of Sport Franchises, Stadia, and Arenas," *Journal of Policy Analysis and Management* 18, no. 4 (1999); Dennis Coates and Brad R. Humphreys, "The Stadium Gambit and Local Economic Development.," *The Cato Review of Business and Government* 23, no. 2 (2000).

40. Dean V. Baim, *The Sports Stadium as a Municipal Investment*, Contributions in Economics and Economic History 151 (Westport. Conn.: Greenwood Press, 1994); Gerald Carlino and N. Edward Coulson, "Compensating Differentials and the Social Benefits of the NFL," *Journal of Urban Economics* 56, no. 1 (2004); Charles C. Tu, "How Does a New Sports Stadium Affect Housing Values? The Case of Fedex Field," *Land Economics* 81, no. 3 (2005); Gabriel Ahlfeldt and Wolfgang Maennig, "Impact of Sports Arenas on Land Values: Evidence from Berlin," *Hamburg Contemporary Economic Discussions,* no. 3 (2007). Apart from major-league sports, Hotchkiss, Moore, and Zobay found significant positive medium-term employment effects on regions in Georgia (United States), that is, those affiliated or close to the Olympic activities of the 1996 Games, but they did not find significant wage effects. Julie L. Hotchkiss, Robert E. Moore, and Stephanie M. Zobay, "Impact of the 1996 Summer Olympic Games on Employment and Wages in Georgia," *Southern Economic Journal* 69, no. 3 (2003). Jasmand and Maennig showed that, for the 1972 Olympic Games in Germany, the sport facilities and the activities in these facilities led to significant income effects for the host regions (but no significant employment effects). Stephanie Jasmand and Wolfgang Maennig, "Regional Income and Employment Effects of the 1972 Munich Olympic Summer Games," *Regional Studies* (forthcoming).

41. Arthur C. Nelson, "Prosperity or Blight? A Question of Major League Stadia Locations," *Economic Development Quarterly* 15, no. 3 (2001).

42. Melaniphy and Santee also argued that stadia in inner cities might be more efficient for the regional development of these cities. John C. Melaniphy, "The Impact of Stadiums and Arenas," *Real Estate Issues* 21, no. 3 (1996); Earl E. Santee, "Major League Cities," *Real Estate Issues* 21, no. 3 (1996).

43. Thomas V. Chema, "When Professional Sports Justify the Subsidy: A Reply to Robert Baade," *Journal of Urban Affairs* 18, no. 1 (1996): 20.

44. Tracy H. Newsome and Jonathan C. Comer, "Changing Intra-Urban Location Patterns of Major League Sports Facilities," *Professional Geographer* 51, no. 2 (2000).

45. Chema, "When Professional Sports Justify the Subsidy," 20.

46. Newsome and Comer, "Changing Intra-Urban Location Patterns of Major League Sports Facilities," 107.

47. Ziona Austrian and Mark S. Rosentraub, "Cities, Sports, and Economic Chance: A Retroperspective Assessment," *Journal of Urban Affairs* 24, no. 5 (2002).

48. Roberto Camagni, "Introduction: From the Local 'Milieu' to Innovation through Cooperative Networks," in *Innovation Networks: Spatial Perspectives*, ed. Camagni (London: John Wiley and Sons, 1991).

49. Roberto Camagni, "Uncertainty, Social Capital and Community Governance: The City as a Milieu," in *Urban Dynamics and Growth: Advances in Urban Economics*, ed. Roberta Capello and Peter Nijkamp, Contributions to Economic Analysis (San Diego: Elsevier, 2004); Roberto Camagni and Roberta Capello, "Urban Milieux: From Theory to Empirical Findings," in *Learning from Clusters—A Critical Assessment from an Economic-Geographical Perspective*, ed. Ron A. Boschma and Robert C. Kloosterman (Dordrecht: Springer, 2005); Roberta Capello and Peter Nijkamp, "The Theoretical and Methodological Toolbox of Urban Economics: From and Towards Where," in *Urban Dynamics and Growth—Advances in Urban Economics*, ed. Capello and Nijkamp (Amsterdam: Elsevier, 2004); Olivier Crevoisier, "The Innovative Milieus Approach: Toward a Territorialized Understanding of the Economy?" *Economic Geography* 80, no. 4 (2004); Jean Rémy, "Villes et milieux innovateurs: Une matrice d'interrogations," in *Les Milieux Urbains: Innovation, systèmes de production et ancrage*, ed. Olivier Crevoisier and Roberto Camagni (Neuchâtel: EDES, 2000).

50. Camagni, "Uncertainty, Social Capital and Community Governance"; Camagni and Capello, "Urban Milieux."

51. Austrian and Rosentraub, "Cities, Sports, and Economic Chance."

52. Robert A Baade, Mimi Nikolova, and Victor A Matheson, "A Tale of Two Stadiums: Comparing the Economic Impact of Chicago's Wrigley Field and U.S. Cellular Field," *AISE Working Paper Series*, no 06-14 (2006).

53. Chema, "When Professional Sports Justify the Subsidy."

54. Newsome and Comer, "Changing Intra-Urban Location Patterns of Major League Sports Facilities."

55. Austrian and Rosentraub, "Cities, Sports, and Economic Chance"; Newsome and Comer, "Changing Intra-Urban Location Patterns of Major League Sports Facilities."

56. Tu, "How Does a New Sports Stadium Affect Housing Values?"; Ahlfeldt and Maennig, "Impact of Sports Arenas on Land Values"; Gabriel Ahlfeldt and Wolfgang Maennig, "The Role of Architecture on Urban Revitalisation: The Case of 'Olympic Arenas' in Berlin-Prenzlauer Berg," *Hamburg Contemporary Economic Discussions*, no. 01 (2007).

57. The federal government wanted to ensure that a second Eastern German city would be a host and decided to contribute US$ 67.8 million to Leipzig in that regard. In Berlin, the Federal Republic owned the rundown Olympic stadium of 1936, and the city of Berlin refused to take possession of the stadium before it was renovated. Rebigianni emphasized that, in addition to direct (and easy to calculate) public subsidies, significant "conspicuous subsidizing" as debt guarantees must be taken into account. He also elaborated on innovative forms of income and financing techniques that might help

to ensure the financial stability of German soccer stadia. Luca Rebiggiani, "Public Versus Private Spending for Sports Facilities—The Case of Germany 2006," *Public Finance and Management* 6, no. 3 (2006).

58. Judith G. Long, "Public Funding for Major League Sports Facilities Data Services (5): A History of Public Funding, 1890 to 2005," Edward J. Bloustein School of Planning and Public Policy, Center for Urban Policy Research Working Paper Series (2005).

59. Calculations on the basis of map24.de and with the help of the official webpages of the transport authorities.

60. In case of Hertha BSC Berlin, some 80 percent of the spectators use public transportation. Information provided by BVG (Berlin Public Transport Agency), Department Marketing from July 11, 2007.

61. Feddersen, Maennig, and Zimmermann found no significant influence of the centrality of sport facilities on the probability of winning an Olympic bid. Arne Feddersen, Wolfgang Maennig, and Philipp Zimmermann, "How to Win the Olympic Games—The Empirics of Key Success Factors of Olympic Bids," *Hamburg Contemporary Economic Discussions,* no. 02 (2007).

62. Jasmand and Maennig, "Regional Income and Employment Effects of the 1972 Munich Olympic Summer Games."

63. Florian Hagn and Wolfgang Maennig, "Employment Effects of the Football World Cup 1974 in Germany," *Labour Economics* (forthcoming).

64. Wolfgang Maennig, "One Year Later: A Re-Appraisal of the Economics of the 2006 Soccer World Cup," *Hamburg Contemporary Economic Discussions,* no. 10 (2007).

65. Florian Hagn and Wolfgang Maennig, "Labour Market Effects of the Football World Cup 2006 in Germany," *Applied Economics* (forthcoming).

66. Chema, "When Professional Sports Justify the Subsidy."

67. Wolfgang Maennig, "Ikonen Statt Schüsseln (Icons Instead of Bowls)," *Immobilienmanager*, nos. 7–8 (2006).

68. For the case of Durban, see Wolfgang Maennig and Florian Schwarthoff, "Stadium Architecture and Regional Economic Development: International Experience and the Plans of Durban, South Africa," in *Major Sport Events as Opportunity for Development*, ed. Diego Torres (Valencia: University of Valencia Press, 2006).

Eight

U.S. Sports Leagues through the Economic Crystal Ball

Rodney Fort

My charge is speculating on the business and economic future of U.S. sports. My expertise is in the North American experience, so speculation is restricted to the four pro leagues and college team sports. The task is undertaken lightheartedly since it makes no difference to me whether I am right or wrong. In this regard, I am rather like Madame Olga telling fortunes on the midway. The fun will be in the eventual unfolding of the explanations offered along with the predictions. And I fully expect to be wrong, quite probably in every instance. In graduate econometrics classes we were warned that forecasting is like driving down a twisty road at sixty miles per hour with nothing but a rearview mirror. Some curves will be successfully negotiated; most will not, so crashes are inevitable.

Because I am an economist I organized the predictions along the economic lines of demand, supply, market structure, and labor and collective bargaining. I could determine no appropriate way to boil down another area for economic forecasting, namely, the future of the relationship between government and the sports business. That set of issues and the background to make them meaningful, in my opinion, requires separate treatment. The issues don't always fit easily into this scheme but, in my opinion, this outline beats a stream of consciousness report. At least I have this much over Madame Olga's approach.

DEMAND

The primary importance of demand in the business world of sports is that it determines revenue. Revenue equals price multiplied by quantity and both of these are on the axes of every graph of any demand function. But more important for crystal-ball gazing are changes in demand determinants that *shift revenues*—income, price and availability of substitutes, population, and, more important for sports than other consumption, preferences.

Income and Population

Prices will continue to increase to sports consumers. As long as incomes and population continue to rise, so will prices to fans. Calculated from the Team Marketing Fan Cost Index data on prices, adjusted for inflation, Table 8.1 shows the real rate of growth in the highest, median, and lowest ticket prices in each of the major pro sports leagues over the last fifteen years (ten years for the NHL). For all leagues except the NHL, these are truly healthy increases compared to the typical 3 percent real annual rate of growth in the economy at large. And it is interesting that this growth occurs for all levels

TABLE 8.1
Ticket Price in North American Major Leagues, 1991–2006 (2004 US$)

League	Price Level	Initial Year	End Year	Growth Rate (%)
MLB	Lowest	$10	$19	5
	Median	$12	$29	6
	Highest	$18	$64	9
	High—Median	$6	$35	13
	Median—Lowest	$3	$10	9
NBA	Lowest	$21	$33	3
	Median	$29	$60	5
	Highest	$65	$109	4
	High—Median	$35	$49	2
	Median—Lowest	$9	$27	8
NFL	Lowest	$25	$54	6
	Median	$34	$81	6
	Highest	$48	$125	7
	High—Median	$14	$44	8
	Median—Lowest	$9	$27	8
NHL	Lowest	$27	$36	3
	Median	$48	$57	2
	Highest	$58	$75	3
	High—Median	$10	$19	6
	Median—Lowest	$21	$21	0

Source: All ticket price levels are from Team Marketing Fan Cost Index ticket prices, http://www.teammarketing.com/fci.cfm.

Note: Initial Year = 1991 for all leagues except NHL (1994); End Year = 2006 for MLB, 2005 for NBA, 2005 for NFL, 2006 for NHL.

of ticket price. If one charts the ticket price data, the upward trend for each level of ticket price is quite apparent. Since this is driven primarily by increasing income and population, it is a pretty safe prediction that this price behavior will continue.

Of course, one of the more interesting issues here is the impact on fans occupying different income levels. Let's suppose fans sort themselves by income across the three levels of prices (low-income fans strive to make the lowest price and so on). First, fans in each sport except hockey have faced truly large increases in ticket prices. Second, the differences between highest and median ticket prices, and median and lowest ticket prices, represent the squeeze on fans at different income levels. The data in Table 8.1 show that the squeeze grew tightest for MLB fans, followed by NFL and NBA fans, with the lightest squeeze on NHL fans. The squeeze grew tighter at the higher ticket prices, as opposed to lower ticket prices, in MLB and the NHL.

As a corollary prediction, typical fans, squeezed out of live attendance, will continue to enjoy more and more of their favorite sports on TV. This will occur because, even though the price squeezes just observed have grown over time, accessibility to live attendance in the four major sports leagues has increased very little through expansion or increases in the number of pro leagues.

There will be a true major college football national championship tournament. Here is why. The top major conferences have already figured out how to exclude all but the very best teams who share nearly all the money through the Bowl Championship Series (BCS). Currently, this occurs by a ranking formula that seeds the top ten teams into what used to be four major geographically determined bowl games plus the BCS Championship game pairing the top two teams. But very soon the best lessons of all from the rest of the NCAA tournaments, similar to tournaments like the Union of European Football Associations (UEFA) Cup in European soccer, will become apparent—(1) letting more teams in does not necessarily reduce the size of the revenue pie for the top teams and (2) fans will pay the most to see a true champion crowned through tournament play. It is a small step from identifying the top ten teams by an artificial ranking scheme to the inevitable, namely, a ten- or twelve-team national championship tournament.

The impending logic is inescapable. The money available for sharing among the teams in a national tournament will more than offset the downside. It is simple statistics to show that the probability of any team winning a true tournament is lower than the probability that a very few teams can win the BCS Championship game. But in every other college sport, and in continental and world competition in soccer, fans are willing to pay the most to see the true champion crowned by play rather than artificial ranking. So, recent champions like Florida, Texas, and Southern California realize the chances of becoming national champion fall, but the overall revenue gain spread among those in the tournament will more than offset. In expected value terms, returns to the top twenty-five are larger under a tournament structure.

This is especially binding logic since there is some evidence of growing parity in the current way that national champions are crowned. First, there are fewer repeat champions. In the 1960s Alabama and Michigan State repeated. In the 1970s Nebraska, Oklahoma, and Alabama repeated. In addition, Alabama won three times in each of those decades. In the 1980s there were no repeat winners, although Miami did have three championships. In 1990s only Nebraska repeated (1994 and 1995) and they also had three championships. In the current decade, so far Southern California is the only repeat winner and the only multiple winner with two. So there is a chance that there will be no three-time champion in the 2000s and even in the event that either Southern California or Florida ends up with three, that will mark the third consecutive decade with a different three-time champion. Teams now realize that the chances for domination are falling, putting even more pressure on a tournament approach that enlarges the pie for all of the teams.

The form the tournament might take isn't difficult to predict given the physical rigors of football. Single elimination has the two finalists each playing four tournament games. Double-elimination makes it no more than seven games for the eventual champion (rising out of the losers' bracket). Single-elimination seems more likely, having the college season, including postseason, just about equal to the length of the regular NFL season.

It wouldn't surprise me if this happened under some form of superconference adjustment. Pressure is building for a superconference in major college football. The top twenty is dominated by pretty much the same teams, year after year so that conference championships are only interesting in so far as they set the stage for postseason play. There are a few million dollars available through conference championships, but this cannot compare to the revenue pot that very soon can be generated by the "next-level" focus of U.S. sports fans. And to lock up that pot of gold, the perennial top twenty can secede, set up their own governing body similar to the NCAA (or similar to UEFA or Fédération Internationale de Football Association [FIFA] for that matter) to continue to maintain adherence to an amateur requirement. They can then use this new structure to set up their own college football championship tournament.

Some will argue this won't happen because a tournament violates the best interests of athletes in their student role, but this is a clear misunderstanding of the current conflict between the student and athlete in "student-athlete."

Participation is already a year-round affair, much the same as a full-time job. Athletes devote as much time to their sport in the off-season as during the season. Game and travel time during the season is just replaced by more time in the weight room and physical therapy getting ready for next season. As a result, adding a few more games will actually make no difference for student-athletes except for the added travel time.

In all other sports, there is a true tournament. Fans want it that way and all other sports happily meet that demand. Major college football is the only exception, not because of tradition or care for the student-athlete but because the highest return to the top twenty still just barely favors the current BCS system. Very soon, the balance will swing toward a tournament. Conference championships, if they even survive, will come to mean about as much as pennant races in baseball or division championships in the NFL. The whole point will be the championship tournament, regardless of the form it eventually takes.

There will be more college football bowl games. Even with a national championship tournament, bowl games will continue to proliferate. Again, the logic is simple and as old as the original motivation for bowl games. A portion of fans of the two teams chosen for the new bowl games will always want to attend. Cities hosting new bowl games will do so for the same reason they always have—the development money associated with that attendance and the entertainment value to the locals who also choose to attend. It also seems clear that even the most minor bowl games attract viewers in sufficient numbers to get aired.

As population and income grow, along with growing economic development imperatives, development officers in an increasing number of locales will invent bowl games and pursue teams to play in them. Remember, these imperatives were the original reason bowl games were invented long ago. Purists decry bowl-game proliferation because the games are meaningless. But they miss the point. These new bowl games will decide nothing, and more often than not will pair middle-of-the-pack teams, but the entertainment will be fun and valuable for the teams, host locations, and broadcasters.

For my personal tastes (for once mirroring the majority), this is just fine. So I'm preparing to sit back and enjoy watching two teams with pretty good records, thus pretty evenly matched, playing in a particularly envious location in the dead of winter, with no implications whatsoever except for the sheer fun of it.

Substitutes

The number of "sports" will grow seemingly without end. Choose any definition of a "sport" and it needs to handle the following question—what is the difference between a world poker challenge and the 100-meter dash? The two share unscripted outcomes but little else. In my definition, one is a sport and the other is not. But I guess as long as the activity is on ESPN, or is reported in *Sports Illustrated*, somebody will automatically add it to an increasingly varied "sports" menu.

This is the essence of creating substitutes, broadly construed. Who cares what happens to NASCAR and Ultimate Fighting Championships? The same people who cared about professional wrestling and the XFL. So as long as an activity falls under the general umbrella of entertainment, without a predetermined outcome, it will almost certainly be labeled a "sport" by someone. The result should be more and more entries on the "sports" program as time goes by and more and more competition for live attendance and TV audience. By the way, the growth of these substitutes will loom large in the revenue and profit discussion below.

Preferences

Steroid use (and worse) will grow, horizontally and vertically in sports. Some would place the steroid issue under a heading below that covers labor and collective bargaining. But it properly belongs under the demand heading because the use of steroids is intimately tied to fan willingness to pay for *both absolute and relative quality*. Fans clearly care about both relative and absolute quality and it is their willingness to pay for it that generates the return to player labor supply decisions including training regimens and the use of performance-enhancing substances.

At any absolute level of play, fans are willing to pay more to enjoy a relatively more competitive team. But fans also are willing to pay more for a higher absolute level of play. Major-league tickets sell for more than minor-league tickets partly based on the different absolute level of play. Partly, absolute quality can change based on player growth, maturity, and the selection process that advances players to higher absolute qualities of play. As players move up the ladder from kids sports, to high school, to college or the minor leagues, and then on to the major leagues, the strength of the players is so much more apparent and only the physically more competitive players advance to higher levels.

But once players have reached physical maturity and honed their skills further, the move to higher absolute levels of quality comes from performance-enhancing activity. Workout regimens are longer and more strenuous and performance-enhancing substances, legal (diet management, for example) and otherwise (steroids), enter the picture. The original performance-enhancing movement came in the move from part-time to year-round workout regimens and diet management. While players originally saw this as gaining a relative advantage, once all players engaged in year-round regimens so as not to be left behind competitively, the absolute level of play increased. All players became stronger and faster.

Without casting any aspersions on their enhancement decisions, think about the following player comparisons. The first Super Bowl champion Green Bay Packers offensive line in 1967 included Forrest Gregg, Jerry Kramer, Fuzzy Thurston, Bill Curry, and Bob Skoronski. This line ranged from 235 to 249 pounds with an average of 245 pounds; all were within fourteen pounds of each other. The largest was Gregg at 6 feet 4 inches, 249 pounds, just edging Skoronski. The most recent Super Bowl champion Indianapolis Colts offensive line included Tarik Glenn, Ryan Lilja, Jeff Saturday, Jake Scott, and Ryan Diem. This line averaged 302 pounds but with a range of forty-two pounds (290 pounds to the 6 foot 5 inch, 332-pound Tarik Glenn). In forty years, Glenn is eighty-three pounds heavier than Gregg and only one inch taller. At the average, the 2007 Colts line is 23 percent heavier than the 1967 Packers line.

The role of illegal performance-enhancing substances is open to speculation. But if they achieve widespread use the result will be the same as the performance-enhancement episode just mentioned. Initially, players are after relative advantages but, as more and more players use these substances, the absolute level of quality increases. Players are even stronger and even faster. And, so far, it appears that this type of outcome hasn't really interfered with fan spending. So the prediction would be that if this type of performance enhancement runs the same course as others that occurred earlier, then fan spending will increase.

Some observers of the sports scene cherish record books and decry performance enhancement as cheating against history. Some fans agree but the vast majority cherishes the spectacle of performance-enhanced competition even more, whether it is gained by year-round workout regimes and diet or by chemistry sets. This leads me to the following prediction: The performance-enhancement movement will expand among pro athletes and among college athletes and right down the line. Future athletes will have to reach an ever-rising bar or miss out on millions of dollars. It seems reasonable to expect that the lure of ever-larger financial return will lead to more of what is already observed on the performance-enhancement front.

Fan-determined halls of fame will compete with the official versions within five years. This prediction is directly related to the performance-enhancement prediction above. The tyranny of record-book gatekeepers, for example, the Baseball Writers of America whose votes determine membership in the Baseball Hall of Fame, will be overthrown by Internet populism. Alternative halls of fame will arise driven by fan voting.

For example, fans will not sit idly by while a player like Mark McGwire (and when they are eligible, quite likely Sammy Sosa and Barry Bonds) is shunned by the voting writers. In McGwire's case, fans cheered him even as he clearly admitted to a performance-enhancement regime (claimed legal by him at the time) during his epic home-run battle with Sammy Sosa in 1998. And those same fans will want his historical accomplishment officially recognized historically. If that does not happen in the current hall, then another, fan-driven hall will satisfy those demands.

While gatekeepers will surely disagree, there actually is an economic justification for this revolt. Fans will always vote for All-Star Game line-ups because the game is purely a fan/TV event and what could be wiser than allowing your audience to actually tell you who they will watch the most? The same goes for a fan-driven hall of fame; it is the fans' game and their pocketbooks have dictated similar changes in other "official" records. Once there was only the *Official Baseball Encyclopedia*. Now there are any number of viable free alternative sources for statistics produced by enthusiasts and the media rather than gatekeepers.

There will be louder shrieking fits about competitive balance. Even though the long-term trend is improved competitive balance in all leagues except, possibly, the NBA, it is reasonable to predict that it will remain the focal point of sports policy in North America. Outcome uncertainty is the essence of what makes sports different than other kinds of entertainment. Academic work has found evidence that fans do prefer more outcome uncertainty to less at the level of close individual games and in determining playoff access. And it is crucial to recognize that attitudes toward outcome uncertainty are strictly a fan preference item. As such, fans can decide to hate any remaining imbalance even more over time, despite the fact that balance has been improving over time!

Fans have always felt an interesting sense of ownership in "their" sports teams; even fans of the relatively hapless Kansas City Royals firmly believe they deserve a better team than they are willing to pay for. As willingness to pay rises over time, fueled by population and income, this sentiment can only be expected to grow. Fans of perennial losing teams will become less and less accepting over time, heedless of the fact that competitive balance may have improved. "Winning isn't everything, it's the only thing"; "Second place is just the first loser"—fans believe it and won't stand for also-ran status like they did in the past, even though they probably get the level of team quality for which they are willing to pay.

A hint of the issue is in Table 8.2. A common measure of regular season imbalance, RSD (explained in Table 8.2), shows that type of imbalance has continually declined in both leagues over the last five years (the period covering the most recent MLB revenue-sharing agreement). The declines are 38

TABLE 8.2
Payroll Rank, League Imbalance, and MLB Playoff Participation, 2002–2006

Year	AL Teams	Payroll Rank	NL Teams	Payroll Rank
2006	Yankees	1	Mets	1
	Tigers	6	Dodgers	2
	Twins	10	Cardinals	7
	Athletics	12	Padres	9
	Average	7.25	Average	4.75
	League RSD	1.88	League RSD	1.27
2005	Yankees	1	Cardinals	3
	Red Sox	2	Braves	6
	Angels	4	Astros	8
	White Sox	6	Padres	9
	Average	3.25	Average	6.50
	League RSD	2.05	League RSD	1.39
2004	Yankees	1	Dodgers	3
	Red Sox	2	Braves	5
	Angels	4	Cardinals	6
	Twins	9	Astros	8
	Average	4.00	Average	5.50
	League RSD	2.11	League RSD	2.20
2003	Yankees	1	Braves	2
	Red Sox	3	Giants	5
	Twins	8	Cubs	7
	Athletics	10	Marlins	14
	Average	5.50	Average	7.00
	League RSD	2.48	League RSD	1.78
2002	Yankees	1	Diamondbacks	1
	Angels	7	Braves	4
	Twins	12	Giants	5
	Athletics	13	Cardinals	7
	Average	8.25	Average	4.25
	League RSD	League 2.69	League RSD	2.06

Source: Payrolls used in this exercise are from *USAToday.com* Baseball Salary Database.

Note: RSD = ASD/ISD; ASD = Actual standard deviation of winning percents in the league, ISD = "Idealized" standard deviation that would occur if the probability that each team could beat the other was 0.5; as RSD rises away from unity, the league is less balanced than the "idealized" league.

percent in the National League (NL) and 30 percent in the American League (AL). But also note the following—the same five teams occupy all the playoff slots in the NL and the same six teams occupy them all in the AL. In addition, the average payroll ranking of the teams in the playoffs declined continually in the AL until jumping up significantly in 2006, while it increased and then fell in the NL. Only once is it greater than 7 (the bottom half) in the AL, and that was in 2002. The average has never been larger than 8 (in the bottom half) in the NL. It seems reasonable that this is the way fans might think about balance and, hence, the prediction.

A smaller-revenue team will always be in the playoff mix. According to the data sources for Table 8.2, in 2006 the Oakland Athletics and New York Yankees made the AL playoffs with payroll rankings of 12 and 1, respectively. The roles were filled in the National League by the San Diego Padres at 9 and New York Mets at 1. The presence of teams ranked low from the revenue perspective often is argued as evidence that revenue variation cannot explain playoff participation. But those adhering to such stories don't understand what business models suggest—typically and on average, the teams with the largest revenue *potential* actually *collect* higher revenues by serving their fans with the best teams, and those teams typically occupy the playoffs. In order to do so they pay the highest payrolls.

But no business observer in his or her right mind would deny the role of uncertainty; the best-laid plans of mice and men often go asunder. In fact, if history is any guide, it will always be the case that *some* team with a smaller revenue potential and the resulting smaller payroll will be in the playoffs. Indeed, that no smaller-market teams would ever be in the playoffs is a pure sucker bet! This is easy to see for baseball over the last five years in Table 8.2.

While, as noted earlier, the average payroll ranking of playoff teams only is large enough in 2002 in the AL to suggest that smaller-payroll teams played an important role, a smaller-payroll team or two is always in the playoffs despite being in the bottom half of the payroll rankings! In the AL we see the Yankees in all five years with the highest payroll each year but there also were two teams ranked 8 or lower in all years except 2005. There are only teams ranked 9 or lower three times in the NL, but the Astros ranked 8 in both 2004 and 2005. So, it is actually a pretty safe bet (especially in the AL) that a smaller-market team will be in the playoffs.

Revenue Results

Revenues will continue to rise in all sports and beat the real growth rate in the economy at large. This is the easiest crystal-ball gazing. Table 8.3 shows the real revenues in each North American league during this decade along with real annual growth rates over the period. All sports beat the typical 3 percent real annual growth rate in the economy at large, all but the NHL easily double that rate, and the NFL leads the way at 8 percent. My crystal ball suggests that this is a safe prediction for college sports as well. Data from the NCAA's own occasional studies, *Revenues and Expenses of Division*

TABLE 8.3
Revenues in North American Pro Sports (In Thousands of 2004 US$)

Year	MLB	NBA	NFL	NHL
2000	$3,456	$2,715	$4,283	$1,961
2001	$3,791	$2,817	$4,531	$2,197
2002	$3,802	$2,833	$5,147	$2,180
2003	$3,952	$2,988	$5,431	$2,281
2004	$4,269	$3,185	$6,029	–
2005	$4,875	$3,468	$6,345	$2,335
Growth	7%	7%	8%	4%

Sources: Compiled from annual revenue reports in *Forbes* magazine's annual team valuation reports.

I and II Intercollegiate Athletic Programs, show revenues growing at about a 5 percent real annual rate over the period 1985-2001.[1]

Remember, this is just about revenues, not profits. There is every reason to believe that profit margins will become tighter and tighter as new and increasing varieties of fan options also proliferate, as discussed above. Revenues will rise, but costs will, too, as inputs to the sports production process are bid up by more and more competitors. It is the essence of economic competition that fans have more choices and bid up the price of inputs to their favorite sports.

Sponsorship will grow in generally predictable ways. Since there is a value to sponsors now, it will surely grow in the future in the same way that ad-space prices continue to grow. More people see each one and the value increases accordingly. But how much they will increase, and in which industries over time, all depends on the economic fortunes of existing firms that advertise in the future and innovative new firms down the road. I won't forecast those (and if I could, I wouldn't report it here, passing up increments to my own income).

Bowl sponsorship values and Super Bowl ad slots are quite nearly sure things. Table 8.4 shows the real increase in the BCS bowls payouts. Again, growth rates are truly telling, except for the Rose Bowl. But we need to remember, and it is easy to see from Table 8.4, that all of the other bowls had to catch up to the traditionally high sponsorship value of the "Grand Daddy of Them All" in the first place. And the Super Bowl is truly astonishing. From data in my textbook, plus reports that thirty-second slots for the 2007 Super Bowl went for about $2.6 million, the annual growth rate was about 5.5 percent adjusted for inflation from 1989 to 2007.[2] As with other revenues, all of these values easily beat the typical 3 percent annual growth rate in the economy at large.

TABLE 8.4
BCS Bowl Payouts, 1989–2007 (In Millions of 2004 US$)

Bowl	1988/89	1997/98	2006/07	Growth (%)
Rose	$9	$11	$18	3
Fiesta	$5	$10	$18	8
Orange	$4	$10	$18	8
Sugar	$4	$9	$18	8
BCS Championship			$18	

SUPPLY

The supply side of sports is all about production, costs, and profits. While profit is not always the ambition in either pro or college sports, in my experience focusing on net return takes us far most of the time. Unfortunately, we don't actually get to see reported owner profits and the nuances of sports accounting make it difficult to figure profits out in the first place. In college sports, where net revenue is not the objective, in addition to learning about costs we also can find the path of revenues through the athletic department expenditure side. Supply, then, covers everything from the actual form of the game that we see, to the endless tensions between fans and players and owners concerning winning and profits, to the value of franchises.

Production

The form of the games will continue to change. Observers all have their pet peeves about the characteristics of play—the designated hitter, uniform styles, realignment, wild card teams, instant replay officiating. But these peeves actually are symptoms of a deeper production choice. The root cause concerning characteristics of play is the changing nature of fans. Not one of the four major sports has ever stayed glued to any generation of fans; the single seat holds the aging fan but those around him are the new generation of fans.

For example, MLB did not stay stuck in the era of eight teams in two leagues, no playoffs (unless a league was tied), wool uniforms, and high socks. Owners choose rules and allow styles in the same way they choose everything else, namely, with an eye toward revenues. Many of us miss the old ways and wax nostalgic, but MLB has always changed to meet changing preferences. It warms the heart of traditionalists when a player tucks his pants up, but newer fans just chuckle at this quirky choice. And it is the newer fans that represent the future economic base.

The same goes for all the other sports, from instant-replay officiating in football and basketball to Dwayne Wade's leggings in the NBA. It is different now because fan preferences are different and fans are differently distributed by income and population. The changes reflect the owners acting together as the league to cater to fan desires—not all fans, but the fans that represent the path to higher future revenues.

Owners will be viewed as uncaring and typically stupid. This is almost as easy a bit of prophesy as revenues continuing to increase. And the prediction rests on very well-known business and economic reasoning. Some observers will always call owners to task using faulty reasoning. First, the vast majority of owners are in it for money, not wins. It seems that fans will never understand that owners are in business, not philanthropy, but analysts should know better. The fact that money and winning are related and owners must write the checks that make winning happen guarantees a fundamental tension between owners and fans unwilling to pay the amounts necessary for a team in contention.

The second reason that many observers typically miss the point concerns a faulty statistical approach to owner choices. The world is an uncertain place, especially in sports production. And while we are all prone to fallacious *ex post* statistical reasoning, many sports writers have it honed to a fine skill. It is invalid to look at owner choices after the fact, point out the good outcomes that a particular owner could have obtained if he or she had only acted like some other owner, and then point out the bad outcomes that that owner could have avoided at the same time.

Here is the statistically valid approach to criticism. At the same time that the owner is making a choice, the analyst points out the predictable errors and makes them public. Then, after the fact, if the analyst is correct, there is something to talk about. Put it in writing, make the prediction, and see if they do any better than management. That is the road to statistical inference, not 20–20 hindsight criticisms.

But it seems we will always see after-the-fact nose-rubbing as in *Moneyball* by Michael Lewis.[3] It is entirely possible that Billy Beane, the Oakland A's GM and subject of Lewis's book, is a genius using tools that other owners ignore. But to then say that other owners should adopt the Beane approach is just bad statistics, silly on the face of it because they are *ex post* assessments of *ex ante* strategy development. And they will invariably be proven so.[4]

Interestingly, stat-heads will follow the likes of Lewis down the yellow brick road because they are terrific at measuring things and then comparing among different measurements *after the fact*. But they still offer no *ex ante* assessment of their measurements. Again, the valid statistical approach is to put it in writing before the fact, make the prediction, and see if they do any better than management. The validity of the approach holds whether the object of analysis is personnel decision by owners or coaching decisions to go for it on fourth down, go for two rather than one point after a touchdown, try on-sides kicks, or steal or bunt more (or less) often.

Among smaller-revenue teams, winning will always cycle. Sports writers will make hay out of this because it means that the larger-revenue teams, with their much larger potential revenue leading to much larger payrolls and level of team talent, do not *always* win. That apparently sells papers but, again, is not really a valid statistical exercise (recall the analysis around Table 8.2 on the MLB playoffs). But those same writers will not be up to the challenge posed earlier—at the *beginning* of the season, predict *which* smaller-market team will be successful in any given year.

Gerald Scully has taken us as far as anybody in his practically forgotten book, *The Market Structure of Sports.*[5] Smaller-revenue teams cycle in clearly detectable ways, but out of sync with one another; rarely will two cycle up at the same time. So fans of smaller-revenue teams need to be patient and their teams will, when their cycle is peaking, compete well with larger-revenue teams. In predicting which smaller-market team will compete in any given season, I have not done any better than the sports writers, but at least I know that Scully has told us why.

Costs

Spending in both pro and college sports will increasingly be viewed as out of control. Every year, there will be articles arguing that spending is out of control in all sports. In pro sports the focus will be spending on players and in college sports it will be on coaches and facilities. But it should be obvious that such spending cannot be out of control. As in all businesses, as long as revenues rise, inputs are worth more and more will be spent on them. Things can only be judged "out of control" if somehow rising costs cannot be covered by rising revenues.

Spending increases in pro sports only reflect the increasing value of talent across leagues and it has already been documented that this increase is quite large. In college sports, the same thing happens but the primary talent input, players, cannot be paid. Since no one is demanding that athletic departments show a net positive on the bottom line, all of the revenues get plowed back into salaries and facilities. Since the increases in revenues again are quite impressive, so will be the increases in spending.

Quite incorrectly, this has been termed the spending "arms race." But technically speaking, an arms race requires very special circumstances that do not hold in either pro or college sports. First, coming in second must be truly tragic so that the decision at the margin is to always up the ante. Second, eventually, we should observe a tragic outcome, that is, one of the pro teams or college athletic departments is driven to economic ruin.

But neither of these circumstances characterizes pro or college sports. Coming in second is neither individually nor collectively tragic in either pro or college sports. No team that has come in well down the line in terms of spending has been in danger of closing up shop since MLB's NL absorbed four teams in 1899 (the Cleveland Spiders, Baltimore Orioles, Louisville Colonels, and Washington Senators). Neither have any truly powerful college sports athletic departments that sometimes falter appear any worse for the wear.

Rather than an arms race, it is correct to simply note that, as in all businesses, as long as revenues rise, rising costs can and will also be covered. So, of course spending on people will increase in the competitive labor markets that characterize pro and college sports. But rather than some ruinous result, teams in pro leagues and college conferences continue to prosper.

Profits

It will always be believed that college athletic departments typically are lucky to break even. So, one may ask, with revenues rising why is it that the NCAA's own commissioned occasional reports cited above show that the majority of teams, by and large (and especially if institutional support is excluded), do not break even? Surely this is the tragic outcome consistent with the arms race explanation?

But the answer actually is quite different because the bottom line in college sports is the wrong place to look for its economic success. There is no incentive whatsoever leading college athletic directors (ADs) to show any positive bottom line! Unlike any other business endeavor, every incentive instead leads college ADs to plow all revenues back into their program. This means that the so-called arms race is actually just an accounting outcome—if no residual claim is there for any positive bottom-line remainder, spending increases will exactly equal all anticipated revenue increases. It can be no other way. We'll see shortly how this plays into truly fascinating talent market outcomes in college sports for both players and coaches.

It will typically be believed that nobody ever makes any money running a pro sports team. Don Fehr, chief executive of the Major League Baseball Players Association (MLBPA), is fond of saying the following come collective-bargaining time, "Owners will always claim two things—there is never enough left-handed pitching and nobody ever made any money owning a baseball team." The former may be lamentable, but the latter doesn't stand up to close scrutiny. Partly, this belief is fostered by how effective owners have been at convincing people they are in it for philanthropy rather than profit. This belief is fostered partly by a misunderstanding of the special tax status of pro sports teams and partly by inherent feelings that players are getting all the money anyway. It is also fostered by a misunderstanding about all of the values of owning pro sports teams.

The issue of making money through sports-team ownership is one of the first puzzles that business analysts came across in sports. How can an asset that never makes any money or, as owners would have it, actually loses money, ever sell for more than it was purchased for in the first place? The price of an asset that loses money continually over time should fall, not rise (barring unsupportable claims of slow Bayesian updaters or speculative bubbles). The answer rests on one of two alternatives. Either they do lose money and consumption is the only possible remaining motive or they don't really lose money in the first place. Now, no doubt there is some consumption value in ownership but there are also three reasons why team ownership really is not a money-losing proposition.

First, the size of the real annual growth rates in sale prices typically is truly remarkable. I have documented this for MLB in the inaugural volume of the *International Journal of Sport Finance*.[6] On average throughout history, the sale value of MLB teams has enjoyed about a 5 percent real annual rate of growth. Large increases, for example, the Mariners in 1992 at about 18 percent, dramatically outweigh the few transactions where prices actually fell (the Angels in 2003, the Marlins in 2002, the Rockies in 2004, and the White Sox in 1981).

Second, it is easy under standard accounting practices to show a paper loss on a sports team that the owner really never bears. Instead, paper losses turn into real income for owners. Under current tax law, the buyer of a pro sports team is allowed to count the entire purchase price of the team as a depreciable asset for a period of fifteen years. For example, Liberty Media just purchased the Atlanta Braves for a reported $450 million. Under a straight line depreciation scheme, that's $30 million per year as a depreciation write-off against taxable team net income. After all other amortization and depreciation, remaining taxable team income is practically eliminated under this tax advantage. And tax advantage it is, since there is nothing in addition to usual capital items that deserves special depreciation treatment of this type.

But that's not the end of the tax advantages. If the owner organizes the team as a pass-through firm for tax purposes (Subchapter S corporation or limited liability partnership, for example), the paper loss on the team goes over to personal 1040 forms to shelter nonsport income. At the current highest tax brackets, this pass-through "loss" saves about thirty-five cents on the dollar.

Finally, focusing on the team as a stand-alone asset ignores all of the other values of ownership. There can be profit-taking on the cost side. The firm must buy services and perhaps it buys them from owners or, as has actually been done, loans to owners can be made at very low interest rates. There also can be spillovers to other endeavors. Team owners are typically "in the loop" on all state and local development decisions. There also can be opportunity to hide revenues through cross-ownership. Suppose the team owner is also part owner of the team's regional cable network. Partial ownership allows the broadcast rights fee to be chosen in order to minimize tax obligations across the two firms.

Forbes *magazine will, on average, undervalue sports teams.* Team valuations in *Forbes* are based on owning teams as stand-alone assets. But following along with the line of reasoning about all of the other values of team ownership, anybody who understands the decision process for buying entire firms understands this is an extremely limited version of value determination. There is the team's own bottom line, with its famous tax advantages, but there also are related business opportunities, profit-taking on the cost side of the firm (done in all corporation structures), and the limited ability to revenue shift in cross-ownership to reduce tax payments.

This all suggests that the estimates in *Forbes* must be lower than the actual sale value, on average, barring any nonrandom errors. And of course, this is easy to see with the last few *Forbes* estimates for the NBA versus actual sale values in Table 8.5. If the *Forbes* estimates are close to the stand-alone asset value, it appears that the values of owning NBA teams in

TABLE 8.5
Forbes **Team Valuations Versus Actual Sale Values, NBA, Since 2000**

Year	Team	Price	Forbes Valuation	As Percentage of Sale Price (%)
2000	Vancouver Grizzlies	$170	$118	31
2001	Atlanta Hawks	$250	$199	20
2002	Boston Celtics	$360	$274	24
2004	New Jersey Nets	$300	$296	1
2004	Phoenix Suns	$401	$356	11

Sources: Various popular publications on sale prices; *Forbes* annual Team Valuation reports.

Note: Only sales that clearly involved only the team and clearly stated partial values are included. Prices in US$ millions.

addition to the team's own bottom line and tax advantages typically (note the Nets) are in the neighborhood of 11–31 percent of sale prices.

MARKET STRUCTURE AND OUTCOMES

Demand and supply do not occur in a vacuum in team sports. Market structure will dictate the actual outcomes. Two things distinguish the market structure of team sports. First, the additional structures of pro leagues and college conferences facilitate team interaction into the organized play most valued by fans. This can be referred to as "single entity" choices required to make play happen. Second, the market structure is characterized by market power, so "joint venture" activity will facilitate profits. Market power follows from the organization in pro sports at the league level and we expect joint-venture choices to make profits happen. But college sports also make use of the NCAA to facilitate an additional layer of careful market-power husbandry.

Never should it be forgotten in thinking about sports that leagues are just the individual team owners putting on a different hat to determine how their sport will be organized for business purposes. Conferences are just individual ADs doing the same, and the NCAA is a more global structure used to subdue and monitor the economically competitive urges of college conferences. This is the essence of joint-venture activity defined by territory definition and maintenance, team location and expansion, and negotiations with host cities, labor, and TV. One last issue is competitive balance, clearly a single-entity concern since leagues are predicted to fold if just a few teams literally win all the games.

Single-Entity Impacts

Rules will be changed according to how it pays. Related to the observations above under production, the actual rules of the games also are a matter of choice. In *The Business of Major League Baseball*, Gerald Scully analyzes the impact of rule changes.[7] The easiest to see is rule changes that have narrowed the strike zone (although Scully covers many more). The result is that hitting is favored relative to pitching, for instance; batting averages should rise along with earned run averages. Indeed, that is precisely what happened in 1969. Scully goes on to point out that this also has economic implications for team revenues and, after that, players' pay. Again, it is easy to see the implications for the record books and the relative value of hitters compared to pitchers.

In my work with Young Hoon Lee on the behavior of competitive balance in pro sports leagues, we find a structural break in the behavior of competitive balance, statistically speaking, around rule changes from the late 1960s through the early 1970s in the NFL.[8] During this time, sudden death was added, the goalposts were moved back, kickoffs were moved back, missed kicks outside the twenty were taken back to the line of scrimmage, downfield contact was increasingly restricted, and the holding penalty was reduced from fifteen to ten yards. Shortly thereafter, the "in the grasp" quarterback rule was put in place. All of these were expected to create more offensive excitement, putting weaker defensive teams in the running. As Scully originally observed, all of this also changes the relative values of different players.

Even hockey, perhaps the most reluctant of all leagues to embrace any changes at all, is not immune. A rule change in place for the 1999-2000 season gave the losing team in overtime one point, rather than zero previously, and overtime is played with four players, plus the goalie, rather than five plus the goalie. According to Abrevaya, there has been a reduction in the number of overtime ties and more aggressive offensive play during overtime as a result of the change in the point system.[9] It is too soon to tell whether this plays out into actual changes in attendance results, but the important observation is that owners will be altering the rules when it suits fan preferences and revenue purposes. The upshot of all this is that we should expect owners, acting as a league (or athletic departments acting through the NCAA), to alter the rules in the direction of higher revenues.

Schedules and the structure of playoffs will be changed according to how it pays. Increasing the number of playoff rounds reduces the chance that the season-winning percent champion will eventually become the playoff champion. For example, switching from a four-team playoff to an eight-team playoff reduces the chance that a season winning percent of 0.800 even makes the championship game from 68 to 58 percent.

To the extent that fans prefer closer outcomes, greater playoff access for any given team, and more equally balanced playoff outcomes once a team is in, then changing the schedule and playoffs to more layers makes sense. Again, in my work with Lee, shortly after the structural change in NFL competitive balance in the early 1970s, the season was increased to sixteen games and the second wild card was added. Balance improved corresponding to this choice.[10]

One would expect this type of alteration in season length and playoff access to be increasingly adopted as leagues continue to expand slowly. Of course, the tradeoff is in regular season revenues. But the increasing nationalization of audiences through television will determine this choice. There are only roughly thirty teams in any league, so the vast majority of fans enjoy the sport through TV and their willingness to pay reasonably can be expected to be more generally aimed at playoff enjoyment.

Joint Venture Impacts

There will be more territory conflicts between teams in the same league. The most recent territorial conflict involved Baltimore Orioles owner Peter Angelos. MLB at large had purchased ownership of the Expos and, after shopping a few alternatives like Puerto Rico, the league decided that the Expos should be D.C.-bound and renamed the Nationals. The resulting "negotiations" to protect the territory of the Orioles owner saw the local TV revenue from the Nationals going to Angelos for a specific period of time.

And we should expect more of the same. Increasingly, the most valuable new locations for teams are in areas already hosting teams—the Eastern seaboard, the southeast, and southern California. When any given owner decides to move his or her team, invariably an owner already in the vicinity will claim a conflict. The fact that any move into any reasonably sized area also butts into regional cable viewing areas makes this nearly a dead certainty.

Fewer and fewer teams will want to move in any given league. Relative to the value that individual owners place on moving their teams, the size of expansion fees will dictate that the league is better off expanding rather than moving. I document that MLB expansion fees have increased at a real annual rate of 7 percent over the thirty-seven years where expansions have occurred, even including a 9 percent decline in 1976![11] A quick check of expansion fees in other leagues shows real annual growth rates of 5, 4, and 1 percent in the NBA, NFL, and (ever the tail-dragger) NHL, respectively. Further, the inevitable territory conflicts that will become more likely over time will also push leagues toward expansion rather than team relocation. The millions earned by each owner from expansion make revenue impacts due to a new neighbor easier to swallow.

There will be an expansion football league within five years. Currently, the NFL walks a tightrope. Keeping Los Angeles open as a believable relocation threat surely is good for owners negotiating with their host communities for increased subsidies from their current city hosts. But the downside is the revenue and TV contract plum hanging in L.A. just waiting to be plucked by a rival league. So, more formally, either there will be an NFL expansion team in southern California or there will be a new rival pro football league.

This is not the longest of shots. The NFL has failed to avert rival league formation in the past—the American Association and the fourth version of the AFL. If the NFL miscalculates, given the terrific dollar amounts in involved and the accumulating capital in sports management firms, starting another league becomes very attractive with an open anchor market like L.A.

There will be two major college conference realignments within ten years. There is nothing sacrosanct about conference alignments, as witness the recent shuffle in the Big East/ACC. Conference membership depends on conferences facilitating the needs of individual athletic departments. Notre Dame will join the Big Ten, bringing membership to twelve teams, dictated by two factors. First, Notre Dame still has its national audience, but no longer outcompetes the remaining big-time football programs for incoming talent. Their recent record in bowl appearances makes this painfully clear. So, one of the advantages Notre Dame previously enjoyed as an independent is reduced. Second, the lure of conference playoff money in football will lead the current eleven teams in the Big Ten to sweeten the pot to get Notre Dame to join. This is exactly what happened when Miami was lured into the Big East originally years ago.

Similarly, BYU and Boise State will bring Pac-10 membership to twelve teams, facilitating a conference playoff in football. The remaining Mountain West and WAC teams are highly likely to rejoin into two cumbersome seven- or eight-team divisions but eventually will reduce membership to twelve as well. Again, twelve is the natural number for a viable conference playoff championship (until big-time football switches to the tournament structure mentioned in an earlier prediction).

Competitive Balance

In pro sports, races for the playoffs will become tighter. While fans will be increasingly unsatisfied with any remaining competitive imbalance over time as discussed above, nonetheless playoff uncertainty will improve. This outcome will have more to do with the narrowing of potential revenue differences across locations over time than with league attempts to improve balance. Put simply, as population and income growth equalize across the larger metropolitan areas, relative team quality will also become more equal.

Whenever balance improves, it is tempting to attribute it to policy choices made by leagues. But there is nearly no evidence that such is actually the case. My work with Jim Quirk years ago, and now with Lee, shows this to be true. Eckard has a similar view.[12] None of the major policy alterations by leagues (drafts, free agency, salary caps, or revenue sharing) has had anything to do with any statistically detectable alteration in competitive balance in any of the major pro sports leagues.

A simple demonstration appears in Figure 8.1, where decade averages for the popular RSD measure of competitive balance are portrayed for all four major sports leagues. Only the NBA shows even a small increase in imbalance over time for this measure, although the AL in MLB bears watching into the future. Since the factors underlying these trends will continue, namely, equalization of revenue potential across major metropolitan areas, so

FIGURE 8.1
RSD through the Decades

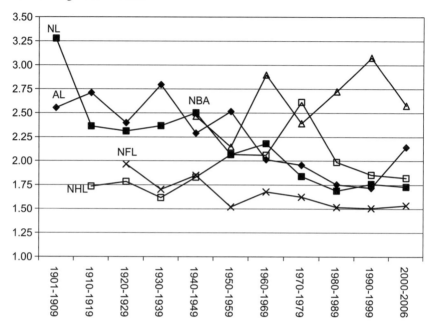

Source: Table 6.3 in R. Fort, *Sports Economics*, 2nd ed. (Upper Saddle River, N.J.: Prentice-Hall, 2006), augmented to 2006.
Note: Averages for the most recent decade include all seasons in all leagues that began in 2006. Calculation of RSD is explained in Table 8.2.

will improvement in competitive balance. To see that this is tied to revenue imbalance, the data in my textbook show that the Gini coefficient of revenue dispersion in all leagues except the NFL improved from the decade of the 1990s through the current decade.[13]

The Yankees and Braves will make the playoffs in each of the next five years but no other league will see the same dominance. Table 8.6 shows access to the playoffs at the division level for MLB, the NBA, and the NFL and at the conference semifinal level for the NHL. The basis for comparison is the last five years (2002–2006) and the five years before that (1997–2001). For example, for the AL 1997–2001, eight different teams appeared in the playoffs. During this period, the Yankees appeared every year and the Indians four of the five possible times.

For MLB, one thing is clear. The Yankees and Braves always make the playoffs. In addition, comparing across the two five-year periods, raw access to the playoffs has worsened in MLB (for example, eight different AL teams appeared in the first period while the number falls to six in the second period)

TABLE 8.6
Playoff Appearance Counts, All Leagues, 1997–2001 and 2002–2006

		Teams in Playoffs		
Championship	League	1997–2001	2002–2006	New Qualifiers
MLB division championship	AL	8 (New York Yankees 5; Cleveland Indians 4)	6 (New York Yankees 5; Minnesota Twins 4)	Minnesota Twins, Detroit Tigers, Los Angeles Angels of Anaheim
	NL	9 (Atlanta Braves 5; Houston Astros 4)	5 (Atlanta Braves/ St. Louis Cardinals 4)	Los Angeles Dodgers
NBA division championship	Eastern	9 (Detroit Pistons 5; New Jersey Nets 4)	9 (New York Knicks 4; Indiana Pacers/ Philadelphia 76ers 3)	New Jersey Nets, Detroit Pistons, Cleveland Cavaliers, Washington Wizards, Boston Celtics
	Western	6 (San Antonio Spurs 5; Dallas Mavericks 4)	9 (Los Angeles Lakers 5; Utah Jazz 4)	Portland Trailblazers, Utah Jazz, Houston Rockets
NFL division championship	AFC	11 (Miami Dolphins 3; many other teams 2)	10 (New England Patriots 4; Indianapolis Colts 4)	San Diego Chargers
	NFC	12 (Minnesota Vikings 4; many other teams 2)	12 (Philadelphia Eagles 4; many other teams 2)	Carolina Panthers
NHL conference semifinals	Eastern	10 (Buffalo Sabres 4; many other teams 3)	8 (Ottawa Senators 3; many other teams 2)	Carolina Hurricanes, Tampa Bay Lightning
	Western	8 (Colorado Avalanche/Dallas Stars/Detroit Red Wings 4)	10 (San Jose Sharks/Colorado Avalanche 3)	Calgary Flames, Minnesota Wild, Vancouver Canucks

Sources: Playoff histories are at Wikipedia.com.

Notes: Entry example. AL 1997–2001, eight different teams appeared in the playoffs. During this period, the Yankees appeared in each of the five possible division championships and the Indians appeared four of the five possible times. The final column lists teams that appeared in the playoffs in 2002–2006 but not in 1997–2001.

and remains about the same in both the NBA Eastern conference (with a bit of improvement in the NBA Western conference) and across the NFL. Hockey is a tougher comparison since the entire season including all postseason play was lost to the lockout of 2004/05. So we can't be sure if the reduction in the NHL Eastern conference is due to simply fewer playoff chances but clearly things are better in the West even with fewer playoff chances.

No other league is dominated in the same way that the Yankees and Braves dominate MLB. Thus, there may be some cause for hopefulness if one looks at which teams dominate in terms of playoff access and the amount of turnover. Even in MLB, the teams that came in second in number of playoff appearances changed from Cleveland to Minnesota in the AL and from Houston to St. Louis in the NL. This in part documents what Scully showed us about cycles among teams others than those in the largest markets, discussed above. And things are even more hopeful from this perspective in the remaining leagues. Only the NHL Western conference shows any repetition at all and then only at the top with the repeat appearances for Colorado. The leaders and other top finishers change completely in the Eastern conference and other top finishers change substantially in the Western conference.

Table 8.6 also shows that, while the same number of different teams typically occupies the playoffs in the two five-year periods, the composition of those teams does change some in all leagues except the NFL and the NL. All other divisions and conferences showed multiple team turnover, and up to a five-team turnover in the NBA Eastern division. Over the entire five-year period, there were twenty chances in the NBA at the division level so this is a 25 percent turnover. A two-team turnover would be 10 percent and a three-team turnover would be a 15 percent turnover.

In college sports, games will become more closely contested but not the championship. While the same bunch of teams will flirt with the top twenty-five, it will become nearly impossible to break into the top twenty. Success is expected to change over time depending on changes in the factors that determine willingness to pay for college sports. Unlike pro sports, where fortunes can change with population and income, college sports fortunes change with the number and income of its alumni and other boosters. And this factor makes it nearly impossible for newcomers to join the ranks of the college sports elite. Further, college athletic departments are place-bound in a way that does not characterize pro sports teams. Finally, there always remains the underlying threat of a top twenty breakaway if a few colleges ever do muster the wherewithal to vie for the top spots. Currently, the BCS structure keeps them down on the farm and if there ever are new upstarts, the top twenty can simply form its own exclusive club by actually forming a superconference.

So, football teams like Kansas State and South Florida will always arise. And occasionally fringe teams from the past will appear again. But the true ability to vie for top spots is limited both by the form of college sports demand and by the current structure governing the distribution of the revenue among current top twenty teams. Those outside the top twenty will get better but not in the sense of becoming viable championship contenders. The 1990 season may be the last time this system faltered, with the championship shared by Colorado and Georgia Tech.

There will never be a contraction of the number of teams in a major pro league. The last contraction of a major pro league occurred when MLB's NL shut down four teams in 1899. And that episode gives us the situation where we might expect another contraction—increased competition from a truly viable rival league (the AL in this particular historical instance) raises the price of talent and drives marginal teams in the older league to the economic brink. It seems nearly impossible that the situation will ever reoccur. Even if there actually is a new rival league (for example, for the NFL as predicted above), subsequent rival leagues after the NL–AL conflict have always seen their most viable teams join the older major league. Single-league dominance is the rule in pro sports.

In addition, in the modern case, there are two other mitigating factors. First, it should be expected that both state and federal antitrust authorities will at least investigate any such attempted contraction. Such intervention, even if it did not stop a contraction, would surely raise the cost of doing so to any league. Second, franchises are simply too valuable to just close them down. Despite threats of contraction at about the same time, MLB chose to buy back the Expos franchise rather than just let it dissolve or, more telling, sell to another potential buyer. The league paid about $120 million including lease buyouts for the franchise in 2002 and then sold it to the Lerner group in D.C. for $450 million in 2006. Ignoring inflation, the other twenty-nine owners enjoyed a cool $11.4 million each on the transaction.

THE LABOR MARKET AND COLLECTIVE BARGAINING

In a competitive world, the last unit of sports talent hired in the market gets paid its "marginal revenue product," or MRP. Since the supply of talent slopes up, all other sports talent in the market makes more than their next best option. MRP is the product of two components. The talent input makes a contribution in addition to the rest of the team called its "marginal product," or MP. But owners also are able to sell this MP and earn additional or "marginal" revenue (MR) from the sale. So the most that any owner would pay for that unit of talent is MRP = MP × MR.

It is common for some observers of the sports scene to forget that both components are important, MP and MR. For example, while player MP may not change over time, the value of that contribution has continually risen over time. "Average" performance players make millions not because they have a greater MP than their predecessors but because MR has risen over time. Fans are willing to pay much more even for players with MP at the league average. This same logic also shows why a player with the same MP at two different locations can make more money in one of the locations—the fans in one location can simply value that MP more than fans in the other location. The same 0.500 lifetime pitcher can be worth millions more in one market over another.

Now, if competition is not so brisk, then player pay can be less than MRP. This was precisely the situation historically in pro leagues under reserve option clauses prior to free agency. And it is reality in college sports, facilitated by the NCAA amateur requirement. College athletes do receive some compensation through their grant in aid (room, board, books, and tuition). For some players, this compensation approximates their MRP. But stars generate millions for their athletic departments and the value of their compensation is less than their MRP.[14]

One other important element of the labor market in sports also causes some observers to stumble in their assessment of owners and player personnel directors. Sports performance and the value that fans put on that performance are both fraught with uncertainty. Athletes do not perform at their historical averages year after year. Indeed, it is common for "career years" to cause this flow of service to be quite difficult to estimate. In addition, willingness to pay by fans is subject to changes in the determinants of demand listed earlier; incomes may rise or fall, the rate of population growth is uncertain, and changing fan preferences over time are difficult to predict.

So, owners must make their best estimate of MRP and offer pay to players accordingly. As with all areas of uncertainty, sometimes owners and player personnel directors will estimate correctly and sometimes they will not. One thing is certain. They will be wrong occasionally about bargains and busts alike. But here is one of the most interesting cases of invalid expectations on the part of sports fans and sports writers. How often should owners and personnel directors estimate the performance and value of players correctly? From the purely statistical standpoint, of course the answer is neither "never" nor "always," but somewhere in between. Yet fans and sports writers typically expect the miraculous and judge the results after the fact—players hired on the basis of expected results then end up to be bargains or busts and observers judge owners and player personnel directors on the basis of their errors with *both* type of player.

But this is a statistically illegitimate *ex post* judgment, that is, 20-20 hindsight. The valid statistical exercise is to assume the place of owners and personnel directors *ex ante*, that is, *at the time the decision was made*. If there are consistent errors from this perspective, using only the information that was available at the decision point in time, then there is bias in the talent market. In such a case, owners and personnel directors can do better than they have been with their difficult task. But if there isn't any such bias, then the *ex post* mistakes that are found simply reflect the degree of difficulty in the process. Hitters typically fail two-thirds of the time. Owners do better than that in the talent market. And both are doing the best that anybody can do given the uncertainty surrounding their difficult tasks.

Turning to collective bargaining, labor negotiation processes can be viewed as efforts by labor to accomplish two things. First, players wish to make sure their pay is closer MRP rather than below MRP. This is an ongoing concern because owners are able to act in concert in their treatment of players in the absence of vigilance on the part of players and their union representatives. Second, in all leagues except MLB, players must negotiate the share of league revenues that goes to players under so-called (and poorly named) salary caps. Properly, these are revenue-sharing payroll caps. Owners and players bargain over the share of league revenues that will go to players. Then that amount is divided by the number of teams to determine the cap on any given team's payroll. Clearly, players have a vested interest in the determination of the amount that is shared in the first place.

Marginal Revenue Product

Professional player salaries will continue to rise into the foreseeable future. I am often asked, "How long can player salaries continue to increase?" There is no reason in the world that pro player salaries cannot continue to rise indefinitely and I predict they will. Since a previous prediction is that revenues in pro leagues will continue to increase, then so will the MR part of player MRP. Remember, players do not have to get better at what they do over time in order to receive higher pay. From this perspective, there will be multimillionaire second-string defensive backs in the NFL. By the same token, there will also be millionaire kicking coaches.

Table 8.7 shows average payrolls in the four major pro sports leagues. This is a measure of the pay per player across the teams in each league, that is, average player salary. Real annual rates of growth here are truly astounding, easily doubling the 3 percent real annual rate of growth in the economy at large. NBA players have always been the highest paid and simple extrapolation into the future predicts they will continue to dominate the salary landscape. Interestingly, average NHL player pay has recently overtaken that of NFL players. It will be interesting, given hockey's declining TV and attendance interest, if this continues into the future.

Division I-A football and basketball coaches will always make more than anybody else on campus. In the first place, these coaches do generate

TABLE 8.7
Average Pay Per Player in Pro Sports (2004 US$)

Year	MLB	NBA	NFL	NHL
1970s	$205,307	$386,514	$141,400	$228,801
1980s	$631,889	$680,428	$321,942	$260,783
1990s	$1,503,383	$2,319,320	$843,451	$941,602
2000s	$2,446,179	$4,356,385	$1,199,984	$1,797,983
Growth	7%	7%	6%	6%

Source: Author's calculations from the *USAToday.com* Salary Data Base.

significant amounts of revenue so their MRP is higher than nearly everyone else on campus. And we should never forget that the athletic department, under the NCAA amateur requirement, does not have to pay its most important input, namely, college athletes. Since the athletic department only pays the tuition of some of their athletes, plus room and board for those same athletes, substantial revenues are left over to be collected by other inputs. Competition will decide which of the other inputs earns these portable revenues. Lately, it appears that the answer is coaches and ADs. Coaches and ADs receive a "double whammy" since their pay increases both because fans value their MP more and because fans value the MP of athletes more. But the athletes are not allowed to receive their share of the increase.

Coaches and ADs have been bouncing from team to team since the term "big-time college sports" came into use. At this writing, Nick Saban was offered in excess of $4 million on average annually to move from coaching the NFL's Miami Dolphins to coach at Alabama. Barring any change in the amateur requirement, or any uniform action by college presidents through the NCAA to take a share of this revenue increase, there will be a college football (or basketball) coach paid $10 million annually within the next five years.

Fans will continue to lament "overpaid" rookies and free agent "busts." The reason for this is that fans and sports writers are avid practitioners of the invalid statistical approach described in the introduction to this section. They continually employ invalid *ex post* judgment of the difficult talent value estimation process confronting owners and personnel directors. Again, it is invalid to look at hiring choices after the fact and point out the bargains that could have been obtained or identified after the fact the busts that occurred. The valid approach is to predict these at the same time that the owner is making his or her choice, pointing out predictable errors at that decision point in time. That is the road to statistical inference in place of 20-20 hindsight criticisms.

And there are many factors suggesting that outside analysts will do no better than owners are able to do. First, many observers have only a limited take on the data available as owners and personnel directors make these choices. For example, a common lament concerns rookies: "How can they be paid millions without ever having worn a pair of pro sneakers?" This criticism ignores that all rookies have been relentlessly scrutinized they were in junior high school. Once they enter the top ranks of college competition, the basis for comparison includes hundreds of players in a given year and thousands of players historically speaking. Further, historically, there have been literally thousands of players that were once rookies and their eventual performance as pros also is known. This includes those playing right now that are quite similar in ability, outcome, and value. Owners and personnel directors can clearly make comparisons and estimates of future value based on a wealth of data.

Will there be incorrect judgments? Absolutely. But whether critics or analysts who evaluate the criticism will ever be able to do any better is the important question. In addition to the data advantage that owners and personnel directors enjoy, the experience advantage also lies with them. Most have grown up in their game; all have access to the ongoing scouting and development function of their teams. And all teams in each league have access to each other's assessments of talent to a certain extent. As a final consideration, nobody has any greater incentive to minimize mistakes than owners. The penalties for error are steep and fall directly on their shoulders.

In any situation governed by uncertainty, there will be some unhappy results. The issue isn't that personnel directors will be wrong about particular players; that will happen with certainty. The issue is whether another approach can do better. So far, while analysts offer criticisms, none has actually come forward, bought a team, done better, and reaped the rewards of his or her superior insights. It could be that, given the size of any possible bias, costs of ownership preclude entry by those who have ferreted out the bias. In this case, the level of bias is efficient. But it could be that critics never had superior insight in the first place and simply offer 20-20 hindsight.

Young people will increase their investment in athletic skill, especially those with the lowest opportunity costs. The incentive to do so will do nothing but increase and young athletes will respond. Further, those with the lowest opportunity costs will face the larger net incentive in percentage terms. For example, if ethnic youth continue to have limited career opportunities, they will invest the most in athletic talent. In addition to the sheer enjoyment of playing, the *net return* is larger for them. This is an obvious outcome dictated by comparative advantage. Those with the lowest opportunity costs often have the greatest net return.

To the extent that these investment choices by young people are perceived as a problem, the problem will grow. The recourse is to alter the opportunities to those youth currently facing limited career choices. Otherwise, we all will watch increasingly honed athletes that, in all likelihood, come from very similar socioeconomic backgrounds.

Collective Bargaining

In less than five years, the draft will be extended to all foreign-born players in all leagues. North American pro leagues are characterized by a high degree of overt cooperative behavior among league members (individual team owners). There is absolutely no reason for owners to continue to allow competition over foreign-born players. Such competition results in very high payments to those players, or the foreign-league owners holding their contracts, as they enter their respective leagues. The main purpose of a draft is to redirect payments from players or their current contract holders to the owners in the league. Extending the draft to foreign-born players is a natural.

Take the case of Daisuke Matsuzaka. He entered MLB with a $50-million payment to the owner of Nippon Professional Baseball League's Seibu Lions. The reason this amount was so high is because unfettered competition made the Boston Red Sox the *highest bidder* for these rights. In the presence of a draft, 2006 bottom-dwellers like the Cubs in the NL or the Devil Rays in the AL would have had the rights to bid for Matsuzaka. Surely, the payment to the Lions' owner would have been much smaller when only the worst teams in the league are able to bid. Ultimately, the Cubs or Rays would have moved Matsuzaka on to his higher valued use in the league, apparently, to Boston. The difference between Boston's $50 million and the fee paid to the Lions' owner by the Cubs or Rays would stay with the Cubs or Rays owner.

When foreign-born players are drafted, lower-revenue teams will bring in exciting international talent, enjoy the returns of that talent in their own market for a short while, and then send the talent on to the teams that currently are paying much more for the very same players. Values will be redistributed from incoming foreign-born players to lower-revenue teams. This is the lesson from the institution of all drafts for domestic talent.

The first baseball lockout in history will occur within the next five years. There have been baseball strikes, but never a lockout. To see why one will occur soon, let's develop a little logical exercise. Suppose MLB owners are considering a lockout. If the lockout is successful, the owners get a gain against players, G. This gain would be in terms of lower overall compensation to players. In addition, owners will enjoy their next best alternative during the lockout, A. The variable costs of running the season would be spent on some other endeavor generating this return. In the past, this has included a season with replacement players but other options surely exist, including simply putting those funds in the bank. But owners will also sacrifice profits from their baseball operations, a loss L. Finally, owners may incur a cost associated with later fan wrath, F. These are all difficult calculations since they (1) occur at future dates requiring some forecasting and (2) may be difficult to measure in the first place. In any event, a successful lockout is yields $(G + A - L - F)$.

If the lockout is unsuccessful, all is the same except there is no gain against the players. Failure brings $(A - L - F)$. If P is the probability of success then the expected value of the lockout is:

$$EV = P \times (G + A - L - F) + (1 - P) \times (A - L - F)$$

Simplifying and rearranging gives the following expression diagrammed in Figure 8.2:

$$EV = (A - L - F) + P \times G$$

$(A - L - F)$ is the "y-intercept" of the expected value function and G is the slope. Also displayed in Figure 8.2 is P_{BE}, the "breakeven" probability. P_{BE} is the value of P such that $EV = 0$. Owners must asses P, but P_{BE} establishes an important benchmark for their consideration. As long as $P > P_{BE}$, then $EV > 0$ and owners can at least entertain the idea of a lockout. If P_{BE} is quite low, owners may not have to spend as much time fine-tuning their guesses about P. Owners, of course, are free to adjust the formula for such things as their aversion to losses, but the EV depicted here generally sums up the elements in their decision process. Let's suppose that the current situation is subscripted "0" in Figure 8.2.

So, as long as $EV > 0$ is large enough, a lockout is a money-making proposition. If so, given the subjective probability of winning a lockout and owners' aversion to losses, it would make sense to work the negotiation process within the letter of the law but bring about a stoppage. And here is why it will happen in MLB. The academic analysis of fan wrath makes it pretty likely that $A - F \geq 0$. Work stoppages do not engender much fan wrath at all and the next best alternative is positive.[15] Further, while revenues have been increasing steadily, the same is not necessarily so for profits, so L has also been declining at least for some teams. This suggests that the entire EV function has been shifting up parallel for MLB owners via the y-intercept term toward the situation subscripted "1" in Figure 8.2. Note that this means that P_{BE} has fallen from P_{BE}^0 to P_{BE}^1 smaller and smaller probabilities of success are needed over time in order to generate $EV > 0$. Even for a given G, the chances for a lockout are increasing over time.

FIGURE 8.2
Expected Value of a Lockout

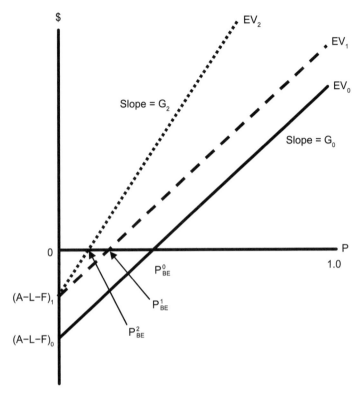

But this is not the end of the changes that make a lockout more likely. The gain to be had against players, G, also has been increasing steadily; MLB shares the highest real annual payroll growth in Table 8.7 with the NBA. So the slope of the EV function also has been increasing, depicted by $G_2 > G_0$ further adding to the fall in P_{BE} to $P_{BE}^2 < P_{BE}^1$ Owners have to actually assess P, but whatever their assessment, if P_{BE} continues to fall, eventually their assessed P will exceed P_{BE} and the lockout will have a large enough positive expected value to make it a reality.

College athletes will never get play for pay and gender equity will never be achieved. The barrier stopping star college athletes from obtaining their MRP is the NCAA amateur requirement. That requirement has created fabulous returns for college ADs and coaches so they will not change anything on their own. Indeed, it should be expected that ADs and coaches will bring the full force of NCAA enforcement to bear on this issue. Court action has also proven ineffectual. In my opinion, the only avenue open for college stars to obtain compensation closer to their MRP is through collective bargaining. In a rough parallel, MLB players did not earn free agency through the courts but through collective bargaining. And that seems the only path open to college athletes.

But here is why it is extremely unlikely that college athletes will ever be able to bargain collectively and, thus, why stars will never obtain their MRP. In order to be able to bargain collectively under U.S. labor law, college athletes must be employees of their universities. Examination of the Internal Revenue Service guidelines strongly indicates that athletes are employees. But thus far, there has been extremely limited success in establishing this through the courts. Let's look at the guidelines and then the reasons why this failure to establish employee status is predicted to continue into the future.

According to the Internal Revenue Service: "In determining whether the person providing service is an employee or an independent contractor, all information that provides evidence of the degree of control and independence must be considered." And: "A general rule is that anyone who performs services for you is your employee *if you can control what will be done and how it will be done*."[16] The emphasis is in the original text! The list includes three elements. First, there is behavioral control. The following lists are quoted directly from the IRS Web page:

- When and where to do the work.
- What tools or equipment to use.
- What workers to hire or to assist with the work.
- Where to purchase supplies and services.
- What work must be performed by a specified individual.
- What order or sequence to follow.

Surely this describes the requirements for participation dictated to college athletes by their coaches. Also under behavioral control is training: "*Training that the business gives to the worker.* An employee may be trained to perform services in a particular manner. Independent contractors ordinarily use their own methods." Again, the emphasis is in the original text and surely describes training for college athletes.

The second element in the IRS determination of an employer-employee relationship is financial control. The following would all suggest less of that control and more likely an independent-contractor relationship:

- The extent to which the worker has unreimbursed business expenses.
- The extent of the worker's investment.
- The extent to which the worker makes his or her services available to the relevant market.

- How the business pays the worker.
- The extent to which the worker can realize a profit or loss.

On these dimensions, the balance for college athletes would seem to swing away from independent-contractor status and, thus, in favor of employee status. To argue against employee status on the basis of the last two is disingenuous since the absence of pay, profit, or loss for the athlete is governed by NCAA rules in the first place.

Third, and finally, other contractual characteristics of the type of relationship are a determining factor:

- Written contracts describing the relationship the parties intended to create.
- Whether or not the business provides the worker with employee-type benefits, such as insurance, a pension plan, vacation pay, or sick pay.
- The permanency of the relationship.
- The extent to which services performed by the worker are a key aspect of the regular business of the company.

Certainly the first sounds exactly like the NCAA "letter of intent" signing while the last is just an undeniable fact—it is doubtful that any fans would come to games or tune in on TV to watch administrators administer, or coaches coach. The athletes perform the key services. Further, to argue that they receive no benefits is disingenuous since that happens by NCAA rules in the first place.

All in all, then, a strong case can be made that college athletes are employees, and both academicians and lawyers have given it the old college try.[17] For some purposes like workers' compensation athletes have been found to be employees while not for other purposes (a nice list of cases is in Davis and Parker).[18] But why hasn't there been a more successful general finding for college athletes?

The answer appears to be twofold. First, the expected result if they are found to be employees in a general context, of course, is what we have already seen from organized labor in pro sports leagues. College athlete employees using collective bargaining will push compensation toward MRP. It seems inevitable that under collective bargaining star college athletes would eventually earn a salary in addition to the other compensation they currently receive under their "grant in aid" (room and board, books, and tuition), investment returns from sports participation, and value of educational attainment. Some would find this excessive on the face of it and it is commonly read and heard that "They get enough with their shot at the pros and the value of their education." Of course, this steamrolls right over the issue that nearly no college athletes actually have a shot at the pros and that the value of their education is subjective, more valuable to some and much less valuable to others.

The second part of the answer seems to me to be the power of play-for-pay myths strongly maintained by ADs and coaches. Top stars are generating literally millions each for their athletic departments.[19] And neither coaches nor athletic directors will entertain the idea of the pay cut they themselves would have to take in order to pay athletes. So they employ powerful myths to protect their pay—richer schools will get some advantage under pay for play; nearly no athletic department has any positive balance at the end of the year so where will the money come from? It is the stuff of undergraduate textbooks that these are myths, but they persist and remain effective.[20] Given this power on the part of athletic departments, through myth and NCAA enforcement, arguments that players are employees have failed to carry the day. Since there is no reason to suspect this will change, employee status will not be achieved and, without it, compensation closer to MRP will remain unattainable.

Gender equity will not be achieved in college sports. Gender equity hasn't been achieved in the thirty-five years since the institution of Title IX (Educational Amendments of 1972) and nothing about why that is true has changed. So there is no reason to suspect it will happen in a subsequent equal period of time. The NCAA and college athletic directors trot out the same myths in this case as in the case of play for pay. Richer schools will get some advantage and where will the money come from? There is the additional unsubstantiated claim that "nonrevenue" sports will kill revenue-generating sports. And some ADs have even chosen to kill minor sports (ironically, including minor women's sports!) in the name of Title IX compliance. But that is a choice that protects coaches' and athletic directors' pay, not a certainty that must happen in order to achieve gender equity. While there is no basis in fact to any of these myths, they remain powerful. Since they are unlikely to be overcome, gender equity will remain elusive.

CLOSING

Rather than summarize the many predictions made above, let's return instead to the caveats. First, "it makes no difference to me whether I am right or wrong." Second, prediction is an inherently difficult (perhaps even objectionable) endeavor so "I fully expect to be wrong, quite probably in every instance." There is nothing riding on these predictions for me so it will simply be fun to see if any come to pass. If they don't come to pass, at least there are explanations put forth that may aid in the assessment of those eventual outcomes—either there is faulty reasoning or unforeseen other changes will undo the predictions.

I leave the reader with one last sure-thing prediction. *Serious sports business analysts will always have jobs.* Applying sound statistical inference apparently is so difficult, or so injurious to the self-interest of some observers, that serious analysts always will have a teaching job to do if nothing else. This is clear to me in the case of criticism of owners' bottom-line decisions under a fair amount of uncertainty and in the case of talent decisions made under even more uncertainty.

In addition, serious analysts also can make a job of debunking myths. This is clear to me in the case of the arguments by ADs and coaches against play for pay and gender equity. Cutting through myths separates the self-interested motivations of the mythmakers from possibilities that are purposefully hidden by their myths. So as long as there is weak statistical inference to criticize and self-interested mythmakers to debunk, serious analysts will always have a job. Now, Madame Olga is tired and must retire to the dark reaches of her tent.

NOTES

1. R. Fort, *Sports Economics,* 2nd ed. (Upper Saddle River, N.J.: Prentice-Hall, 2006), 463.

2. Ibid., 57.

3. Michael Lewis, *Moneyball: The Art of Winning an Unfair Game* (New York: W. W. Norton, 2003).

4. As with J. K. Hakes and R. D. Sauer, "An Economic Evaluation of the *Moneyball* Hypothesis," *Journal of Economic Perspectives* 20 (2006): 173–185.

5. G. W. Scully, *The Market Structure of Sports* (Chicago: University of Chicago Press, 1995).

6. R. Fort, "The Value of Major League Baseball Ownership," *International Journal of Sport Finance* 1 (2006): 9–20.

7. G. W. Scully, *The Business of Major League Baseball* (Chicago: University of Chicago Press, 1989).

8. R. Fort and Y. H. Lee, "Structural Change, Competitive Balance, and the Rest of the Major Leagues," *Economic Inquiry* (forthcoming).

9. J. Abrevaya, "Fit to Be Tied: The Incentive Effects of Overtime Rules in Professional Hockey," *Journal of Sports Economics* 5 (2004): 292–306.

10. Fort and Lee, "Structural Change, Competitive Balance, and the Rest of the Major Leagues."

11. Fort, "The Value of Major League Baseball Ownership."

12. J. Quirk and R. D. Fort, *Pay Dirt: The Business of Professional Team Sports* (Princeton, N.J.: Princeton University Press, 1992); Fort and Lee, "Structural Change, Competitive Balance, and the Rest of the Major Leagues"; E. W. Eckard, "Baseball's

Blue Ribbon Economic Report: Solutions in Search of a Problem," *Journal of Sports Economics* 2 (2001): 213–227.

13. Fort, *Sports Economics,* 172.

14. R. W. Brown and R. T. Jewell, "Measuring Marginal Revenue Product in College Athletics: Updated Estimates," in *Economics of College Sports,* ed. J. Fizel and R. Fort (Westport, Conn.: Praeger, 2004), 153–162; Brown and Jewell, "The Marginal Revenue Product of a Women's College Basketball Player," *Industrial Relations* 45 (2006): 96–101.

15. M. B. Schmidt and D. J. Berri, "The Impact of Labor Strikes on Consumer Demand: An Application to Professional Sports," *American Economic Review* 94 (2004): 344–357.

16. Internal Revenue Service, "Independent Contractors vs. Employees," http://www.irs.gov/businesses/small/article/0,id=99921,00.html.

17. A. L. Stack and E. J. Staurowsky, *College Athletes for Hire: The Evolution and Legacy of the NCAA's Amateur Myth* (Westport, Conn.: Praeger, 1998).

18. T. Davis and T. Parker, "Student-Athlete Sexual Violence against Women: Defining the Limits of Institutional Responsibility," *Washington and Lee Law Review* (Winter 1998): 1–55.

19. Brown and Jewell, "Measuring Marginal Revenue Product in College Athletics: Updated Estimates"; Brown and Jewell, "The Marginal Revenue Product of a Women's College Basketball Player."

20. Fort, *Sports Economics.*

Nine

The Big Business of College Sports in America

Daniel F. Mahony and Timothy D. DeSchriver

In July 2006 University of Louisville football coach Bobby Petrino signed a contract extension for $25.5 million over ten years, which made him among the highest-paid coaches in college football.[1] While Petrino had been successful at the University of Louisville, the school had never played in a bowl championship (BCS) game and had finished the season in the top ten only once in its history. Questions emerge, such as how does a university justify paying a coach over four times as much as the university president and how did the value of the university football coach go from $800,000 in 2002 to $2.5 million in 2006? At least part of the rationale presented in the local paper was that to be a top-ten program in college football, the university has to pay its head coach a top-ten salary.[2]

In other words, the University of Louisville had to pay so much for its football coach because that is what other top programs were doing. In fact, both the local paper and the university's athletic director suggested that to be a "major player" in college football, the university must first be a "major payer." While $2.5 million to coach an "amateur" sports team may seem like a lot, it is important to note that several coaches were paid comparable salaries and some were even higher.[3] The increases in salaries and the large amounts of money being paid to keep up with other universities suggest the existence of an "arms race" in which universities rapidly increase their spending in college athletics in order to be successful. While many universities appear to participate in this arms race, it is still unclear to many whether it is worth it.[4] This chapter will examine early perspectives on college athletic economics, the current financial trends, some of the more controversial issues relative to economic decision-making in college athletics, and where the current trends may be taking us.

HISTORICAL PERSPECTIVES ON COLLEGE ATHLETIC ECONOMIC BENEFITS AND COSTS

Early college athletics were activities started by students for students. The earliest games involved groups of students from one university playing against each other. University officials not only did not see the potential economic benefits from athletics, they often tried to stop them. Once university teams started to travel to play against one another, many university officials' concerns increased. The games were often seen as excessively violent and the officials felt that they were distracting students from focusing on their academic responsibilities. Some officials tried to limit college athletics or even ban them. While some people at universities still have these concerns today, many top university officials began to change their perspective on college athletics during the later part of the nineteenth century. The highly competitive higher education marketplace and the instability of resources in higher education led these officials to look more closely at the potential economic benefits of college athletics.[5]

In general, it was believed that successful teams could benefit the university in several ways. As college athletics, football in particular, became more popular, it was clear that many fans were willing to spend a lot of money on tickets. The hope was that the money from these games would not only support the team, but "extra" money could be used to address other university needs. However, many of the benefits that were perceived to have the greatest potential were less direct. Universities at that time and today rely heavily on revenue from alumni donations, student tuition, and, for public institutions, state subsidies. Successful teams were seen as having a positive benefit on each of these revenue sources.[6] First, alumni who were happy with the team's success would be more likely to donate large amounts of money to the general university fund. Second, legislators happy with the team's success would be more willing to appropriate state resources to the university.[7]

Finally, for numerous reasons, students would be more attracted to the university if its football team was successful. The presence of a successful team would make the college environment more enjoyable. Also, many universities believed students, as well as others, judged the quality of the university by the success of its teams.[8] In an era before university and academic program rankings and in which good data on institutional quality was rare, many universities saw athletic success as the best way to increase institutional prestige. For example, when President William Rainey Harper was seeking to build the prestige of the University of Chicago, one of his first steps was to hire Amos Alonzo Stagg as the football coach. Harper told Stagg to go recruit the best players and gave him access to the Rockefeller trust fund to pay these athletes.[9] Although in the 1930s the university took the unusual step of dropping football, the focus on football to build prestige in the early years of the university was not unusual.[10]

However, the question still remains whether universities truly got the economic benefits they were seeking in the early days of college athletics. No academic research was being conducted to investigate possible relationships between athletic success and alumni donations, state subsidies, student enrollment, or institutional prestige. It is likely, therefore, that the perception that such relationships were or would be strong was based more on anecdotal evidence than on anything that would be considered very strong. In fact, it does not appear that any studies were done on college athletic finances until the 1920s. The most famous study in the early days of college athletics, the 1929 Carnegie Report, suggested that college athletics was in good financial shape. However, there are questions about whether that conclusion was accurate.[11] The main problem then, as it is now, is how to determine the true profitability of college athletic programs.

FINANCIAL TRENDS

Initially it would appear that measuring the true financial position of a collegiate athletic department should not be difficult. Unfortunately, this is not the case. Due to the various accounting methods used by colleges and universities, there is no such thing as "generally accepted accounting practices" in college sports. For example, how are revenues generated from concession sales at athletic contests accounted for? If the concession stand is operated by the university's food services department, those revenues may not be credited to the athletic department. However, on another campus those revenues may end up in the athletic department coffers. Another example may be the cost of athletic grants-in-aid (i.e., scholarships). Should the athletic program cover full cost of an athletic scholarship? At some universities this is true, while other universities provide financial waivers to the athletic program to cover the cost of these grants-in-aid. Just from these two examples, one can see that accounting practices across intercollegiate athletic departments may vary greatly.

The topic of finances in college athletics has become so important that the National Collegiate Athletic Association (NCAA) established a Presidential Task Force to examine the issue of fiscal responsibility. One of the task force's recommendations was to set up common accounting practices across its members. This would allow for "apples to apples"-type financial information to be shared across institutions.[12]

Despite the lack of common accounting practices, some attempts have been made to examine the current financial situation in college sports. As part of a 1998 congressional amendment to the Higher Education Act of 1965, the U.S. Department of Education, Office of Postsecondary Education is required to collect financial information on men's and women's intercollegiate sports and make it available to the public.[13] Unfortunately, the information that must be provided is quite general in nature. The financial data is provided for overall spending by sport, men's and women's, along with the overall coaching salaries by sport. Thus, very little may be learned about individual areas of revenue and expense such as ticket sales, media rights, or travel costs. Another source of financial information on collegiate athletics is a voluntary survey that is distributed by the NCAA to its members. Since the 1960s, the NCAA has asked its members, at all division levels, to voluntary provide financial information.[14] For the last decade, this data has been compiled and reported on by Dr. Daniel Fulks, a professor of accounting at Transylvania University in Lexington, Kentucky. However, it should be noted that all of the individual institutional data is kept confidential and results are reported in a cumulative fashion. Thus, it is impossible to determine the individual levels of costs and revenues for specific colleges or universities. Despite this, the Fulks reports do provide us with some enlightening information on the financial trends in collegiate athletics.

There are many different sources of revenue for a collegiate athletic department. The most recent report on the Revenues and Expenses of Intercollegiate Athletics Program (referred to as the Fulks report in this text), completed for the 2002-2003 academic year, stated that the average Division I-A athletic department generated $29.4 million in revenue annually. Perhaps even more important, this represented a 17 percent increase from 2001, only two years prior. The highest reported Division I-A revenue level was $87.8 million.[15] As one can see, the largest collegiate athletic programs in the United States generate a substantial amount of revenue each year.

By further examining the Fulks report, we can also see the importance of various streams of revenue for Division I programs. The largest stream of revenue for a Division I-A athletic program is ticket sales. On average, 27 percent of a Division I-A program's revenue comes from ticket sales, totaling over $7.8 million annually. The second largest source of revenue, at $5.271 million or 18 percent of total revenue, is fundraising/donations from boosters and alumni.[16]

As Table 9.1 indicates, several sources of revenue in intercollegiate athletics are quite different from traditional professional sports leagues. First,

TABLE 9.1
Operating Revenues for Division I-A Athletic Programs, 2003

Source	Dollar Amount (in thousands)	Total Revenues (%)
Ticket sales	$7,854	27
Fundraising/donations	$5,271	18
Institutional support	$3,029	10
NCAA and conference distributions	$2,641	9
Radio/television	$2,118	7
Miscellaneous	$2,096	7
Student activity fees	$1,854	6
Signage/sponsorship	$1,259	4
Postseason competition	$898	3
Guarantees and options	$1,043	3
All other sources		6

Source: D. L. Fulks, *Revenues and Expenses of Divisions I and II, Intercollegiate Athletics Programs* (Indianapolis: National Collegiate Athletic Association, 2005).

fundraising and donations are a major part of the financial landscape in college sports. Athletic departments rely on sizable donations from boosters and alumni. Sometimes these donations can be in the millions of dollars. For example, billionaire T. Boone Pickens recently donated $165 million to the athletic department at Oklahoma State University in Stillwater, Oklahoma.[17] This was easily the largest single donation made in the history of collegiate athletics. The money will be used to finance the construction of new campus athletic facilities.

Another unique form of revenue for college sports is the distributions that individual programs receive from the NCAA and the conferences. The NCAA owns the rights to all NCAA championships. By far, the most popular of these championships is the men's basketball championship, known as March Madness. The NCAA has sold the media and marketing rights for March Madness to CBS through the year 2011. The average annual price tag for these rights is just over $500 million. A large portion of this revenue is distributed by the NCAA to its member institutions through several different programs. Additionally, most Division I-A institutions are members of a conference like the Big Ten, Atlantic Coast (ACC), or Southeastern Conference (SEC). These conferences have the ability to sell media rights to intraconference contests. The profits from these media rights deals, conference sponsorship contracts, and conference championship events are also distributed to individual institutions. For the 2005-2006 academic year, the SEC distributed $116.1 million across its twelve members.[18] In comparison, just ten years prior in 1996, the SEC distributed only $45.5 million.

While sponsorship and signage make up only 4 percent of the average total revenues for a Division I program, it is a revenue stream that has shown growth in the past decade.[19] In a fashion similar to professional sports, collegiate athletic departments are becoming more active in attracting corporate sponsors and selling the naming rights of facilities and events to corporations. For example, the University of Maryland opened a new 17,950-seat, on-campus basketball arena in 2002. Comcast purchased the naming rights for the facility at a price tag of $20 million for the next twenty-five years.[20] Other recent naming rights deals have included Value City and United Supermarkets purchasing the naming rights for the arenas at Ohio State University and Texas Tech University, respectively.

Another area of growth for collegiate athletic programs is the addition of premium seating areas in facilities and the sale of personal seat licenses. Traditionally, many large Division I athletic programs have required those who wish to purchase tickets for premier events such as football and men's basketball to make large donations to the athletic department in order to have access to these highly coveted seats. In the past decade, we have seen this practice become more prevalent. In addition, programs have added luxury seating options such as hospitality suites and club seats. These luxury seating areas come at a considerable price. Universities such as Florida State, Ohio State, and Penn State have all undertaken major renovations of their football facilities within the past ten years. The inclusion of luxury seating areas has been a major component of these renovations At Ohio State, the new club seats sold for between $2,000-$3,000 and purchasers were required to sign a five- to seven-year lease. Access to these seats requires the purchaser to be a member of the Buckeye Club and make a minimum annual donation of $2,500 during the life of the club seat contract.[21]

Similar to collegiate athletics revenues, the story for college athletics expenses is one of large annual increases. In part, this is due to the very nature of college sports. Collegiate athletic departments are nonprofit organizations. Therefore, unlike traditional for-profit businesses, their financial goal is to maximize revenues so that they can reinvest in the organization. The more money they make, the more money they spend. This is somewhat different from the traditional for-profit business model of maximizing profits by increasing revenues while limiting expenses.

As one can see in Table 9.2, the two largest areas of operating expenses for a Division I-A athletic program are salaries/benefits and grants-in-aid (i.e., scholarships).[22] Together, they comprise 50 percent of all operating expenses for Division I-A programs.

A recent trend within the salaries and benefits area is the large increase in salaries for coaches in football and men's and women's basketball.

TABLE 9.2
Operating Expenses for Division I-A Athletic Programs, 2003

Source	Dollar Amount (in thousands)	Total Expenses (%)
Salaries and benefits	$8,640	32
Grants-in-aid	$4,743	18
Team travel	$1,988	7
Contract services	$1,345	5
Equipment/uniforms/supplies	$1,179	4
Guarantees and options	$1,181	4
Recruiting	$541	2
Fundraising	$299	1
Game officials	$250	1
Sports camps	$235	1
All other	$6,792	25

Source: D. L. Fulks, *Revenues and Expenses of Divisions I and II, Intercollegiate Athletics Programs* (Indianapolis: National Collegiate Athletic Association, 2005).

Recently, coaches such as Urban Meyer, Charlie Weis, Rick Pitino, Roy Williams, Pat Summitt, and Geno Auriemma have signed multimillion-dollar contracts. For example, in the middle of his first season at Notre Dame, head football coach Charlie Weis signed a ten-year contract extension that was reportedly worth between $30-40 million.[23] In 2001 the University of Louisville signed its new head coach, Rick Pitino, to a six-year deal, valued at about $12.25 million, that has since been renegotiated for even more money.[24] While head-coaching salaries in these three sports are much larger than those in the other sports, large percentage increases are not limited to these head coaches.[25] This will be addressed again later in this chapter.

With respect to grants-in-aid, the primary challenge facing college athletics programs is the spiraling cost of tuition and living expenses at many universities. As the cost of attending an institution increases, the cost for an athletic department of providing a full grant-in-aid for a recruited student-athlete also increases. In football alone, the NCAA permits a Division I-A program to provide as many as eighty-five grants-in-aid. If the average annual price tag of a grant-in-aid for a public institution is $15,000, the annual cost of grants-in-aid for the football program is $1.275 million. As the Fulks report states, the average Division I-A program is spending over $4.7 million annually on grants-in-aid and it appears that this amount will only increase in the foreseeable future. It should be noted that the percentage of total expenses going to cover grant-in-aids is not increasing, so this increase is not unique. In fact, the trend is for these increases to occur across most areas of spending for athletic programs. Line items such as transportation, equipment, hotels, and meals have all increased over the past decade.[26] In order to maintain the same number of sports and athletes, athletics administrators fight a continual struggle to generate revenues to cover these costs.

On a sport-specific level, most college athletic programs look to football and basketball to be their revenue generators. According to Fulks, the average Division I-A football program generates about $13 million in revenue annually, while the average men's basketball program produces about $4.3 million each year. On the women's side, women's basketball is the largest revenue producer with annual average revenues of $500,000.[27] There are some institutions where other sports may be significant revenue generators. For example, schools like the University of Miami and Louisiana State University have traditionally generated significant revenues from baseball, while the University of Minnesota and the University of Maine have made ice hockey into a profitable sport. However, at most Division I-A institutions, football and basketball are the primary drivers of revenue for the athletic program.

Another distinction that must be made when discussing the business of collegiate sport is the major financial differences that appear across divisions. While most of the media and fan attention is devoted to Division I-A, the majority of NCAA members compete at the Division II or III level. At these levels, the revenues and expenses are much smaller. Additionally, these programs offer fewer or no grants-in-aid to their student athletes and the coaches' salaries and benefits are much lower. According to Fulks, the average Division II athletic program, with football, has only $2.56 million in total revenues with the largest reported level of revenues being $8.33 million. The average level of expenses for a Division II athletic program that has a football team is $2.74 million, with the largest expense level being reported at $8.33 million.[28] Thus, the average Division II institution has a deficit of about $180,000.

At the Division III level, the average annual expense level is just over $1.5 million per year for those institutions with football and under $1 million for those without football.[29] As one can see, this number is significantly less than the corresponding revenues for Divisions I and II. The primary reason for this is that Division III programs are not permitted to provide grants-in-aid for student-athletes. While student-athletes may be provided need or academic-based aid at the Division III level, the costs of these grants are usually not included as a cost for the institution's athletic department.

From a financial standpoint, another important area that must be addressed is the disparity in revenues and expenses between men's and women's sports. For example, the Fulks report shows that men's sports at the average Division I-A athletic program in 2003 generated $18.6 million annually. In comparison, the average women's program had about $1.8 million in annual revenues, with another $9 million in revenues being classified as nongender On the cost side, the average I-A women's program had annual expenses of $5.4 million, while the average annual expenses for a men's program was $12.5 million with another $9.8 million being again classified as nongender.[30] These numbers clearly show that more money is being both generated and spent on the men's side. However, while the picture may appear dark for women's athletics, the financial numbers do show promise for the future. The $1.8 million in average annual revenues generated through women's sports is three times greater than the $600,000 in revenues that occurred in 1995.[31] Thus, in just eight years, the average I-A women's sport program has tripled its level of annual revenues. Additionally, the NCAA Women's Basketball Championship has become a sizable revenue generator. The event is now played in major arenas and is sold out months in advance. Every game of the sixty-four-team championship tournament is also televised live by ESPN.

PROFITABILITY OF COLLEGE ATHLETIC PROGRAMS/DEPARTMENTS

Many of those outside of college athletics look at the rapidly increasing revenues from television contracts, sponsorships, and ticket sales for both regular season and postseason games and assume this translates into profitability for most athletic departments. However, that ignores the rapidly increasing expenses discussed earlier in this chapter. As anyone who examines organizational finances knows, increased revenues do not automatically translate into profitability and this is certainly possible in this case. So, the question that remains after examining revenues and expenses is: do athletic departments typically have annual net profit or an annual net loss?

While the question is obvious, the answer is much less clear. As previously discussed, the NCAA has conducted a number of surveys over the years that give us a little insight into this answer. According to the responses to the NCAA surveys, most programs appear to be losing money. With the exception of Division I programs, a very large percentage of schools report financial losses in their athletic departments. Even at the Division I-A level, approximately 30 percent of the athletic departments report a loss. However, the average profit at this level was reported to be $2.2 million in 2003, which would seem to suggest good profitability for some programs.[32]

However, the situation is less clear than these figures would suggest. There are two major problems. First, there are a number of related-party transactions that may result in the athletic department appearing to be profitable when it is actually losing money.[33] A related-party transaction is a transaction that involves two entities who are both under a larger entity. For college athletic departments, the related party is the university. The university can support athletics in a variety of ways and easily make a loss look like a profit.

Some of this can be seen in the NCAA data set. For example, the average athletic department in 2003 received approximately $3 million in direct institutional support. In other words, on average, the parent university provided its athletic department with a direct appropriation of $3 million to help meet the operating expenses of its sports programs. Most would argue that this subsidy is not truly revenue earned by the athletic department and represents a loss to the institution of resources that could have been used for academic purposes. If that $3-million direct subsidy is removed from total revenues, then the reported $2.2-million average profit becomes in reality a loss of $800,000.[34]

Other items should also be examined more closely. Athletic departments receive over $400,000 in direct government support and $1.85 million in student fees, both of which are also questionable as revenue generated by athletics.[35] In fact, a recent NCAA task force indicates that 18 percent of the total revenue at Division I-A comes from "allocated funds" (i.e., direct institutional support, student activity fees, and government support); this percentage climbs to 70 percent for schools in Division I-AA and Division I-AAA.[36] In addition, the NCAA data reports that approximately $3 million was also paid annually for debt service and capital expenditures for athletics, but these items are not included in the total expenses.[37]

While these examples are identified in the NCAA data, a number of related party transactions are not always as clear. For example, the university could waive the cost of tuition for certain athletes, pay the costs of operating a football stadium, pay for an academic support unit for athletes, pay some or all of the salary of an athletics department employee, or pay for the maintenance costs of an athletic facility.[38] The existence of such costs for the university would not be included in the NCAA data, so the true costs of the athletic department to the university may be even greater than this data set suggests.

The second problem when relying on the NCAA data, or any other financial data related to college athletics, is that athletic departments do not all report their data in the same manner.[39] For example, the president's office may pay a large sum of money to the athletic department for season tickets and a luxury suite at the stadium. Some universities may report this as ticket sales, while others may report it as direct institutional support. In addition, an athletic department in which the electrical bills are paid for by the university could report the electrical costs as an expense and the revenue from the university to cover that cost as direct institutional support.

However, they could also ignore it completely on the athletic department's financial statements and only record it as an expense for the university. Because there are no "rules' that must be followed, athletic departments and universities may handle related party transactions in a variety of ways, which makes it impossible to make comparisons across universities, or to combine the data and reach definite conclusions.[40]

While there is no clear answer, the evidence we do have suggests that very few athletic departments produce a profit and most lose money. However, this does not mean it is impossible to produce a profit, or that universities have stopped pursuing this goal.[41] The problem seems to be that whenever an athletic department experiences an increase in revenue, this incremental income is quickly spent.[42] If a football team has a successful year and makes it to a major bowl game, they will likely spend whatever bowl proceeds they receive on taking a large entourage to the bowl game, including the band, major donors, and senior university officials. And, of course, most coaches' contracts stipulate major salary bonuses as a result of just appearing in a postseason bowl game.[43] Typical of the contracts of head football coaches at major institutions, Ty Willingham, at the University of Washington, is guaranteed a bonus of $75,000 if his team appears in a postseason BCS bowl game and an additional $100,000 if his team is selected to play in the BCS championship game. It becomes easy to see that increases in revenues can lead to increases in costs, so this leads to little or no profitability.

FAIRNESS OF THE DISTRIBUTION OF FINANCIAL RESOURCES AND THE IMPACT OF TITLE IX DISTRIBUTIONS

While the true profitability of college athletic departments may be questionable, the data does indicate the top programs generate large amounts of revenue. The question that naturally follows is: how should that money be distributed? This has been a great source of controversy and involves examining the purpose of college athletics and what is a fair distribution of financial resources given that purpose. While gender equity has had an impact on these discussions, as well as the distributions, the controversy over resource distributions far precedes Title IX. In fact, in the early 1900s minor sports leaders at Yale University complained to the athletic director and head football coach Walter Camp that too much was going to his football team and more should be given to their sport teams. Not surprisingly, Camp disagreed and refused to change the distributions.[44]

In order to examine the fairness of resource distributions in college athletics, researchers have built on research on distributive justice in the organizational behavior literature. Deutsch identified three distribution principles: (a) equity or contribution (those who contribute more should receive more of the resources), (b) equality (everyone should receive the same distribution), and (c) need (those with greater needs should receive more of the resources).[45]

The principle used is often related to the organization's purpose. Equity or contribution is more often used as a basis for making distributions in organizations in which economic success is the primary goal. Organizations in which cooperative relations are fostered, in which maintaining positive social relations is important, in which there is a high level of cohesion, and in which there is a sense of a common fate are more likely to distribute resources based on equality. Finally, researchers have suggested that need is most often the basis for distributions in organizations in which both fostering personal growth and the survival of group members is a top priority.[46]

Depending on what one perceives as the purpose of college athletics, it is possible that any of these principles could be seen as fair and/or be used in making distributions. If, as some have argued, big-time college sports are being operated like big business and are following a corporate model, then contributions based on equity or contribution should be perceived as most fair and used in making distributions.[47] However, given that "fostering personal growth" is listed as the first goal by the NCAA, need-based contributions would appear to be most closely aligned with the stated purpose of college athletics.[48]

In the initial study on college athletics, Hums and Chelladurai found that college athletic coaches and administrators were more likely to perceive equality and need as fair.[49] While there were some differences across NCAA divisions, the preference for these principles was consistent. Subsequent studies on top college athletic administrators and students also found a preference for equality and need over contribution based distributions (i.e., equity).[50] The only difference was that the administrators tended to prefer need over equality. This was true even when the source of the resources was from higher-than-expected revenue production from the football team.[51] Moreover, the administrators also said they were more likely to make distribution decisions based on the principles of need and equality. The preference for need and equality would suggest that the values of the employees and their actual decisions are synchronized with the purpose of college athletics as professed by the NCAA.

The problem is there does not seem to be much support for this when actually examining college athletic financing. Mahony and Pastore examined financial distributions in the twenty years after Title IX was passed and did not find strong support for need- and equality-based preferences or decisions.[52] In general, they found that distributions in big-time college athletics were more often based on revenue production and spectator appeal. The largest portions of the budget continued to go to football and men's basketball. While some of the football budgets could be related to the naturally high cost of operating these teams (such as more players, more expensive equipment), the rapid increases in these budgets would appear to be more likely related to their contribution through spectator appeal and revenue production.

A couple of other facts seemed to refute the finding in other studies that need and equality were perceived to be more fair or were used to make actual distributions. In particular, a historical analysis of the distribution of resources to women's sport teams supports such a conclusion. Mahony and Pastore suggest the distribution patterns toward women's sports seemed to be more closely related to legal obligations to move toward equality as opposed to the perceived fairness of equality.[53] The passing of Title IX brought a large increase in opportunities for women athletes and in resources for women's sports. However, by the mid-1980s these distributions were far from equal. After the Supreme Court decision in the *Grove City v. Bell* case, Title IX no longer applied to college athletics.[54] Mahony and Pastore found that over the next few years the percentage of the budget going toward women's sports was no longer increasing and athletic departments stopped moving toward equality.[55]

This changed again after the passing of the Civil Rights Restoration Act in 1988, which made it clear that Title IX was going to apply to college athletics. After that, universities began to shift more resources toward women's sports. This shift, however, did not mean that resources were taken from the traditional revenue-generating sports (i.e., football and men's basketball). In fact, during the period of 1989–1993 women's sports had the highest percentage increase in the budget, but the absolute dollar increase in the football budget alone was about twice the increase in all women's sports budgets combined.[56]

These results suggest a few things relative to resource distribution in college athletics. First, any move toward equality appears to be more likely a result of legal pressures than because of a general belief that distributing resources equally is perceived as fair by those working in college athletics. Second, despite the strong support for distributing resources to programs that currently lack resources, there is little evidence that this is used as a basis for distributing resources. Mahony and Pastore found that as resources were shifted toward women's teams, they did not come from programs with more resources.[57] Instead, the resources were taken from men's nonrevenue sport teams. In some cases the teams were eliminated completely, which would be an unusual decision for organizations focused on personal growth and survival of group members.

One theory for why the distributions are based on revenue production when many say they believe equal and need-based distributions to be fairer is that many in college athletics are defining "need" differently.[58] One of the need-based subprinciples that was often supported by those at the Division I level was need-related to competitive success. In other words, some teams need more resources to compete with the other schools. This brings us back to the impact of the college athletics' arms race on the distribution of resources. For example, as an administrator I may believe that I must spend a lot of my resources on football and men's basketball because everyone else is doing so and if I do not, these teams will not be successful, will generate less revenue, and all of my teams will be negatively impacted. The problem becomes that unless an institution decides to opt out of the arms race, no one knows for sure what the impact of reduced spending would have on team success and in the budget.

DISTRIBUTIONS TO STUDENT ATHLETES

In addition to the disagreements over how the resources should be distributed among teams, there is also controversy over the share of the resources provided to the student-athletes. For many years, athletes have been limited to an athletic scholarship (e.g., tuition, room, board) and the percentage of the budget at Division I schools spent on scholarships has not increased, while the revenue generated relative to their performance has grown enormously.[59] Some would argue that this appears to be unfair. Generally in a capitalist society, those responsible for generating revenue for an organization are not limited to their share of the resources. In fact, a group of economists in the early 1990s suggested the limit placed on athlete compensation by the NCAA was the most obvious monopoly-like activity in the United States.[60] This group of economists is hardly alone in suggesting that the NCAA operates like a monopoly or, more accurately, as a cartel.[61] This raises the question: why are athletes not allowed to receive a greater share of the resources they help generate?

There are really two sets of answers to this question; one suggests the current approach is important for maintaining the purpose of college athletics, while the other suggests the approach benefits the university and those in charge of college athletics. Those who are in charge of college athletics obviously agree with the first answer. Their argument starts with the importance of amateurism. Amateurism is what makes college athletics special and if athletes were to be paid, this would make them no different than professional sports. They also argue the current approach keeps people focused on the "student" part of "student-athlete." If athletes were to be paid, they would not focus on the true value of the college experience—their education. Those on this side will also point out the value of a college degree and that because of this value the scholarship is worth far more than most believe. Finally, they will argue that since college athletics does not make a profit in most cases, any move toward paying athletes would have a huge impact on the university and the nonrevenue sport teams.[62] This is especially true because they believe that the payments could not be limited toward those who generate the revenue and athletes in all sports would need to receive the same amount.

Those on the other side of this controversy would quickly refute many of these arguments. First, they argue that amateurism died in college sports a long time ago. Once scholarships were allowed by the NCAA, college athletes were being paid to perform and, thus, were not amateurs. Those in charge have maintained the myth of amateurism for a couple of reasons. Some fans believe that because college athletes "play for the fun of the game" and not for pay, that college athletics is special. Also, by creating the myth of the student-athlete and amateurism, college officials avoid all of the implications of athletes being labeled as employees, including worker's compensation and payroll taxes. Second, they would argue that despite the public relations campaign by universities, the priority for many athletes is their sport and not their education and this emphasis also comes from their coaches. The impact of this is that student-athletes do not get the same quality of education as the other students and many, particularly in the "revenue" sports (i.e., football and men's basketball), will not graduate.[63]

Finally, they will argue that there is nothing in the law that would suggest that athlete-employees must all receive the same payment. Just as the typical medical school or law school faculty member makes much more than the average professor of English, a football player could be given more than a swimmer, so the cost may be less than estimated. Moreover, they will argue that athletic departments could still break even if they controlled their costs in other areas (e.g., coaches and administrator salaries, recruiting). Overall, they will argue that the NCAA and the universities understand that the payment of athletes would lead to a shifting of resources and that is their main reason for opposing it. The current approach leads to large salaries for coaches and athletic directors along with sponsorship and endorsement deals for coaches and universities. If athletes were allowed to negotiate for more money and endorse products and services, this would change the distributions.

POSSIBLE FINANCIAL BENEFITS OF COLLEGE ATHLETICS FOR THE UNIVERSITY

As discussed earlier, many have argued that while universities do not generally receive direct financial benefits from college athletics and may even need to supply some of the resources needed for them to break even, that there are still indirect financial benefits for the university. First, many people believe that a successful athletic program will result in increased donations to the general university. The problem is while some studies have reached a more positive conclusion, much of the research dating back to the 1930s would suggest that increased athletic success does not lead to increased donations to the general university and may even have a negative impact in some cases.[64]

Although this appears illogical at first, a closer examination of university fundraising suggests it might be quite logical for a couple of reasons. While some alumni attend games and follow the team closely, not all alumni are sport fans. In fact, when they are asked to list the most important priorities for the university, athletics ranks very low, while undergraduate program quality ranks high.[65] In other words, those who give to the university or one of its academic programs do so to improve the quality of the academic programs, not because they are happy about the performance of the football team. In fact, we would expect that those who are happy about the performance of the football team will instead donate directly to the athletic department, which is supported by prior research.[66] So, in general, it appears those focused on academics give to academics and those focused on athletics give to athletics. Although it goes against the common belief about the impact of athletics, this all makes intuitive sense.

The second manner in which athletics is expected to benefit the university financially is by attracting more students. This is often referred to as the "Flutie Factor" after former Boston College quarterback Doug Flutie. After Flutie won the Heisman Trophy, student applications to Boston College increased by 25 percent.[67] While anecdotal stories such as this are common and there is some research to support a positive relationship between athletics and student applications, many have questioned the magnitude of the impact of athletic success on tuition revenue for several reasons.[68] First, many of the examples supporting a positive impact results from examinations done immediately after great athletic success at universities that had not traditionally been successful in athletics.[69] The problem is it does not appear that these spikes in applications are sustained, so the impact may often be short-lived. In fact, at Boston College the increase related to the Flutie Factor lasted only one year and they actually experienced a dip the following year.[70] In addition, such dramatic changes in success are actually not that common in college athletics, as the status quo is more typical.

Second, an increase in applications does not necessarily have any financial impact. For example, Northwestern University had a large increase in applications following a significant improvement in their football team's success. However, Northwestern is not seeking to enroll more students, so the increase in applications did not change enrollment or the related tuition dollars. The same issue emerges when arguing the financial impact of the athletes themselves. Some may argue the athletic scholarships paid by athletic departments to universities represents a financial benefit to the university. However, if the university has a limit on enrollment and is able to reach this limit each year, then the tuition paid by athletics is simply a substitute for tuition that would have been paid by other students, so the financial impact is nonexistent.

If there is no financial benefit from increased tuition dollars, then the main benefit of an increase in applications is an improvement in the quality of the students. However, this improvement also appears to be short-lived, the magnitude of the change may be small—such as a 1.7 SAT point increase for each additional round played in the NCAA men's basketball tournament—and some of the research even suggests that there is no lasting positive impact at all. In fact, there is some evidence that while athletic success may have more of an impact on what schools students will consider, it has much less of an impact on which school they choose to attend.[71] Moreover, even if successful athletic teams have a mild positive impact on the admissions scores of students at the university, this is likely more than offset by the lower scores achieved by many of the athletes who enroll at the university.[72] Overall, when examining the impact of athletic success on student enrollment and donations, Frank concluded that it was not clear such impacts exist and if they do, they are very small.[73]

The final way in which public universities have been hypothesized to benefit from athletic success is through increased appropriations to the universities from the state. While this possibility has been discussed for many years, it has largely been ignored by researchers. Humphreys recently examined this theory and reached some interesting conclusions.[74] First, institutions with Division I-A football programs did receive larger appropriations after controlling for some institution-specific factors. However, greater athletic success (e.g., national rankings, bowl game appearances) did not lead to any increases in appropriations. This latter finding would appear to refute that theory that state legislators will give more money to institutions because they are happy with their success on the field. Still, the first finding provides at least initial support for some indirect financial benefits for the university from the athletic program. It is still not very clear why simply having a

Division I-A team would have such an impact and whether this relationship may have resulted from other factors that were not controlled for in Humphreys's study. Therefore, this remains an area worthy of additional research.

THE IMPACT OF ARMS-RACE RELATED SPENDING

While the financial benefits of athletic programs for the university may indeed be overstated in many cases, that does not mean people do not believe the benefits are there and spend accordingly. In fact, spending on athletics has grown more rapidly than spending on other areas of the university in recent years. Because spending on players is controlled by the NCAA, universities have increased spending in other ways. Whether this is part of an arms race is open to debate.[75] However, the rapid growth in spending does suggest there is at least some effort to keep up with other universities. While there are a number of areas that we could discuss, we will focus on two that are particularly expensive.

The first is athletic facilities. One of the ways that universities can attract athletes and coaches is by providing them with top-notch facilities. This includes both game facilities and practice facilities. While practice facilities rarely are expected to generate much revenue to cover their operational or construction costs, the hope is often that the new or remodeled game facilities will pay for themselves, or at least cover a lot of their costs. Determining whether this is true is often difficult for a few reasons. First, while the revenue generated by the facility generally stays with the athletic program, some of the expenses may be covered by the university.[76] For example, if the university pays for things such as maintenance and utilities, a facility may appear to be profitable when it is actually losing money. In addition, most of the facilities are not paid for upfront, so there is a debt that must be paid over time. Again, the university may pay this debt for the athletic department, which would also result in the facility appearing more profitable. This is particularly true for multiuse facilities (i.e., a facility that may house an academic department or a student affairs division).

Second, in some cases there is another entity involved in the construction of the facility. The state and/or city may also contribute resources to build the facility, which further complicates the process of determining the true cost-benefit ratio associated with the facility. Third, the methods of paying for the facility may result in hidden opportunity costs for the university. For example, if student fees are used to help pay for the facility, the university could have used this money for other purposes. In addition, if a donor makes a large contribution for the facility, the university may decrease its ability to obtain money from this individual for other future projects.

The second rapidly growing cost is employee salaries, particularly those of the coaches and athletic directors. The theory is that good coaches are critical to financial success and they are worth what they are paid. However, research suggests this may not be the case. The problem appears that many make the mistake of looking only at the total revenue generated by the team and fail to examine the marginal revenue generated by an excellent coach.[77] For example, there are many top football programs that would likely sell out every game regardless of the coach. In addition, the television contract for the football games are generally negotiated at the conference level, so the quality of the coach at a given institution may not have much impact on this revenue source either. It is easy to see that a certain amount of the revenue generated by top teams is relatively stable and signing a better coach will not have much impact.

However, this does not mean a great coach cannot have any impact on marginal revenue. For example, a great coach can allow the program to go to bowl games, the NCAA tournament, or raise ticket prices. The difficult questions to answer are how much marginal revenue is actually generated by a great coach and is this marginal revenue enough to justify the large salaries. While this has not been examined in the literature a lot, Zimbalist did estimate the marginal revenue for excellent coaches and found that it (i.e., $121,000—$172,000) was far short of justifying the large salaries. Moreover, this analysis focuses only on excellent coaches. As Zimbalist explains in his book, even coaches who are not great and appear to generate no marginal revenue still get large salaries. While there appears to be no good economic justification for this practice, it appears to result from a combination of ignoring the concept of marginal revenue and focusing instead on total revenue and of believing to be a "major player," you have to be a "major payer." In fact, the large salaries go to all coaches of the "revenue" sport teams, even if the coach is unproven.[78]

In addition, it is important to note that the head coaches of the "revenue" sports are not the only ones receiving the larger salaries. An increasing number of head coaches are also working to increase the salaries of their assistants so they are among the best paid. If the marginal revenue produced by a great coach was not enough to justify the head coach's salary, it is hard to imagine that it can justify large salaries for an entire coaching staff. In addition, these large salaries are not limited to just coaches of the "revenue" sport teams. Large salaries in the "nonrevenue" or "Olympic" sports are also becoming more common.[79] While there is potential for marginal revenue in those sports (i.e., less likely to sell out consistently regardless of the coach), it is not clear that the decisions to increase these salaries are based on sound economic reasoning either.

The last issue related to coaches' contracts that leads to problems for universities is their length. The conventional wisdom is that for coaches to be able to recruit, the players must believe the coach will be there for their entire career. This means the university must have the coach signed for a contract length of five years or more. While they may justify this length based on the notion that a long contract means the coach's job is safe, the reality is the university may still fire them after any season. However, the university must then pay the coach for the remaining portion of the contract. In other words, they pay them not to coach the team anymore. While the university may be lucky enough to hire a new coach who produces enough marginal revenue to justify his contract, they are less likely to hire someone who makes enough to justify both contracts. In fact, some universities have had to pay as many as three head coaches at once—the current coach and two coaches who were fired. When this is all taken together, the current spending patterns appear to lack good economic sense and do not appear to lead to positive economic results. In fact, recent research found that a one-dollar increase in spending in college athletics leads to a one-dollar increase in revenue. In other words, the net effect is zero.[80]

CONCLUSION

The business of college sports has seen some dramatic changes over the past several decades. For example, major investment has been made in facilities such as stadiums, arenas, practice fields, and weight rooms, just to name a few. A great deal of this growth has been financed through state/institution support, private donations, and corporate sponsorship. As we look to the future, it will be interesting to follow the facilities arms race. Will the investment in sports facilities continue? If it does, what form will it take? In 2050 will the University of Michigan be playing in a 150,000-seat stadium that has 500 hospitality suites and 5,000 club seats? Will the owners of those seats be paying $500,000 per year for access to these preferred seating opportunities? Will corporate sponsor banners be consistently placed on the players' uniforms, on the field of play, and across the stadium's facade? Will the fabled Michigan Stadium be renamed the Pepsi Stadium after the corporation agrees to give the university $500 million over the course of twenty years?

With respect to the involvement of corporations, most universities have made a concerted effort to attract corporate sponsors, while also attempting to minimize their influence on the overall administration of the institution. It will be interesting to see how this plays out in the future with respect to collegiate athletics. In order to generate more revenue, will athletic programs provide corporations with additional opportunities to associate their products with college sports? For example, the NCAA currently allows only one corporate logo on athletic uniforms. Under financial pressure, will there be a movement to loosen these restrictions? Will the 2050 Duke basketball uniform look more like a European soccer uniform with the "DUKE" logo being replaced by a corporate brand? College sports properties such as conference tournaments, bowl games, and individual games already have corporate sponsors attached to them. Additionally, coaches such as Bob Knight at Texas Tech have corporate sponsor patches on their game clothing. Perhaps the logical next step is for the corporate name to replace the team name. Instead of the Duke Blue Devils, it could be the Bank of America Duke Blue Devils, or the Duke Blue Devils presented by Bank of America. While this may seem blasphemous, if it generates needed revenue, some athletic administrators may approve of this action.

Another interesting financial area to follow in the future is the investment into women's sports. Since the passage of Title IX, college athletics programs have invested millions of dollars in developing sports opportunities for women. The results of this investment have been impressive. Women are participating in sports in large numbers and some women's sports have seen tremendous gains in popularity. We have also seen women's college sporting events such as the Women's Final Four and the College Softball World Series attract significant media attention. ESPN televises all the games in these two championship tournaments. However, as more college athletic programs become compliant with Title IX, it will be interesting to see if the investment in women's sport continues. Is there perhaps a possibility that college athletic administrators may become somewhat complacent once they are compliant with Title IX?

Another area that has received significant attention recently is the tax-exempt status of the NCAA and its members. In the fall of 2005, the U.S. House of Representatives Ways and Means Committee addressed the issue. In a letter to NCAA President Dr. Myles Brand, U.S. Representative Bill Thomas from California asked, "Why should the federal government subsidize the athletic activities of educational institutions when that subsidy is being used to help pay for escalating coaches' salaries, costly chartered travel, and state-of-the-art facilities?"[81] Mr. Thomas believes that the NCAA and its members must make a better case for how college sports contribute to the educational mission of colleges and universities. While the outcome of this congressional inquiry is in doubt, it does raise a serious question. Should the NCAA, with its annual revenues in excess of $475 million, receive tax-exempt status from the federal government?

The House Ways and Means Committee is also interested in the recent trend of some Division I-A sport conferences starting their own TV networks. For example, in 2007 the Big Ten Conference started its own for-profit all sports TV network known as the Big Ten Network. The Southeastern Conference has plans to start its own network in the future as well. While these networks will be taxed, the lucrative rights fees that the conferences receive for the airing of their games will remain tax-exempt. Some House Ways and Means Committee aides have initiated discussions with conference commissioners, such as Mike Slive of the SEC, concerning how these TV revenues are used and if they should be considered tax-exempt.[82] It will be interesting to see how this situation plays out in the future.

Since the inception of collegiate athletics, there has been one guiding theme. Those persons who compete in sports are considered amateurs. Student-athletes are permitted to receive only the value of a grant-in-aid, which generally is defined as housing, meals, tuition, and books. Despite the fact that some major universities generate tens of millions of dollars through the sports in which these athletes compete, they are not permitted to be paid like professional athletes. This system has worked for the best of collegiate sports for the better part of a century. Will this system continue to be the best model for the future? Will student-athletes in sports such as football and basketball apply pressure to collegiate sport and higher education administrators for the need for additional financial remuneration? While it is highly unlikely that college sports will be managed in a manner similar to professional sports where athletes are paid a salary, will some other form of payment occur? For example, is it possible for the grant-in-aid to include a stipend such as those received by graduate students at universities across the United States? If so, how are issues related to Title IX, worker's compensation, and health benefits managed once student-athletes begin to receive a monetary payment above the traditional value of a grant-in-aid?

The financial aspects of modern day collegiate athletics are quite complex. Colleges and universities strive to maximize revenues while maintaining some level of amateurism as well as integrity. University presidents and athletic administrators are constantly attempting to reach a delicate balance between the two.

NOTES

1. Eric Crawford, "Petrino Gets $25.5 Million Extension," *Courier Journal,* July 14, 2006, A1, A12.

2. Eric Crawford, "Major Payer and 'a Major Player,'" *Courier Journal,* July 14, 2006, C1–C2.

3. Ibid.

4. Ibid.; Robert E. Litan, Jonathan M. Orszag, and Peter R. Orszag, *The Empirical Effects of Collegiate Athletics: An Interim Report* (Indianapolis: National Collegiate Athletic Association, 2003), 22–28.

5. Ronald A. Smith, *Sports and Freedom: The Rise of Big-Time College Athletics* (New York: Oxford University Press, 1988), 18–23, 118–133; Donald Chu, *The Character of American Higher Education and Intercollegiate Sport* (Albany: State University of New York Press, 1989), 9, 17, 27, 54.

6. Chu, *Character of American Higher Education,* 31–34; Smith, *Sports and Freedom,* 78–82.

7. Chu, *Character of American Higher Education,* 31–34, 88; John R. Thelin, *Games Colleges Play: Scandal and Reform in College Athletics* (Baltimore: John Hopkins University Press, 1994), 3.

8. Chu, *Character of American Higher Education,* 25–27; Thelin, *Games Colleges Play,* 3.

9. Smith, *Sports and Freedom,* 163, 188–189.

10. Thelin, *Games Colleges Play,* 42–43.

11. Ibid., 25, 169–171.

12. Michael Smith, "NCAA Wants Schools to Square Up Accounting," *Sports Business Journal* (September 18–24, 2006).

13. U.S. Department of Education, Office of Postsecondary Education, "Equity in Athletics Disclosure," http://ope.ed.gov/athletics (accessed October 15, 2006).

14. Daniel L. Fulks, *2002–03 NCAA Revenues and Expenses of Divisions I and II Intercollegiate Athletics Program Report* (Indianapolis: National Collegiate Athletic Association, 2005); Fulks, *Revenues and Expenses of Divisions I and II Intercollegiate Athletics Programs: Financial Trends and Relationships—2001* (Indianapolis: National Collegiate Athletic Association, 2003); Fulks, *Revenues and Expenses of Intercollegiate Athletics Programs: Financial Trends and Relationships—1997* (Overland Park, Kan.: National Collegiate Athletic Association, 1998); Fulks, *Revenues and Expenses of Intercollegiate Athletics Programs: Financial Trends and Relationships—1993* (Overland Park, Kan.: National Collegiate Athletic Association, 1994); Mitchell H. Raiborn, *Revenues and Expenses of Intercollegiate Athletic Programs: Analysis of Financial Trends and Relationships, 1985–1989* (Overland Park, Kan.: National Collegiate Athletic Association, 1990); Raiborn, *Revenues and Expenses of Intercollegiate Athletic Programs: Analysis of Financial Trends and Relationships, 1981–1985* (Overland Park, Kan.: National Collegiate Athletic Association, 1986); Raiborn, *Revenues and Expenses of Intercollegiate Athletic Programs: Analysis of Financial Trends and Relationships, 1977–1981* (Overland Park, Kan.: National Collegiate Athletic Association, 1982); Raiborn, *Revenues and Expenses of Intercollegiate Athletic Programs: Analysis of Financial Trends and Relationships 1973–77* (Overland Park, Kan.: National Collegiate Athletic Association, 1978).

15. Fulks, *2002–03 NCAA,* 23, 24.

16. Ibid., 45.

17. "Pickens Sets Record with $165M Oklahoma State Gift," ESPN.com, January 10, 2006, http://sports.espn.go.com/ncaa/news/story?id=2286820 (accessed October 4, 2006).

18. 2005–06 SEC revenue distribution, http://www.secsports.com (accessed October 17, 2006).

19. Fulks, *2002–03 NCAA,* 45.

20. Manuel Perez-Rivas, "Sale of Naming Rights Hits Amateur Fields," *Washington Post,* June 18, 2000, http://www.commondreams.org/headlines/061800-02.htm (accessed October 5, 2006).

21. Bill Estep, "University Offers New Stadium Seat Program," *On Campus Online*, 29, no. 12 (January 13, 2000), http://oncampus.osu.edu/v29n12/thisissue_2.html (accessed October 10, 2006).

22. Fulks, *2002–03 NCAA*, 46.

23. "Notre Dame Extends Weis through 2015," ESPN.com, October 20, 2005, http://sports.espn.go.com/ncf/news/story?id=2207478 (accessed November 1, 2006).

24. "Pitino Can't Say 'No' to Louisville," March 28, 2001, http://espn.go.com/ncb/news/2001/0321/1159280.html/ (accessed October 1, 2006); "UofL Extends Pitino's Contract through 2010," UofL Sports, March 4, 2004, http://uoflsports.cstv.com/sports/m-baskbl/spec-rel/030404aaa.html (accessed November 13, 2006).

25. "Coaches' Salary Growth Outpacing Revenue Increases," Collegeathleticclips.com, March 29, 2005, http://www.collegeathleticsclips.com/archives/000496.html; Andrew Zimbalist, *Unpaid Professionals: Commercialism and Conflict in Big-Time College Sports* (Princeton, N.J.: Princeton University Press, 1999), 74–89.

26. Fulks, *2002–03 NCAA*, 46; Fulks, *Financial Trends and Relationships—1993*.

27. Fulks, *2002–03 NCAA*, 35.

28. Ibid., 90.

29. Ibid., 17.

30. Ibid., 30.

31. Fulks, *Financial Trends and Relationships—2001*.

32. Fulks, *2002–03 NCAA*, 23, 25; Fulks, *Financial Trends and Relationships—2001, 1997,* and *1993;* Raiborn, *Analysis of Financial Trends and Relationships, 1985–1989, 1981–1985, 1977–1981,* and *1973–1977*.

33. Zimbalist, *Unpaid Professionals,* 149–165.

34. Fulks, *2002–03 NCAA*, 25, 45.

35. Ibid., 45; Murray Sperber, *College Sports, Inc.: The Athletic Department vs. the University* (New York: Henry Holt, 1990), 82–91.

36. "The Second-Century Imperatives: Presidential Leadership—Institutional Effectiveness," http://www2.ncaa.org/portal/legislation_and_governance/committees/future_task_force/final_report.pdf (accessed November 1, 2006).

37. Fulks, *2002–03 NCAA*, 45–46.

38. Zimbalist, *Unpaid Professionals,* 152–157.

39. Ibid.

40. Litan, Orszag, and Orszag, *Empirical Effects of Collegiate Athletics,* 13–15; Zimbalist, *Unpaid Professionals,* 152–157.

41. Brian Goff, "Effects of University Athletics on the University," *Journal of Sport Management* 14 (2000): 85–104.

42. Murray Sperber, *Beer and Circus: How Big-Time College Sports Is Crippling Undergraduate Education* (New York: Henry Holt, 2000), 216–229; Rick Telander, *The Hundred Yard Lie* (New York: Simon and Schuster, 1989), 123–139.

43. Sperber, *Beer and Circus,* 222–225.

44. Thelin, *Games Colleges Play,* 19–20.

45. Morton Deutsch, "Equity, Equality, and Need: What Determines Which Value Will Be Used as the Basis of Distributive Justice?" *Journal of Social Issues* 31 (1975): 137–149.

46. Ibid.; Blair H. Sheppard, Roy J. Lewicki, and John W. Minton, *Organizational Justice: The Search for Fairness in the Work Place* (New York: Lexington, 1992).

47. Nand Hart-Nibbrig and Clement Cottingham, *The Political Economy of College Sports* (Lexington, Ky.: D. C. Heath, 1986); Sperber, *College Sports, Inc.*

48. *NCAA Division I Manual* (Indianapolis: National Collegiate Athletic Association, 2000), 121.

49. Mary A. Hums and Packianathan Chelladurai, "Distributive Justice in Intercollegiate Athletics: The Views of NCAA Coaches and Administrators," *Journal of Sport Management* 8 (1994): 200–217.

50. Daniel F. Mahony, Mary A. Hums and Harold A. Riemer, "Distributive Justice in Intercollegiate Athletics: Perceptions of Athletic Directors and Athletic Board Chairs," *Journal of Sport Management* 16 (2002): 331–357; Ian S. C. Patrick, Daniel F. Mahony, and Joseph M. Petrosko, "Distributive Justice in Intercollegiate Athletics: Perceptions of Equality, Revenue Production, and Need," *Journal of Sport Management* (in press); Daniel F. Mahony, Harold A. Riemer, James L. Breeding, and Mary A. Hums, "Organizational Justice in Sport Organizations: Perceptions of Student-Athletes and Other College Students," *Journal of Sport Management* 20 (2006): 159–188.

51. Patrick, Mahony, and Petrosko, "Perceptions of Equality, Revenue Production, and Need."

52. Daniel F. Mahony and Donna L. Pastore, "Distributive Justice: An Examination of Participation Opportunities, Revenues, and Expenses at NCAA Institutions—1973–1993," *Journal of Sport and Social Issues* 22 (1998): 127–148.

53. Ibid.

54. *Grove City v. Bell*, 465 U.S. 555 (1984).

55. Mahony and Pastore, "Distributive Justice."

56. Ibid.

57. Ibid.

58. Daniel F. Mahony, Mary A. Hums, and Harold A. Riemer, "Bases for Determining Need: Perspectives of Intercollegiate Athletic Directors and Athletic Board Chairs," *Journal of Sport Management* 19 (2005): 170–192.

59. Fulks, *2002–03 NCAA*; Fulks, *Financial Trends and Relationships—1994.*

60. Robert J. Barro, "Let's Play Monopoly," *Wall Street Journal,* August 27, 1991, A12.

61. Timothy D. DeSchriver and David K. Stotlar, "An Economic Analysis of Cartel Behavior within the NCAA," *Journal of Sport Management* 10 (1996): 388–400; Arthur A. Fleisher, Brian L. Goff and Robert D. Tollison, *The National Collegiate Athletic Association: A Study in Cartel Behavior* (Chicago: University of Chicago Press, 1992).

62. Zimbalist, *Unpaid Professionals,* 51–53.

63. Allen L. Sack and Ellen J. Staurowsky, *College Athletes for Hire: The Evolution and Legacy of the NCAA's Amateur Myth* (Westport, Conn.: Praeger, 1998), 43–50, 80–93, 99–109; Telander, *The Hundred Yard Lie,* 39–77, 81–120; 2005 Federal Graduation-Rates for NCAA Division I Schools, National Collegiate Athletic Association, http://www.ncaa.org/grad_rates/2005/d1_school_data.html (accessed September 8, 2006).

64. Goff, "Effects of University Athletics on the University," 85–104; Paul W. Grimes and George A. Chressanths, "Alumni Contributions to Academics: The Role of Intercollegiate Sports and NCAA Sanctions," *American Journal of Economics and Sociology,* 53 (1994): 27–41; Jeanne E. Budig, "Relationship among Intercollegiate Athletics,

Enrollment, and Voluntary Support for Public Higher Education," Ph.D. diss., University of Michigan, 1977; James Frey, "The Winning Team Myth," *Currents* 15, no. 1 (1985): 33–35; John F. Gaski and Michael J. Etzel, "Collegiate Athletic Success and Alumni Generosity: Dispelling the Myth," *Social Behavior and Personality* 12, no. 1 (1984): 29–38; Judy Grace, "Good Sports? Three Studies Examine Athletic Fund-Raising Programs," *Currents* 14, no. 7 (1988); Litan, Orszag, and Orszag, *Empirical Effects of Collegiate Athletics,* 6; Arnaud Marts, "College Football and College Endowment," *School and Society,* July 7, 1934; Jonathan M. Orszag and Peter R. Orszag, *The Empirical Effects of Collegiate Athletics: An Update* (Indianapolis: National Collegiate Athletic Association, 2005), 7–8; Allen L. Sack and C. Watkins, "Winning and Giving: Another Look," in *Sociology of Sport: Diverse Perspectives: 1st NASS Annual Conference Proceedings,* ed. Susan L. Greendorfer and Andrew Yiannakis (West Point, N.Y.: Leisure Press, 1981), 173–180; James L. Shulman and William G. Bowen, *The Game of Life: College Sports and Educational Values* (Princeton, N.J.: Princeton University Press, 2001), 205–226; Lee Sigelman and Samuel Bookheimer, "Is It Whether You Win or Lose? Monetary Contributions to Big-Time College Athletic Programs," *Social Science Quarterly* 64, no. 2 (1983): 347–359; Lee Sigelman and Robert Carter, "Win One for the Giver? Alumni Giving and Big-Time College Sports," *Social Science Quarterly* 60, no. 2, (1979): 284–294; Sarah E. Turner, Lauren A. Meserve, and William G. Bowen, "Winning and Giving: Football Results and Alumni Giving at Select Private Colleges and Universities," *Social Science Quarterly* 82, no. 4 (2001): 812–826.

65. Chu, *Character of American Higher Education,* 89; Shulman and Bowen, *Game of Life,* 217–219.

66. Cletus Coughlin and O. Homer Erkeson, "An Examination of Contributions to Support Intercollegiate Athletics," *Southern Economic Journal* 51 (1984): 180–195; Sigelman and Bookheimer, "Is It Whether You Win or Lose?"; Jeffrey L. Stinson and Dennis R. Howard, "Scoreboards vs. Mortarboards: Major Donor Behavior and Intercollegiate Athletics," *Sport Marketing Quarterly* 13 (2004): 73–81.

67. Sperber, *Beer and Circus,* 60–61.

68. Goff, "Effects of University Athletics on the University"; Franklin G. Mixon and Rand W. Ressler, "An Empirical Note on the Impact of College Athletics on Tuition Revenues," *Applied Economics Letters* 2 (1995): 383–387; Robert G. Murphy and Gregory A. Trandel, "The Relation Between a University's Football Record and Size of Its Applicant Pool," *Economics of Education Review* 13 (1994): 265–270.

69. Zimbalist, *Unpaid Professionals,* 167–171.

70. Jennifer Jacobson, "Success in College Sports Has Only a Tenuous Tie to More Gifts and Applicants, Report Says," *Chronicle of Higher Education,* September 17, 2004, http://chronicle.com/weekly/v51/i04/04a03502.htm.

71. Franklin G. Mixon, "Athletics versus Academics? Rejoining the Evidence from SAT Scores," *Education Economics* 3 (1995): 277–304; Robert H. Frank, "Challenging the Myth: A Review of the Links among College Athletic Success, Student Quality, and Donations," 2004, http://www.knightcommission.org/about/frank_report/; Irvin Tucker and Louis Amato, "Does Big-Time Success in Football or Basketball Affect SAT Scores?" *Economics of Education Review* 12 (1993): 177–181; Zimbalist, *Unpaid Professionals,* 169–171.

72. Shulman and Bowen, *Game of Life,* 29–58.

73. Frank, "Challenging the Myth."

74. Chu, *Character of American Higher Education,* 31–34; Brad R. Humphreys, "The Relationship Between Big-Time College Football and State Appropriations for Higher Education," *International Journal of Sport Finance* 1 (2006): 119–128.

75. Litan, Orszag, and Orszag, *Empirical Effects of Collegiate Athletics,* 2; Orszag and Orszag, *The Empirical Effects of Collegiate Athletics: An Update,* 2.

76. Zimbalist, *Unpaid Professionals,* 152–157.

77. Ibid., 74–89.

78. Ibid., 86, 225–226; Sperber, *College Sports Inc.,* 149–153; Zimbalist, *Unpaid Professionals,* 74–89.

79. Zimbalist, *Unpaid Professionals,* 74–89; "Coaches' Salary."

80. Litan, Orszag, and Orszag, *Empirical Effects of Collegiate Athletics,* 4.

81. Paul Fain, "Congressman Sends Letter Grilling NCAA on Tax-Exempt Status of College Sports," *Chronicle of Higher Education*, October 5, 2006, http://chronicle.com (accessed on November 2, 2006).

82. Brad Wolverton, "Congress Broadens an Investigation of College Sports," *Chronicle of Higher Education*, September 22, 2006, http://chronicle.com (accessed November 5, 2006).

Ten

Sport in the Digital Domain

Paul Swangard

Any attempt to accurately capture the current and future economic opportunities in sport's digital domain must first come with a disclaimer: the opportunities have already changed since this sentence was written. Just consider three of the most recent examples of emerging technologies and their meteoric rise to economic prosperity: in 2005 the News Corporation purchased the social networking Web site MySpace for $327 million; in 2006 Google purchased YouTube, a Web site for user-generated video content for $1.65 billion; and in 2007 satellite broadcaster EchoStar purchased Slingbox, a company that developed a platform for place-shifted video content for $380 million. In all three cases, few people could have predicted the incredible growth curve and subsequent financial windfalls for the company and its founders. Yet, for the purposes of this chapter, all three do represent success stories in the digital space that are all at least due in part to a longstanding symbiotic relationship between sport and the growth of new forms of media and technology.

This chapter provides the reader some overall context to the role of sport in the digital domain with particular focus on how sport properties have leveraged these new opportunities to fuel economic growth while attempting to enhance fan loyalty and fan satisfaction. Showcasing efforts by Major League Baseball (MLB) and the National Hockey League (NHL) provide both a taste of the current success and future possibilities for sport organizations in the digital space. The chapter concludes with a brief summary of emerging technologies that currently sit in the incubator stage of development but might offer a glimpse of what the next generation of sport "killer applications" might look like.

SPORT AS AN ADOPTION DRIVER

Perhaps no two industries have been as mutually dependent on the other's success as sport and the media. In his 1989 essay on the subject, Robert W. McChesney noted that "virtually every surge in the popularity of sport has been accompanied by a dramatic increase in the coverage provided sport by the media. Furthermore, each surge in the coverage of sport has taken place during a period in which the mass media have sharply increased their penetration into the nooks and crannies of American social life."[1] For newspapers, radio, and eventually television, sport became a key driver of demand and adoption of these new channels of content distribution. In return, sport benefited from lucrative rights fee arrangements that, for properties like the National Football League (NFL), became their single biggest source of revenue. Where there were no rights fees involved, sport still enjoyed the benefits of free media coverage that helped to engrain it into the fabric of American culture.

The relationship appears unchanged despite the rapid proliferation of new media in the last twenty years of the twentieth century and the early years of the twenty-first century. As television evolved from a three-channel broadcast network model to an infant cable model, ESPN's arrival in 1979 ushered in an era of both national and regional sports cable networks (Versus, CSTV, Fox Sports Net, Comcast SportsNet) and in recent years individual sports cable networks (NBA TV, NFL Network, Golf Channel, Tennis Channel). The increase in airtime provided both established and fledgling sports properties access to viewers and potential fans and generated significant revenues for all involved where subscriber or viewership reached viable levels.

Even as rights fees have skyrocketed for some of the marquee properties, new entrants to the media landscape continue to invest in sport, often using the content acquisition as a loss-leader strategy. After an unsuccessful bid for the Monday Night Football package in 1987, the Fox Broadcasting Company returned to the NFL and outbid CBS for the rights to air National Football Conference (NFC) games beginning in the 1994 season. In conjunction with acquisitions of key local television groups giving the network a legitimate national footprint, Fox leveraged paying a significant premium for the NFL rights ($395 million per year vs. $290 million per year on CBS) by aggressively cross-promoting its non-NFL programming on football broadcasts and building a viable network-sized audience. In 2005, having spent less than twenty years on the air and competing against the long-established established networks (CBS, NBC and ABC), Fox won its first-ever Nielsen Ratings period bolstered in large part by its exclusive coverage of Super Bowl XXXIX.[2]

As television transitioned to its own digital age, DirecTV (ironically now owned by News Corporation, the parent company of the Fox Broadcasting Company), followed a similar strategy to build a subscriber base for its digital broadcast satellite service (DBS). Paying $150 million a year annually beginning in the late 1990s, DirecTV was given exclusive rights to show out-of-market NFL broadcasts on its fledgling platform, providing a key distinct product from cable and other DBS competitors. When the contract was renewed for $400 million per year in 2004, there were estimates that every dollar DirecTV generated from selling pay-per-view subscriptions to the service (called the Sunday Ticket package) went to pay the NFL contract. The return on investment came from the increased subscriber base that paid for non-NFL programming the other seven months of the year. Any questions about DirecTV's satisfaction with the partnership were answered when they extended the deal again in 2006 for $700 million per year through the 2010 NFL season.[3]

SPORT ENTERS THE INTERNET AGE

Much of television's growth, expansion, and evolution would have happened with or without the Internet, yet the arrival of the digital backbone signaled a fundamental shift in both the ways consumers (in this case fans) accessed content and communicated as well as the ways leagues, teams, events, athletes, and brands interacted with their markets. During its initial growth and development, the World Wide Web was bolstered by strong sports brands embracing the space, including ESPN, which launched its first Web site in 1995, as well as upstart brands that recognized they could link consumers to desirable content efficiently and cost-effectively.

AudioNet (later known as Broadcast.com) provided one of the best early Web success stories. Founded in 1992 by Chris Jaeb, but whose most well-known employee was entrepreneur Mark Cuban, AudioNet provided Internet users the chance to listen to live radio programming over their low-bandwidth connections. Featuring a myriad of sport-related offerings including both college sports, the NFL and the National Basketball Association (NBA), AudioNet went from a dot-com startup to an initial public offering darling (setting an at-the-time one-day record 250 percent increase from its opening price) to eventually being acquired in a $5-billion dollar stock deal with Yahoo![4]

Unfortunately, for every AudioNet success story there were dozens of failed digital efforts tied to the promise of marrying technology and sports. Dot-com darlings included Quokka.com (live-event streaming), MVP.com (sport product and apparel e-commerce) and Athlete Direct (athlete home pages) that all failed to establish a viable and sustainable business model despite millions in venture capital and the buzz that existed in the marketplace at the time. In hindsight, much of the failure can either be attributed to an overheated investment environment or just good ideas and poor execution.

But the evolution of the Internet had a significant role to play in stagnating much of the growth of sport-related businesses. On one hand, sport properties grappled with control issues over their content, pointing to the growth of Napster, Kazaa, and other peer-to-peer file-sharing services that were enabling unprecedented levels of copyright infringement. Perhaps the more important bottleneck was, literally, the bottleneck of getting affordable high-speed Internet access into homes. As Figure 10.1 shows, sport organizations historically got rich selling their content rights to broadcasters who enjoyed wide distribution. However, sport organizations found themselves waiting for a bigger pipeline to the desktop early in the digital era. While Internet usage was surging, a lagging broadband penetration rate meant the on-line experience was a bit static. While consumers clamored for content, many found early Web sites totally devoid of high-quality multimedia. It was the promise of that broadband connectivity, and a growing body of research that showed broadband homes consumed more media than dialup homes, that fueled optimism about the future of the on-line sports world.

FIGURE 10.1
Growth in U.S. Broadband Subscribers

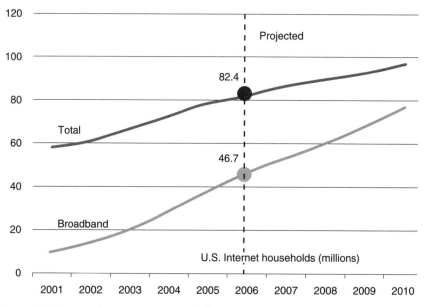

Sources: FCC, PricewaterhouseCoopers LLC, Wilkofsky Gruen Associates.

By 2003 the dot-com bust had cleared away and the survivors appeared to have more realistic expectations about the growth and evolution of the Web, given its reliance on faster connection speeds to offer consumers more compelling on-line experiences. ESPN.com, a clear winner in the on-line sport world having consistently ranked at or near the top of most Web traffic reports since its inception, provided mainstream sport audiences their first real taste of the broadband promise. ESPN Motion, launched in February of 2003, pushed video clips to the desktop using the PC's idle connectivity to the Internet. Near-television quality content could be downloaded over a period of the computer's inactivity (overnight), allowing the fan to enjoy better content regardless of the speed of their Internet connection. By mid-2003, 1.6 million users had installed the service and about half of them were watching content daily. Along with proving there was clear demand for richer multimedia sport content on the Web, ESPN Motion also proved there was a viable business model with brands like Gatorade and Lexus stepping up to pay in some cases twenty-five dollars per thousand people who watched their commercials embedded into the video clips.[5] That cost per minute (CPM) rate was in line with what brands were paying for spot advertising on network television and well above industry averages for standard banner and Web advertising which had fallen to CPM rates of about one dollar after enjoying television-like pricing in the late 1990s.

BASEBALL HITS A HOME RUN

During a time when some traditional broadcasters like ESPN were quick to "get" the Internet and build a viable new distribution channel for their sports content, perhaps the most intriguing storylines emerged when sport organizations themselves began to consider their own emerging digital opportunities. Most leagues, teams, and even athletes were quick to establish a presence on the Web during the 1990s; all suffered like everyone else with the narrowband connection speeds and limited content. But what existed then held true even after the dot-com bust—the Internet provided a vehicle through which the sport brands could communicate and transact directly with their fans. In this newly wired world, sport organizations didn't necessarily need a distributor to get content out to their fan bases.

Based on this vision, the leadership of MLB set out to design a structure for how the sport would embrace the digital age. In the 1990s owners were given the autonomy to go out and strike their own Internet deals just as they've traditionally done with their local media rights. It mimicked a proven strategy, but also perpetuated the inequities built into baseball's economic model. Larger markets would be clear winners by aggregating larger audiences for potential partners and generating larger revenue streams. If the on-line world proved to have enormous upside, the structure would have made the Yankees and Red Sox richer and the Royals and Expos poorer.

But in 2000, in the wake of the dot-com collapse, MLB commissioner Bud Selig and team owners revisited the largely on-your-own structure of its digital strategy. Convinced that there were both efficiencies and opportunities to combine efforts, owners agreed to combine all existing Internet operations under one roof. The creation of Major League Baseball Advanced Media (MLBAM) would be funded through annual $1-million investments by individual teams over four years; in return, the teams would share equally in the profits. It was no different than when the NFL owners in 1960 agreed to share equally in the sale of their collective television rights. MLB owners would hope running the same play four decades later in a digital world would yield the same benefits.

It perhaps made more sense for baseball, than any other major professional sport, to centralize its efforts since the Internet provided a way to push more content through the distribution system. With 162 games played by each team plus spring training and the playoffs, baseball boasted the most content, much of which was never seen outside of its local market. The Internet removed those regional barriers and could conceivably provide every baseball fan who had a browser with almost limitless access to the content they wanted, when they wanted it, and how they wanted it.

This evolution of delivering sports content opened up whole new way for fans to consume their favorite sports. Targeting a largely younger, more tech-savvy fan who grew up on ESPN SportsCenter highlight shows, MLB was quick to recognize simply offering games on the Web would ignore changing consumption habits. As *Wired* magazine put it in a 2007 cover story, there was an emerging "snack culture" seeking tastes of content rather than meals.[6] Why buy the CD when I can just buy the song? And in the sport context, why watch or listen to the entire game if I only want the good stuff? Digital video recorders and digital music players all rose to success seeking the "snackers" and MLBAM would be a trendsetting player in the sport category.

The early MLBAM offerings targeted two core consumer segments: displaced fans seeking access to live radio broadcasts of their favorite team and the baseball fanatic who wanted to tap any game on any night plus gain access to exclusive content from the MLB archives. The offerings included:

- Gameday audio—Fans could listen live to every broadcast of an MLB game.
- Game video—Fans could watch archived broadcasts of every MLB game.

- Condensed games—The first of MLBAM's snack services, games were condensed into twenty-minute versions featuring only those plays that led to a hit, run, or out.

- Highlights direct/custom cuts—Fans are empowered to select longer highlight reels from the season or create customized reels that could be accessed on demand.

Layered on the foundation of an MLB Web presence similar to what other pro sport leagues were offering, the multimedia tier added a subscription-based service to the package and gave MLBAM an early success story; 125,000 fans paid either monthly or yearly subscriptions for the service in year one, accounting for the largest portion of MLBAM's $36-million 2001 revenues.[7] Tracking the growth of broadband penetration, MLB began offering limited live video in 2002 and saw the subscriber base grow to 500,000. When all games were offered live in the 2004 season MLB saw its subscriber base top one million with revenues surging to an estimated $265 million.[8]

IT'S NOT ALL ABOUT MEDIA

The success of MLBAM's content platform certainly validated the model, but its recent growth and prospects for future growth seem tied to other uses of the digital domain. Often lost in the discussion of the digital opportunity is how other standard sport consumer transactions were also made more lucrative by the Web. The year 2005 marked two key service additions to MLBAM. First, the site enhanced its e-commerce offerings for licensed merchandise in response to growing consumer acceptance of on-line purchases. Adding to the standard array of clothing and logoed items, the league also launched an auction site featuring exclusive game-worn and signature items through an eBay-like service to a known community of baseball enthusiasts. In essence, MLBAM was taking validated Web usage models and simply folding them into the existing enterprise. MLBAM reportedly generated $25 million from the sales and auctions of licensed merchandise and collectibles in 2005.[9]

The more significant deal leveraged MLB's inventory advantage over other professional sports leagues. This time, instead of media inventory it was ticket inventory. The acquisition of Tickets.com gave MLB the backend system to sell tickets for all teams to the growing MLB.com audience. After witnessing on-line ticket sales grow from 4.4 million in 2003 to 11.4 million in 2004, MLBAM's market entry was perfectly timed to meet consumer demand and provided a new level of convenience to potential ticket buyers.[10] MLBAM eventually expand the ticket-sales engine into the minor leagues. Recent years have brought added features including virtual ticketing on mobile phones as well as a partnership with StubHub to capture a lucrative share of the on-line secondary ticket market while providing season-ticket holders a way to fill unneeded ticket inventory. Many have wondered how in the midst of so many scandals MLB has been able to enjoy record attendance levels. MLBAM's ticketing engine might just be the reason there have been more butts in seats than ever before.

Fast-forward to 2007, and MLBAM is considered the industry standard for taking full advantage of the digital domain. Once considered an initial public-offering candidate and valued at close to $2 billion, the operation has remained private and has returned all of the initial investments made by the teams.[11] With annual revenue now exceeding $450 million per year, MLBAM has also diversified its interests.[12] With unique expertise in video streaming, it has assisted nonbaseball clients, including the U.S. Figure Skating Association and CBS with its first foray into streaming NCAA Basketball Tournament Games on-line.[13] At the same time, they continue to ride the technology adoption curve. In 2008 they will double the video quality of live games on MLB.tv and the Extra Innings out-of-market television package will move exclusively to satellite. Those cable subscribers missing their baseball will only be one click away from the content with MLBAM standing to benefit by aggregating more of their fans in a baseball controlled on-line world.

WHERE THE PUCK IS GOING

Major League Baseball's digital success has been driven largely by adopting technologies that have moved past the lead-adopter stage of the development curve and were heading for Main Street. While MLBAM demonstrates that baseball is open to embracing technology, it hasn't exactly been on the leading edge of new innovation. That's where hockey comes in.

Once asked by a reporter what made him a great hockey player, Hall of Fame legend Wayne Gretzky responded, "I skate to where the puck is going, not to where it is." Those who follow the sport understand the idea of anticipating how and where the play would develop but one could argue "The Great One" might have also been a visionary in helping the National Hockey League understand how it might approach the emerging digital era.

The National Hockey League might provide the most intriguing case, as it is the only one of the major four U.S. professional sports leagues that has had significant struggles on television. Television ratings for the NHL have been a fraction of its peers and regular season games have routinely been outwatched by lesser-known sports, including professional bowling and

TABLE 10.1
NHL Regular Season Ratings

Year	Network	ESPN/Versus	ESPN2
05/06	1.0	0.2[a]	
04/05		No season due to lockout	
03/04	1.1	0.47	0.24
02/03	1.1	0.46	0.23
01/02	1.4	0.49	0.23
00/01	1.1	0.59	0.25
99/00	1.3	0.62	0.29
98/99	1.4	0.59	0.32
97/98	1.4	0.67	0.38

[a]Versus became the cable partner of the NHL in 05/06, replacing ESPN/ESPN2.

Note: Cable ratings are coverage-area figures.

Source: Nielsen Media Research.

figure skating (see Table 10.1). In perhaps its lowest point in television history, the NHL 2007 All-Star Game lost a ratings battle with reruns of *The Andy Griffith Show*, which wrapped up production in 1968, the same season the league expanded from its original six to 12 teams.[14]

While television remains a huge economic engine for sport, it won't have to be for the NHL. After a nasty labor dispute that canceled the entire 2004/05 season, the league reached an agreement with the players' union that better tied player salaries to league revenue. Whether or not the league gets millions in television dollars, the players now receive 54 percent of league revenues for their compensation. The agreement gave the league some flexibility in developing new initiatives, particularly in areas like digital, where the investments did not require compensating the players until there was a demonstrable return on the investment. It also meant that, while many of the competitive sport league brands were trying to embrace the opportunity of the digital space without angering their traditional broadcast partners, the NHL was in a great position to progressively seek out new ways to reach and engage their current and potential fan base. For the most part, traditional broadcasters would pay little attention.

The NHL's existing fan demographics also enhance its digital strategy. Since the early days of the Internet, the league has had a tech-savvy consumer base and an ESPN poll suggested that among those who use a personal computer to get sports information, hockey fans are most likely to turn to the Web.[15] Just as Gretzky had predicted, NHL fans were way ahead of their fellow sport fans in embracing the on-line world. It would be a key component both during and after the lockout. The league used its

Web presence to communicate directly with fans trying to gain their bargaining position with the players' union. And in the wake the of the lost lockout season, the league aggressively pushed on-line audio and video content, including the first live free streaming of games through Comcast.net. Though television ratings remained relatively stagnant, the NHL reported increases in attendance and Web traffic in the post-lockout year and achieved revenues of $2.1 billion, which were in line with pre-lockout revenue levels.[16] Not bad for a league that had shut its doors for a full year, potentially alienating much of its fan base.

Having recaptured much of its core consumers, the league has now set out on an ambitious plan to stake a leadership position in next-generation digital distribution channels. A review of agreements signed in 2007 send a clear message to other sport organizations that the digital opportunities continue to expand, and given the ever-accelerating speed of consumer adoption, managers must be ready to embrace these innovations as they will forever change the way fans consume sport.

NHL Digital Media Agreements Signed in 2007

Amazon.com Unbox: In conjunction with the start of the 2007 playoff season, the NHL announced a deal with Amazon.com to sell downloads of regular-season and playoff games as well as classic games from the league archives. The services provide the league a way to monetize decades of video assets while giving consumers the choice of what they want to watch.

Exponentia PlayAction: An effort to capitalize on the growing revenue pie presented by wireless services, the league joined forces with Exponentia to offer mobile gaming during the 2007 Stanley Cup Playoffs.

Joost: A content-distribution system developed by the founders of the popular Kazaa file-sharing program and Internet telephony service Skype, Joost offers users a "Telewebbing" experience by marrying video content with other interactive Web 2.0 features like instant messaging, message boards, and news feeds.

MySpace: Part of the growing genre of user-generated content and social networking, MySpace joined forces with the league to provide content to users of the on-line community either through an NHL branded profile or through embedded content that MySpace users could place on their own page. In this case, the league was empowering its fans to be brand ambassadors in a modern twist to ways in which fans could demonstrate their team or league allegiance.

SlingMedia Clip+Sling: Embracing a device that some sport organizations considered illegal, the league teamed up with the makers of the Slingbox to give users the power to record and share broadcast NHL content. Created by a San Francisco Giants fan who traveled frequently and wanted to access games on his laptop, the Slingbox allows users to access and control their home-video sources (TV, DVR, satellite, digital cable, and so on) remotely. With Clip+Sling, NHL fans can choose portions of broadcasts to share on a Web-based portal.

XM Radio: The NHL was no stranger to satellite radio having already been on both XM and rival Sirius™ for several years. The exclusive partnership in 2007 ($100 million over ten years) includes access to live out-of-market audio broadcasts but also pushed the league into other nongame programming, including having a dedicated NHL channel that features the first weekly show cohosted by a major pro sports league commissioner.

NeuLion: The league's new video-distribution partner provides the backbone for a wide array of video programming, including the on-line version of the out-of-market Center Ice package, team-generated content, and a customizable portal, giving fans the ability to organize and share content globally.

Gydget: Like the deal with MySpace, the league's partnership with Gydget is all about turning existing fans into brand ambassadors. Available for use on almost any social networking blog or Web site, Gydget's widgets give the league a way to virally expose consumers to hockey content through key influencers by pushing updated hockey content to all sites that embed the service.

These deals represent seven months of announcements covering digital usage models ranging from video streaming to social networking. It might appear too aggressive to some, but reinforces the reality, as well as the opportunity, that the digital world represents. In one early validation of the NHL's success, the Vancouver Canucks solicited user-generated fan videos to post on their website as part of their "Ultimate Canucks" promotion. The content (showcasing fan avidity for the team) generated an incremental one million page views on the Canucks.com website. Along with generating increases in Web-based ad revenue for the team, team president Chris Zimmerman noted the initiative helped engage fans who might never see the team play live, creating wonderful new options to build and retain a fan base in a virtual world.

WHERE DO WE GO FROM HERE?

In reviewing a snapshot of deals across a broad spectrum of properties, it is clear that MLB and the NHL are certainly not alone in the digital space (see Table 10.2). For each property there are a unique set of opportunities and challenges. For the NFL, driven to such a large degree by national

TABLE 10.2
New Media Rights Deals

	NFL	MLB	NBA	NHL	NASCAR	NCAA	OLYMPICS
MOBILE Video (Live Games)	ESPN *Monday Night Football* starting in 2006	MobiTV, three-year deal through 2007; ESPN (as part of network feed)	None	None	None	Rights held by CBS, NCAA	N/A
Video (Highlights)	Sprint, $600-million, five-year deal through 2009	Cingular, Sprint via MobiTV, three-year deal through 2007	Nokia	Airborne Entertainment	Turner distributes race previews and weekly reviews to Cingular Wireless	Rights held by CBS, NCAA	N/A
Audio (Live Games)	Sprint, highlights only	Cingular, Sprint via MobiTV, three-year deal through 2007	N/A	In negotiation	Turner distributes with partner Digital Orchid to multiple carriers	Rights held by CBS, NCAA	N/A
Data	Sprint NFL Fantasy, screensavers and ringtones	Multiple carriers	T-Mobile, Nokia, THQ	Airborne Entertainment	Turner and partner Digital Orchid distribute "NASCAR.com To Go" to major carriers	Rights held by CBS, NCAA	N/A
Games	EA Mobile, THQ	EA Mobile, THQ	EA Mobile, THQ	Amiga, EA Mobile, THQ, Global, TIRA	N/A	Digital Chocolate (men's basketball) Cingular (football)	

	NFL	MLB	NBA	NHL	NASCAR	NCAA	Olympics
INTERNET Web (Official Web site)	In-House	MLB Advanced Media, which controls all MLB interactive rights	In-House	In-House	Turner Interactive, extension signed in July 2006 through 2008; NASCAR has options through 2010	SportsLine.com (NCAAsports.com) through 2013	NBC Universal, NBCOlympics.com
Streaming Video (Games)	None	ESPN markets MLB.TV as part of an eight-year, $240-million deal	No Live Games	Select games on Comcast.net	None	N/A	N/A
Streaming Video (Highlights)	In-House	AOL and MSN, $49 million combined for live games and highlights. Comcast, Charter Communications, Cablevision	NBA.com, ESPN.com, AOL	Comcast, other deals being finalized	Turner Sports Interactive NASCAR.com Trackpass	SportsLine.com (NCAA sports.com)	NBC offered limited downloads in 2006
Streaming Audio	NFL.com Field Pass, $9.95 per month during season	MLB.com Gameday Audio, $7.95 per month	NBA Audio League Pass on NBA.com, $19.95 per month	NHL.com	Turner Sports Interactive NASCAR.com Trackpass	Individual schools can provide with NCAA approval	N/A

(*Continued*)

TABLE 10.2
(Continued)

	NFL	MLB	NBA	NHL	NASCAR	NCAA	OLYMPICS
OTHER Video Games	EA, $300-million, five-year deal through 2009; children's product with Atari through Humongous	Take-Two Interactive, beginning in 2006; platforms allowed to make their own games	EA, Take-Two Interactive, Midway, Sony, Atari	EA, Take-Two Interactive, Sony	EA through 2009	Collegiate Licensing Company sublicense to EA, 2K Sports	International Sports Multimedia
Fantasy	Licensees, with rights granted through Players Inc.	17 licensees, most have only right to carry MLB.com games. ESPN.com, Pro-trade.com, Yahoo! and SportsLine.com have additional licenses	NBA.com, plus licenses ESPN, AOL, Yahoo!, Sporting News, SportsLine.com	League, NHLPA has 10 licensees	Turner Sports Interactive	N/A	NBCOlympics.com
Real-Time Data	Licensed to Stats LLC, Sportsticker, all broadcasters		NBA.com, ESPN.com through 2007–2008, Yahoo!, AOL, Sportsticker	Stats LLC	NASCAR.com Trackpass and Sportsvision	SportsLine.com	NBC Universal-NBCOlympics.com

Source: Sports Business Journal (2006).

television contracts, there is still no way for fans to watch games on-line. In contrast, the Olympic Games will shepherd in a new era in 2008 when NBC will broadcast 3,600 hours of online coverage, including 2,200 hours of live streaming footage, giving consumers unprecedented access to events that would otherwise be ignored given the limitations of traditional broadcast media.[17]

There have also been success stories that reinforce the idea that technology must ultimately enhance the fan experience. Sport Vision and Princeton Video Image were early innovators in virtual signage technology, making the yellow first-down line a must have on any television football broadcast. For NASCAR, the introduction of TrackPass and PitCommand showcased the ability to repackage existing information for the Web. Taking telemetry data that had always been transmitted from individual race cars to the pit area, NASCAR now offers fans the chance to view the same information real-time on an on-line digital dashboard. Users can choose to follow a customizable set of drivers while monitoring their car diagnostics. The service reportedly had 300,000 subscribers in 2006 paying $9.99 per month or $64.95 a year.[18]

Table 10.2 also provides a basic framework for how to view the digital rights world beyond television and radio. While both television and radio have their own digital dynamics, the most exciting innovations are happening in mobile, on-line, and other products like video games and fantasy leagues that are changing the way fans interact with sport.

Mobile phone opportunities in the United States have been hampered by the same broadband bottleneck that existed on-line. Most phone users subscribe to services that would have difficulty delivering a rich digital content experience. Success so far has been through data services like score updates, and downloads like ringtones, games, and screensavers. Only recently have wireless providers begun rolling out third-generation network infrastructures. 3G brings broadband connectivity to the masses and is expected to scale to more than 500 million users globally by 2008 (see Figure 10.2). The arrival of these high-speed services will mark yet another opportunity for sport organizations to help these carriers deliver compelling and desirable content to drive adoption.

Branded websites, e-commerce, and audio/video streaming have matured to a point where the Internet sector delivers good economic value. Still to be determined is how Web 2.0 services like social networking will produce financial returns. The next-generation Web serves more as a tool to connect to fans and allow them to champion (or, some would say, potentially damage) the brand. Early examples, though, do show promise. Nike might expect to pay $200,000 to produce a television commercial and another $20

FIGURE 10.2
Worldwide 3G Users (In Millions)

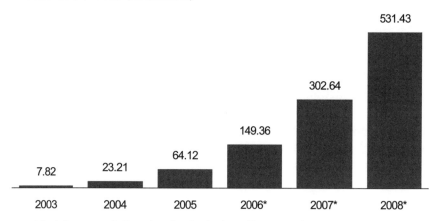

Note: Third-Generations (3G) is a broadband technology offering a standard set of high-speed services to mobile computer and phone users no matter where they are located in the world.
Source: Adapted from *Street and Smith's Sports Business Journal 2007 Resource Guide and Factbook.*

million to place it in traditional broadcast rotation. As part of its new media strategy they have created long-form viral videos and uploaded them directly to YouTube for free. Brand loyal fans generate the buzz and link to the video on-line, offering us a glimpse at the organic way sport marketing might be successful in the future.

Video games have been around for several decades but have also reached a point where the category has become both a key source of revenue for the properties and a key fan-development tool. In yet another example of the role of sports in technology and media adoption, EA Sports' Madden National Football League game was the top-selling game of 2006, grossing more than $100 million in its first week of sales.[19] For its part the league receives $60 million per year for use of its trademarks and venues in the game although it comes nowhere near the $700 million Fox Broadcasting Company currently pays for the live product. For properties seeking a larger share of sport marketplace, video games have provided a new vehicle to expose potential fans to the sport. New video-game titles featuring Arena Football and Bass Fishing are banking on converting a game player into a game watcher. A sport without a video game seems symbolically out of touch with the next generation of fans.

With so many ways in which in which to consume sport and more of it, sports properties also found a great incentive tool in fantasy gaming. A pre-Internet activity that was connected largely to baseball, fantasy league fans draft their own team of players and compete against other fans based on statistical achievements. Unlike following a single favorite team, a fantasy player might need to follow several games on a given day or might be compelled to watch a losing team because it could affect the outcome of his fantasy competition. Building a fantasy fan base was a perfect strategy to develop a market for multiplatform and comprehensive content services. An engaged fantasy fan would want access to all the games, on any device, home or away.

The Fantasy Sports Trade Association (FSTA) released a study in 2007 that reveled 19.4 million people are actively playing fantasy sports games in the United States and Canada with more than 34 million people having at least played a fantasy sports game.[20] The same study revealed two million of those active players are teenagers who tend to be more comfortable with new technology and new devices than their elder peers. It would suggest that as the fantasy sector grows, demand for sport content including customizable highlights, real-time audio, video, and statistics will grow with it.

CONCLUSION

In his landmark 1995 book *Being Digital*, MIT Media Lab's Nicholas Negroponte framed the digital transition as a transition from atoms to bits. "World trade has traditionally consisted of exchanging atoms," he said. In the sport context, fan purchased paper tickets to sit in a physical seat to watch a live game. Television and radio, leveraging early analog technologies, were able to extend the experience outside the venue, but being digital wasn't about extending a traditional broadcast-to-the-masses model. Added Negroponte, "Mass media will be redefined by systems for transmitting and receiving personalized information and entertainment."[21]

What has emerged is certainly a validation of Negroponte's vision. The digital age for sport is about putting control in the hands of the fans, giving them full access and letting them choose how to connect, consume, and communicate with sport. The traditional experiences of attending a game live or watching it or listening to it from start to finish are now just among a range of options. For MLB, success has come from adding convenience and connectivity to fans with ever-dwindling discretionary time but it is still all about driving people back to the ballpark. For the NHL, the strategy has more to do with fan development seeking the ways in which technology can help overcome the league's limited exposure on television.

In summary, the power of the digital opportunity for sport organizations is to put its best content "always within an arm's length of desire," a mantra coined successfully by Coca-Cola in building its distribution infrastructure in the twentieth century. With expansion of digital technologies across traditional mediums like television and radio, as well as new media platforms like wireless, the Internet, and video gaming, sport enjoys the historical success of helping to drive adoption of these platforms. In a world where content is king, sport has a lucrative seat at the throne.

NOTES

1. Robert W. McChesney, "Media Made Sport: A History of Sports Coverage in the United States," in *Media, Sports, and Society* (Thousand Oaks, CA: Sage Publications, 1989), 49.

2. R. Kissell, "Fox, Idol Find Sweeps Groove," *Variety,* March 1, 2005, http://www.variety.com/article/VR1117918745.html?cs=1&s=h&p=0.

3. S. Donohue and M. Reynolds, "Ticket Too High, Cable Punts on Pricey NFL Slate," *Multichannel News,* November 15, 2004, http://www.multichannel.com/article/CA480250.html.

4. S. Junnarkar, "Broadcast.com's Bang-up IPO," News.com, June 17, 1998, http://www.news.com/Broadcast.coms-bang-up-IPO/2100-1001_3-213462.html; S. Junnarkar, "Yahoo! Completes Broadcast.com Acquisition," News.com, July 20, 1999, http://www.news.com/2100-1023_3-228762.html

5. S. Olsen, "Disney to "Push" ABC Over the Net," News.com, June 12, 2003, http://www.news.com/2100-1025_3-1016486.html?tag=cd_mh.

6. "Snack Attack," *Wired Magazine,* March 2007, 124–135.

7. N. Mitsis, "Major League Baseball: Profiting Beyond the Ballpark with Satellite," *Satellite Today,* March 1, 2005, http://www.satellitetoday.com/sbs/casestudy/5328.html.

8. S. Levingston, "Online Overtime," *Washington Post,* January 29, 2006, F1, http://www.washingtonpost.com/wp-dyn/content/article/2006/01/28/AR2006012800143.html.

9. M. Brown, "MLBAM: The Stealthy Money Machine," *The Hardball Times,* December 5, 2005, http://www.hardballtimes.com/main/article/mlbam-the-stealthy-money-machine.

10. Mitsis, "Major League Baseball."

11. Brown, "MLBAM."

12. E. Fisher, "Payoff Time for MLBAM Investment," *Sports Business Journal* (November 19, 2007): 6.

13. E. Fisher, "Score Another for MLBAM," *Sports Business Journal* (February 19, 2007): 15, 18.

14. M. Hiestand, "It's All Super Bowl All Week Long on Sports Networks," *USA Today,* January 28, 2007, http://www.usatoday.com/sports/columnist/hiestand-tv/2007-01-28-hiestand-weekend_x.htm.

15. M. Hiestand, "NHL Tries to Lure Fans to Watch Playoffs," *USA Today,* April 10, 2001, http://www.usatoday.com/sports/hockey/cup01/bonus/hiestand.htm.

16. "NHL Agents Get Good News on Revenues," TSN.ca, May 31, 2006, http://tsn.ca/nhl/news_story/?ID=167508&hubname=nhl.

17. H. Sanders, "Olympic Dream$," *New York Post,* November 14, 2007, http://www.nypost.com/seven/11142007/business/olympic_dream_738145.htm.

18. C. Mayberry, "Gearheads in All Their Glory," *Hollywood Reporter*, August 29, 2006,   http://www.hollywoodreporter.com/hr/search/article_display.jsp?vnu_content_id =1003053677.

19. M. Wong, "Madden Video Game Posts Record Sales," Associated Press, September 1, 2006.

20. Press release, August 2007, http://www.fsta.org.

21. N. Negroponte, *Being Digital* (New York: Random House, 1996), 4, 6.

About the Editors and Contributors

Brad R. Humphreys is the Chair in the Economics of Gaming and an associate professor in the Department of Economics at the University of Alberta in Edmonton, Alberta, Canada. He holds a Ph.D. in economics from the Johns Hopkins University. He was previously an associate professor at the University of Illinois at Urbana-Champaign and the University of Maryland, Baltimore County. His research on the economic impact of professional sports, the economic determinants of participation in physical activity, and competitive balance in sports leagues has been published in scholarly journals, including the *Journal of Urban Economics,* the *Journal of Policy Analysis and Management*, the *Journal of Economic Behavior and Organization*, the *Journal of Sports Economics*, and *Contemporary Economic Policy*. His research has been featured in numerous media outlets, including *Sports Illustrated*, the *Wall Street Journal*, and *USA Today*. In 2007 he testified before the U.S. Congress on the financing and economic impact of professional sports facilities.

Dennis R. Howard is the Philip H. Knight Professor of Business at the Lundquist College of Business, University of Oregon. He joined the Lundquist College in 1997 after serving six years as the director of the Graduate Program in Sport Management at Ohio State University. He has published numerous articles on the marketing, financing, and management of sports in such journals as the *Journal of Sport Management*, *Marketing Management*, and *Sport Marketing Quarterly*, and is coauthor of the textbook *Financing Sport*. He is the founder and editor of the *International Journal of Sport Finance*.

Adam Antoniewicz is the director of marketing partnerships for NBA China. Based in Shanghai, China, he currently helps NBA partners, including Coca-Cola, Nike, Electronic Arts, and McDonald's, to leverage their association with the NBA. He first came to China in 1998. Since then, he has consulted to major multinationals, including Nike, NFL, the U.S. Olympic Committee, Nokia, ESPN, and Shui On Properties. He has an MBA from the University of Oregon's Warsaw Sports Marketing Center, where he was the valedictorian of his class. He has been featured in articles in *USA Today*, *Business Week*, and the *San Francisco Chronicle*, as well as being a key speaker at the Harvard China Review in March 2006. However, one of his most gratifying experiences came when his research team was featured in a cover story for *ESPN* magazine (January 2003) for creating a "Bang for Your Buck" metric to measure fan return on investment for all major professional teams in the United States.

Babatunde Buraimo is a senior lecturer in sports management and sports economics at the University of Central Lancashire, Preston, United Kingdom. He has a doctoral degree from Lancaster University. His doctoral thesis was an empirical analysis of the fundamental conjectures in sports economics. These included the effects of market size in professional team sport and the outcome uncertainty hypothesis. Buraimo has many research interests, including spatial economic analysis, competitive balance in team sports, audience demand in sport, the economics of gambling, and market efficiency. His research has been published in scholarly journals, including the *Journal of Sports Economics*, *Journal of the Operational Research Society*, *Managerial and Decision Economics*, *Scottish Journal of Political Economy*, and *Southern Economic Journal*.

Timothy D. DeSchriver is an associate professor in the Department of Health, Nutrition, and Exercise Sciences at the University of Delaware. He holds an Ed.D. from the University of Northern Colorado, along with an M.A. from Penn State University and a B.A. from Villanova University. Dr. DeSchriver's research interests are in the fields of sport economics, finance, and marketing, specifically in the areas of professional sport and collegiate athletics. He has published articles in the *Journal of Sport Management*, *Sport Marketing Quarterly*, *Eastern Economic Journal*, *International Journal of Sport Management*, *Sport Management Review*, and the *International Sports Journal*. He has also been cited by articles in publications such as the *New York Times*, the *Washington Post*, and the *Hartford Courant*. Dr. DeSchriver is the coauthor of a textbook entitled *Sport Finance* (first and second editions). He also cowrote chapters in *Contemporary Sport Management* (second and third editions), and *Principles and Practices of Sport Management* (second edition). Dr. DeSchriver is a member of the editorial boards for the *Sport Marketing Quarterly*, *International Journal of Sport Finance*, and *Journal of Sport Management*. Dr. DeSchriver has also made numerous presentations at the North American Society for Sport Management and Sport Marketing Association annual conferences. He has also traveled to the nations of South Korea and Turkey as an invited international speaker. Additionally, he has been involved in marketing research projects with organizations such as the National Collegiate Athletic Association, the Anschutz Entertainment Group, Ripken Baseball Incorporated, and the National Steeplechase Association. Prior to joining the Department of Health, Nutrition, and Exercise Sciences at the University of Delaware in the fall of 2004, Professor DeSchriver was on the faculty at the University of Massachusetts from 1998 to 2004.

Arne Feddersen is a postdoctoral research and teaching assistant in the Department of Economics at the University of Hamburg, Germany. His research interests are sports economics, regional and urban economics, and the economics of higher education. He has published articles in the field of sports economics in several books, conference volumes, and scholarly journals including *Journal of Applied Social Science Studies* and the *International Journal of Sport Finance*.

Rodney Fort, a professor in the sport management program at the University of Michigan, is a recognized authority on sports economics and business, both in the United States and internationally. In more than fifty articles and monographs, his work covers sports topics as diverse as cross-subsidies in U.S. sports leagues, predatory behavior by Major League Baseball toward African American baseball leagues during integration, and comparative analysis of North American and world sports leagues. His contributions have appeared in the *American Economic Review*, *Journal of Political Economy*, *Journal of Economic Literature*, *Economic Inquiry*, *Scottish Journal of Political Economy*, *Economic Inquiry*, and the *Journal of Sports Economics*. He also serves on the editorial boards of the *Journal of Sports Economics*, the *International Journal of Sport Finance*, and the *Eastern Economic Journal*, and as a vice-president for the International Association of Sports Economists. Professor Fort is coauthor of the books *Pay Dirt* and *Hard Ball*, both nominated for national awards, and he also recently coedited two volumes, *Economics of College Sports* and *International Sports Economics Comparisons*. His best-selling textbook, *Sports Economics*, is in its second edition. Professor Fort is a regular speaker on sports issues and has been a panelist on sports economics issues at various universities, the Stanford Institute for Economic Policy Research, the Independent Institute, the Marquette Sports Law Institute, the Brookings Institution, and the International Center for Sports Studies in Neuchatel, Switzerland. He has testified before the U.S. Senate Subcommittee on Antitrust concerning competitive balance issues in baseball and before the New Zealand Commerce Commission on the establishment of a Premier Division in New Zealand Rugby Union. Fort has been a keynote speaker at international sports congresses in

Cologne, Germany, Rio de Janeiro, Brazil, and Gijon, Spain. He also frequently renders expert opinion in legal cases concerning sports. In addition, Professor Fort has appeared on the CBC's Hockey Night in Canada and is frequently interviewed on National Public Radio.

Wolfgang Maennig is a professor of economics at Hamburg University. Previously, he was professor at E.A.P. Paris-Oxford-Berlin-Madrid. He was a visiting professor at the American University in Dubai as well as at the Universities Stellenbosch (South Africa) and Istanbul, and at the University of Economics Bratislava. He was also visiting scholar at International Monetary Fund in Washington, D.C., and at Deutsche Bundesbank in Frankfurt. His research concentrates on economic policy, sport economics, transport economics, and real estate economics and has been published in numerous academic journals including *Economic Letters, Regional Studies, Regional Science and Urban Economics, Labour Economics, Applied Economics, Journal of Sports Economics,* and *Contemporary Economic Policy.* Professor Maennig has worked as an expert for many bids of large sport events, including the Olympic bids of Berlin 2000, Leipzig 2012, Munich 2018, and the Athletics World Cup Berlin 2009. He was Olympic Champion (rowing, eight with coxswain) at the Olympics 1988 in Seoul and president of the German Rowing Federation, 1995-2001. In 2000 he received the Olympic Order.

Daniel F. Mahony is a professor of sport administration and the associate university provost at the University of Louisville. He has a B.S. in accounting from Virginia Tech, an M.S. in sport management from West Virginia University, and a Ph.D. in sport management from Ohio State University. Before becoming a faculty member, he worked in both public accounting and intercollegiate athletics. Dr. Mahony is an active researcher in the areas of sport consumer behavior and intercollegiate athletics and has had fifty articles accepted for publication in various refereed journals including *Journal of Sport Management, Sport Management Review, Sport Marketing Quarterly, International Journal of Sport Marketing and Sponsorship, International Journal of Sport Management, European Journal of Sport Management, Journal of Academic Ethics, Journal of Contemporary Athletics,* and *Journal of Sport and Social Issues.* He was also a coauthor for *Economics of Sport.* Dr. Mahony is a NASSM Research Fellow and won the 2007 Earle F. Zeigler Award from the North American Society for Sport Management for his research contributions to the field.

Daniel S. Mason is an associate professor with the faculty of physical education and recreation and an adjunct professor with the School of Business at the University of Alberta in Edmonton, Canada. His research takes an interdisciplinary approach and focuses on the business of sport and the relationships between its stakeholders, including all levels of government, sports teams, leagues, the communities that host teams, agents, and players' associations. His research has been funded by the Social Sciences and Humanities Research Council of Canada and Alberta Gaming Research Institute, and he has published more than forty articles in refereed publications such as *Contemporary Economic Policy, Economic Development Quarterly, European Journal of Marketing, Journal of Sport and Social Issues, Journal of Sport History, Journal of Sport Management, Journal of Urban Affairs, Managing Leisure,* and *Urban History Review*. In 2004 he was named a research fellow by the North American Society of Sport Management.

Victor A. Matheson is an assistant professor in the Department of Economics at the College of the Holy Cross in Worcester, Massachusetts. He earned his Ph.D. in economics from the University of Minnesota. He has published extensively in the field of the economics of collegiate and professional sports including studies of the economic impact of the NCAA Final Four, Major League Baseball's All-Star Game and the World Series, the Super Bowl, the World Cup, and the Olympics. He also works as an intercollegiate soccer referee and has officiated games in the NCAA men's and women's soccer tournaments.

Jane E. Ruseski is an assistant professor in the Department of Economics at the University of Alberta in Edmonton, Alberta, Canada. She earned her Ph.D. in economics at the Johns Hopkins University in 1998. She was formerly an assistant professor in the Department of Kinesiology and Community Health at University of Illinois at Urbana-Champaign and an economist in the antitrust division of the Federal Trade Commission. Her research interests are in health economics, finance, and policy. Her current research focuses on the economic determinants of participation in physical activity and sports and the link with obesity; the effectiveness of policies to promote physical activity; competition and antitrust policy in health-care markets; and the effect of ownership status on behavior and efficiency in health-care organizations.

Rob Simmons is a senior lecturer in economics in the Department of Economics at Lancaster University Management School, United Kingdom. His Ph.D. is from University of Leeds. Simmons's research interests include economics of sports, labor and personnel economics, and economics of gambling. Recent journal outlets include *Economic Inquiry, International Journal of Forecasting, Journal of Sports Economics* and *Southern Economic Journal*. Simmons is a qualified Football Association referee and long-time supporter of Manchester City FC.

Paul Swangard is managing director, Woodard Family Foundation Fellow, James H. Warsaw Sports Marketing Center, University of Oregon. Swangard joined the Warsaw Center in 2001. In his role as managing director, Swangard oversees the day-to-day operations of the nationally recognized center, teaches at both the undergraduate and graduate level, and serves as one of the center's primary industry analysts on sports business issues. His comments on the industry have appeared in numerous national publications including the *Wall Street Journal,* the *New York Times,* and *USA Today.* He has also appeared on ABC's *Nightline,* ESPN's *Outside the Lines,* and CNBC's *Power Lunch.* In addition to numerous consulting projects with leading sports firms, Swangard has participated in executive education programs on sponsorship and sports marketing with the Chinese Olympic Committee in Beijing and Shanghai. In 2006 he was honored as one of the University of Oregon's Outstanding Officers of Administration. Swangard received his MBA with a sports business concentration from the University of Oregon in 1999 and spent two years in consumer and business marketing positions at Intel Corporation. While at Intel, Swangard focused on corporate strategy for emerging technologies in digital media and entertainment. An award-winning journalist, Swangard spent ten years with KEZI-TV in Eugene, serving as the station's sports director from 1994 to 1997. As a freelancer, Swangard has appeared on events airing on ESPN, the Outdoor Life Channel, Action Sports Cable Network, and Fox Sports Net. He earned his bachelor's degree in journalism in 1990 at the University of Oregon.

Andrew Zimbalist is the Robert A. Woods Professor of Economics at Smith College, where he has been in the Economics Department since 1974. He received his B.A. from the University of Wisconsin, Madison, in 1969 and his M.A. and Ph.D. from Harvard University in 1972 and 1974, respectively. He has consulted in Latin America for the United Nations Development Program, the U.S. Agency for International Development, numerous companies, and has consulted in the sports industry for players' associations, cities, companies, and leagues. He has published seventeen books and several dozen articles, including *Baseball and Billions* (1992), *Sports, Jobs and Taxes* (1997), *Unpaid Professionals: Commercialism and Conflict in Big-Time College Sports* (1999), *The Economics of Sport,* 2 vols. (2001), *May the Best Team Win: Baseball Economics and Public Policy* (2003), *National Pastime: How Americans Play Baseball and the Rest of the World Plays Soccer* (with Stefan Szymanski) (2005), *In the Best Interests of Baseball? The Revolutionary Reign of Bud Selig* (2006), and *The Bottom Line: Observations and Arguments on the Sports Business* (2006).

Index

Media (*continued*)
74, 140–42; revenues, 125, 137–40;
sports dependency, 254–55; team
ownership, 49. *See also* Broadcasting;
Internet
Media rights: China Central Television
funding, 75; college sports, 229; sales
and revenues, 137–38. *See also* Tele-
vision rights
Mediated sports, 8–10
Mega-event economics, 81–97
Membership associations, 156
Memberships, 25–26
Men's collegiate sports, 232–33
Men's sports teams (nonrevenue), 237–38
Merchandise, 142–43, 259
Merchandising, 125–26
Metropolitan economies, 91
Milan, Italy, 119
Millwall Football Club, 48
Ming Yao, 67, 73
MLB All-Star Game, 81, 82, 88, 91,
95, 194
MLB.com, 140, 259
MLB Enterprises, 143
MLB Properties, 142–43
Mobile media: data services and content,
267; revenue stream, 140; rights con-
tracts, 264
Mobility of players, European soccer, 53
Models. *See* Business models; Economic
models
Monday Night Football, 254
Monetization, video content, 262
Money-ball (Lewis), 199
Monopolies: Chinese Central, 75; collu-
sive groups, 41; football team owner-
ship in UK, 49; National Collegiate
Athletic Association, 238; owner in-
terest and local, 153; sport broadcast
rights, 138
Monopolies and Mergers Commission
(UK), 49
Montreal, Canada, 96, 102, 144

Montreal Canadiens, 49
Montreal Expos, 206, 211, 258
Moore, Robert, 95
Moral hazards, 53
Moscow, Soviet Union, 115
Mountain West Conference, 207
MSG Network, 147
Multimedia: baseball content, 258–59;
broadband, 257
Multiplier: estimates, 83–84, 111,
112–14; inaccuracy, 88; mega-event
estimates, 90
Multiplier-based economic impact esti-
mates, 113–14
Munich, Germany, 86
MySpace.com, 253, 262
Myths, 222

Nagano, Japan, 103, 106, 120
Nagin, Ray, 85
Naming rights, 133, 134–37; Chinese
Football Association, 64; college
facilities, 229–30
NASCAR: attendance, 7–8; sponsorship
revenues, 143; telemetry data repack-
aging for Web, 267; television audience, 10
Nashville Predators, 145
National Basketball Association (NBA),
139; All-Star Game visitors, 84; audience, 9; China market, 64; China
market approach, 72; European-US
competitive balance, 166–70; expansion revenues, 144, 206; gate receipts,
126; licensing rights, 143; mega-event
stadiums, 88; playoff chances, 209–10;
team valuation, 203–4; ticket
prices, 188–89
National Basketball Players Association,
143
National Collegiate Athletic Association
(NCAA): accounting practices,
227–28; cartel behavior, 238–39;
coach salaries and revenues, 214;

75; content rights, 254; digital media revenue stream, 140; distribution channels, 254–55; Division 1-A sport conferences, 245–46; economic value of listening, 29; English small football team pressures, 47; fans viewing, 189; league expansion and relocation, 206; mega-event tourism, 86; National Hockey League, 260–61; revenue-sharing polices, 38; sports audience, 8–10; sport substitutes, 192

Television revenues: college conferences and taxation, 245–46; English Football League, 46; English Premier League, 40; European trends, 52; league expansion, 144; Olympic Games, 105–6

Television rights: Chinese Football Association, 63–64; European soccer clubs/leagues, 159; National Football League and, 50; Olympic Games, 102–3, 106; sales and revenues, 137–38. *See also* Broadcast rights; Media rights

Telewebbing, 262
Tennis, 9–10
Territories, 206
Texas, 95
Texas Rangers, 49
Texas Tech University, 230
Thurston, Fuzzy, 193
Tiananmen Square, 61, 63
Ticket price forecasts, 188–89
Ticket sales: college athletic events, 226; economic activity, 8; Internet, 259–60; multiplier-based economic impact estimates, 113; Olympic Games, 108–9; premium seating and season, 131–32; spectator sports, 28–29. *See also* Gate receipts
Tickets.com, 259
Time, 8
Time-switchers, 87, 113
Title IX, 221, 235–38, 245

Tokyo, Japan, 115, 116
Total revenues: apparel market, 20–21; college coach contribution, 243; college Division II programs, 232; college program operations, 229; college program subsidies, 234; college sponsorship, 230; cost of talent, 40; equipment manufacturers, 16–17; fitness/recreation subindustry, 14; footwear, 18; golf course/country club, 12; professional sports, 125; supply-side business, 29; ticket revenues, 126
Toronto, Canada, 144–45
Tottenham Hotspur, 40, 48, 158
Tourism: Chinese, 78–80; event estimates, 84; mega-event impact, 86, 87; multiplier-based economic impact estimates, 113–14; Olympic Game host, 66, 108, 110, 115; Olympic Game long-term impact, 117
Trade imbalance, 65
Trade promotion, 66
Traffic, 173
Training of college athletes, 219
Transaction costs, 172
Transfer fees, 53–54
Transportation: European stadiums, 176; Olympic Game construction, 109–10
Transylvania University, 228
Travel, 78–79
Tuition, 231, 240–41
Turkey, 166, 167, 168
Turner, Ted, 146
Turner Broadcasting System (TBS), 139

Ueberroth, Peter, 62, 103
UEFA Champions League (UCL), 41, 54, 154, 165, 170
Uncertainty: outcome, 192, 194, 196, 199–200; player performance, 212; team revenues and competitive, 37; team staffing decisions, 215

GV716 .B89 2008
v.1

The business of sports

2008.

2009 01 08

Due Date	Date Returned
	AUG 0 3 2010
JUL 2 9 2010	AUG 3 1 2010
AUG 1 7 2010	
OCT 2 7 2011 NOV 1 7 2011	NOV 1 6 2011

www.library.humber.ca